Freedom for Ministry

Freedom

for Ministry

Richard John Neuhaus

1817

HARPER & ROW, PUBLISHERS, San Francisco
Cambridge, Hagerstown, New York, Philadelphia
London, Mexico City, São Paulo, Sydney

FREEDOM FOR MINISTRY. Copyright © 1979 by Richard John Neuhaus. All rights reserved. Printed in the United States of America. No part of this book may be used or reproduced in any manner whatsoever without written permission except in the case of brief quotations embodied in critical articles and reviews. For information address Harper & Row, Publishers, Inc., 10 East 53rd Street, New York, NY 10022. Published simultaneously in Canada by Fitzhenry & Whiteside Limited, Toronto.

FIRST HARPER & ROW PAPERBACK EDITION PUBLISHED IN 1984.

The Library of Congress supplied the following Library of Congress Cataloging in Publication Data for the hardcover edition

Neuhaus, Richard John
    Freedom for ministry.

    Includes bibliographical references and index.
    1. Clergy—Office. 2. Pastoral theology. I. Title.
BV660.2.N42 1979   253   78-3352
ISBN 0-06-066094-5

LC# 78–3352
ISBN 0—06—066095–3

84 85 86 87 88 10 9 8 7 6 5 4 3 2 1

Contents

Debts

My uncle, Henry Karau, a good and honorable man who lived his own life in living for others, and Mary Elizabeth, his wife, whose love I continue to cherish.

Clemens Henry Neuhaus, my father and the first pastor I knew, who taught me what ministry is and can be, and the difference between the two.

"The Wednesday Night Group" of practicing clergy, who continue to instruct me on the meaning of ministry.

Thomas and Betty Edge, who offer respite and perspective on ministries quite different from my own.

The gracious folk at the Divinity School of Duke University, who got this book started by inviting me to deliver the Gray Lectures of 1977.

The faculty of Concordia Seminary, St. Louis, now Christ Seminary-Seminex, who took the risk of training and recommending me for the Church's ministry.

Stephen Bremer and Kenneth Runge, outstanding among the

many pastors who have taught me and who, I hope, will recognize their contributions in these pages.

James Finn, Susan Woolfson, and Claire Moise at *Worldview,* and Glenn Stone at *Lutheran Forum,* all of whom are helpful beyond my deserving.

Robert Wilken and Elliott Wright, who gave solid criticisms on the manuscript, and Larry Bailey, who, in addition to that, is my respected pastor and colleague at Trinity Church—Lower East Side.

John Loudon and John Shopp of Harper & Row, the first of whom encouraged and the second of whom both encouraged and patiently edited.

In different ways, they all share responsibility for whatever may be the strengths and weaknesses of this book.

A Word to the Reader

This book is for parish pastors and others in Christian ministry, and for those who would understand what ministry is about, or should be about. It is called "a critical affirmation of the Church and its mission." Both words—*critical* and *affirmation*—are important. There is much here about the theoretical and practical problems of ministry, but always within the context of affirming the urgency and dignity of the calling.

It begins, for reasons that will become evident, with thinking about the Church and the religious situation in which, for better and for worse, we find ourselves ministering. Then there is a discussion of the ways in which the minister is, and is not, a professional. The argument is that there is a necessary awkwardness about Christian ministry because we are ambassadors of a "disputed sovereignty." That necessary—and liberating!—awkwardness informs the discussion of counseling, psychology, the search for community, and the suspect goal called ministerial success. The discussion then moves on to the minister as leader of worship and concludes with two chapters on the art, discipline, and "absurd responsibility" of preaching.

There is a longish final chapter on the pursuit of holiness. It deals with some of the more common moral dilemmas of ministry, with particular reference to ambition, sexuality, and money. The premise is that the minister is to live an "exemplary" life, and the purpose is to inquire as to what that might mean today. One reviewer has suggested that the reader should begin with that last chapter and then go back to the rest of the book. He may have a point, but you can decide that for yourself.

He and *his* are used throughout. Obviously there are women ministers and, if the enrollment in some seminaries is a portent, there will be many more. But both principle and good taste militate against employing *he/she, his/her,* and similar constructions that currently litter the linguistic environment.

This is intended as an ecumenical discussion of ministry. The author is a Christian of the Lutheran species. It is nothing to boast or complain about, but the relevance of the fact is no doubt evident at points. I hope, however, that the ministry described here is recognizable from the diocesan office in Detroit to the revival tent in Georgia, from the New England meeting house to Southern California's spiritual emporiums. More than we might think, we share in common the essential problems and the essential joys of ministry today.

Finally, this book was written in the year after my departure from the Church of St. John the Evangelist in Brooklyn, New York, where I had been pastor for seventeen years. I am grateful to be at Trinity —Lower East Side in Manhattan, but I miss St. John's very much. I had considered writing a chapter on the pains of leaving a people and a parish that, if it is possible, one loves too passionately. But that will have to wait for another time. Enough to say that, no matter how others may cite your successes, you are more keenly aware of what you might have done and might have been. If these pages seem at times to present an impossibly high ideal of Christian ministry, the author acknowledges his complicity in the compromises he deplores. Indeed, it is not uncommon that we most deplore that to which we are most inclined.

A critical affirmation then. It will have served its purpose if people who care deeply about the idea and practice of ministry find in it what they themselves would wish to say, had the writing of books been their vocation.

RJN

New York City
The Ninth Sunday of Pentecost, 1978

1.
The Thus and So-ness of the Church

Times Square, fully lit, would be a magnificent sight, if only one could not read. So said G. K. Chesterton. And so it might be said of the splendidly various, star-spangled, busy, busy business that is religion in America. Visitors from foreign lands regularly exclaim upon what they kindly call the "vitality" of the churches in America. They speculate about the spiritual circuitry and social wiring that maintain this bright spectacle. Explanations range from theories about American voluntarism to the condescending suggestion that Americans, largely untouched by national tragedy and untainted by critical thought, can afford to be as exuberant about their religion as they are about most other things. But whatever the reasons given, we are reminded that, among advanced industrial societies, only in America do the churches seem to enjoy a prosperous present and high confidence about the future.

Many of us who are professionally part of religion in America are less impressed by the bright lights. Perhaps that is because we can read, and we are embarrassed by the messages so garishly proclaimed: Jocks for Jesus, the World's Biggest Sunday School, Possibility Thinking, and the Bishops' Call to Action are all promoted as the formulas for health, wealth, happiness, and maybe even justice. Christianity is packaged for a market that seems infinitely various in its demands. It offers liberation from political oppression and psychological depression. In this supermarket you can pick up tranquilizers in Aisle A and revolutionary engagement in Aisle D, and at the checkout counter they will accept whatever you are moved to give. It is a wondrous system and a cause for amazement on the part of all who have pondered its workings.

It is also the cause of deep uneasiness on the part of those professionally responsible for its working. Whether we are ministers, pastors, priests, presbyters, bishops, or evangelists, we are the functionaries of this enormous enterprise. We do not like to think of ourselves as functionaries, for we are also—more and less, at sometimes more than other times—visionaries. We have read and we have believed that the Church is the Body of Christ, the People of God, the salt of the earth, a light set upon a hill. We have been told and we have solemnly affirmed that we are, in the words of St. Paul, stewards of the mysteries of God (1 Cor. 4).

Stewards of the mysteries are seen as salesmen to the markets, and we are profoundly uneasy about that. The success of the religious enterprise is an embarrassment to those who remember that the Church claims to be a community gathered by the cross, the symbol of offense, of scandal, of life through death. The tension between the theological or spiritual definition of Church and the sociological fact of Church is acutely embarrassing. We have a number of ways of relieving the embarrassment.

CONFUSING COLLAPSE WITH THE CROSS

One way is to deny the sociological fact. Thus some of us look for and warmly welcome signs that the Church is in deep institutional trouble. This response to our embarrassment was very popular during most of the 1960s, following the so-called religious boom of the 1950s. Each time the Gallup Poll reported a percentile's slippage in church attendance, hopes were raised that the Church was finally becoming the minority it is supposed to be in a "post-Christian era."

It seemed that hardly a lecture was given or a book written that did not assert that maybe the Church would have to die before it could rise again to really be the Church. I confess that I was always rather puzzled by this line of argument. It seemed to me that people were confusing institutional decline with walking the way of the cross. Not long ago I was at dinner with a former Roman Catholic priest and his wife. Both were touchingly typical refugees from the sixties. With a perfectly straight face, indeed with high enthusiasm, he told me that he, unlike others, did not leave the active priesthood because of dissatisfaction with what he was doing. To the contrary, he said, "Everything was going great." I and another priest had been in this parish only two years, and already we had cut out two masses, almost nobody was coming to confession, and in another year we would have closed the school." A crisis over celibacy brought a timely end to this success story in Christian ministry.

The instance may seem bizarre, but it is by no means atypical. One could find in all the churches learned theologians who urge that, if the Church were truly faithful to the gospel, she would divest herself of her properties, sell her holdings, disband her organizations (except, of course, for the organizations that promote the right causes; that is, the causes which merit the approval of said theologians) and generally go out of business. There is no doubt that if Christians are radically and relentlessly faithful to the gospel, they will frequently find their public relations damaged and their budgets unbalanced. They may even find themselves persecuted and subjected to sundry unpleasantries such as imprisonment and execution. It has been known to happen.

To the disappointment of many, however, it is hard to get oneself persecuted for being a Christian in North America. I write this as one who has been in and out of jails over the years for actions on behalf of racial justice and peace. I do not have enough virtue that I can afford to be excessively modest about what I have done, and certainly I do not wish to detract from the courage of the brothers and sisters with whom I have done these things. In fact, since I seem to lack the capacity to accept things as they are, I am fully prepared to go to jail again if that seems the appropriate way to advance what I believe right or to resist what I believe wrong. But all this is only ambiguously related to persecution for being a Christian.

Those who stand in truly solitary witness are a case apart. But in the Times Square of American culture and religion it is hard to stand in solitary witness. The crowds are so large and diverse that anyone with an itch for martyrdom can readily find or start a new martyrs' association that will soon have its own newsletter, board of directors, and maybe even a balanced budget. Thus, without ever having involuntarily missed a meal, one has a more or less solid institutional base from which to demand that the churches divest themselves of their institutional trappings. The ability of American culture to assimilate its critics (the word used to be *cooptation*) is a cause of frustration to some and of joy to others. But, at least so far, it has been remarkably successful at such assimilation. The critics become part of the show.

Those who confused signs of institutional decline with the way of the cross, leading, supposedly, to a resurrected and revitalized Christianity, also tended to confuse their own wishes with the institutional facts. While the cover of *Time* magazine asked whether God is really dead, and cultural critics, including theologians, were readying themselves for the autopsy on organized religion, the American people remained remarkably calm in the face of the crisis. The indicators of decline that the pollsters turned up resulted for the most part from institutional adjustments among Roman Catholics to the changes initiated by Vatican II. Some observers contend that the drop-off among Roman Catholics was almost entirely a result of the Pope's unpopular stand on contraception. I suspect that for many Catholics that is only a convenient excuse. But, be that as it may, institutional decline in Roman Catholicism seems to have bottomed out, and there is today a new sense of confidence and even assertiveness about the future of Catholicism in America. While the so-called mainline Protestant churches experienced intermittent pauses and declines during the past decade, these too seem to be turning around toward greater stability and, in some cases, positive growth. And, of course, the big news of institutional expansion and vitality has been coming from the evangelicals (by no means limited to the churches that call themselves evangelical) and from charismatics, both Protestant and Roman Catholic. In short, the lights are not going out on the Times Square of American religion, and those who can read have no choice but to read the messages, both for better and for worse.

The idea that decline or collapse is the prelude to renewal reveals a kind of nostalgia for the catacombs. A return to the catacombs might ever so greatly simplify the vexing problems of Christian identity and discipleship, but it is a solution we are not likely to be favored with in our time. I do not say that this is good; it is simply the way it is and is likely to be for the foreseeable future. In talking about Church and ministry we should show a healthy respect for the way things are, holding our visions of the way things ought to be in tightest tension with existing reality. Only in this way can the existing Church be prodded, urged, seduced, and loved into approximating a bit more closely the Church that ought to be.

The necessary tension is fatally relaxed by those who interpret institutional crisis in terms of cross and resurrection. Such theories have lost touch with the millions of people who actually constitute the church in North America. They are the ones who do the unheroic, routine things like showing up on Sundays, paying the bills, harassing their pastors, saying their prayers, hoping for heaven, and, more often than not, trying to be decent to those both more and less fortunate than themselves. And in the midst of muddling through, there is occasional ecstasy, occasional heroism, the occasional act of self-surrendering love. It is all very human, and any serious conversation about Church and ministry must begin at that very human level. It is unseemly for us to hold ourselves superior to the human in which God invested his very being in Jesus Christ.

I too want to think about cross and resurrection, about Christian radicality, about the revolutionary mandate of the ministry we bear. But first we need to be clear about the concreteness of the Church from which and for which such ministry exists; we want to be clear about its here and now-ness, about its thus and so-ness. Otherwise, all our talk about ministry is a self-indulgent escape, no longer accountable to the empirical fact of Church.

It is in connection with this reality that we must read the gospels and epistles of the New Testament. We cannot here enter into the debate over whether Jesus of Nazareth intended to establish a

Church. I personally am persuaded that he did, and anyway I don't know where one goes with the argument if one concludes that he didn't. We may be less sure about whether Jesus intended the United Methodist Church, or the American Lutheran Church, or St. Stanislaus Polish Catholic Church in Brooklyn. But whether he intended them or not, he got them. Although most of us have, no doubt, eminently sound plans for re-forming the churches in greater conformity with his intention, we are responsible for these mutilated, separated, pedestrian churches that comprise his Church. That is, we are responsible for the millions of people in these churches who are the object of his reckless and redeeming love.

Those who are called "liberation theologians" today tell us that we should read the Bible through the eyes of the poor and oppressed, and they are right. We should also read the Bible through the eyes of the more elegantly and complicatedly poor who make up the churches of North America. It is easier to cheer the liberation struggles in distant lands than to anguish over the liberation of ourselves and others with whom we cross paths and cross words every day. The Church may be the pilgrim people of God on their way to the New Jerusalem, but they are still pedestrians, and it is to the pedestrian Church that we are called to minister.

I do not think we should regret it if this Church is institutionally strong. For the millions of people who support and participate in the churches, it is likely a good thing. To be sure, we all deplore the superficiality, the cheap grace, the caricature of Christian discipleship that mark some of the most successful peddling of the gospel in our time. The hustling that dominates "the electronic church" of religious broadcasting, the mile-long cathedrals of glass made possible by the avoidance of controversy, the multimillion dollar commerce in books that reinforce every prejudice and stereotype—all this is repugaant on many scores. And yet, and yet: through all this, millions of people are receiving a more adequate and truthful view of the world than they might otherwise have. They are introduced at least to the rudiments of the Christian world view: to the Creator God, to the reality of sin, to the redeeming power of God's initiative in Jesus Christ, to the presence of the Spirit, to the ethic of love, to the hope of glory. No matter how bastardized we may think the form of the gospel is, they are at least brought within the circle of Christian discourse where the understanding of the gospel can be deepened and fulfilled in Christian discipleship.

IN SEARCH OF THE AUTHENTIC

We do well to guard against the sin of presumption. Before despising the piety of so many of our brothers and sisters, we should remember that the Spirit blows where he will, works in ways beyond our understanding and beyond the articulation of those with whom he works. Spiritual reality far surpasses the way in which that reality is articulated; and, sad to say, the eloquence of religious articulation may far surpass the spiritual reality. We have biases of our own to which we need to be alert.

Perhaps the point can be illustrated by three expressions of Christian faith, and our different reaction to each. The first comes from an elderly Black woman in a Brooklyn parish. Originally from the South, she has raised six children with several men in New York City. In earlier years she dabbled in prostitution, and today becomes more "spiritual minded" during bouts with alcohol.

She says, "I knows de Lord have hold on me. He knows I be a sinner, but even when I let go o' him, he holdin' on an' holdin' on. So I'm alway sayin', 'Thankyou, Jesus. Thankyou, Jesus.'"

The second expression comes from Paul Tillich, at the end of his *The Courage to Be:*

> The courage to take the anxiety of meaninglessness upon oneself is the boundary line up to which the courage to be can go. . . . Within it all forms of courage are re-established in the power of God above the God of theism. The courage to be is rooted in the God who appears when God has disappeared in the anxiety of doubt.

And the third expression of Christian faith comes from a bigname professional football player in a television interview: "When I accepted Jesus as my personal Lord and Savior, everything changed for me. I knew Jesus was a winner and I wanted to be on his team."

Which of these is the most "authentic" expression of Christian faith? Each can be criticized with ease. The first smacks of cheap grace, laced with revival meeting clichés. Tillich's statement may, upon close examination, turn out to be saying nothing at all, although, to be sure, saying it very elegantly. Our football player's winning formula would not seem to leave much room for the cross. How shall we judge the "authenticity" of such different expressions of the faith? By the coherence of the statements with the lives of those who made them? We are perhaps touched by the woman's troubled experiences, and intimidated by Tillich's erudition, and we are likely put off by the suggestion that Jesus is a fan of the Dallas Cowboys. But finally we have neither moral nor theological nor spiritual tests by which we can judge at all; at least we cannot judge in the sense of excluding any of these speakers from our definition of authentic Christian community. The Church in all its forms and manifestations is profoundly inauthentic; it is made authentic only by the judgment of a gracious God. And each person within this community is a center of mystery deserving of our respect—no, of our reverence.

By asserting that we should suspend judgment, I am not proposing a laissez-faire attitude toward the Church, nor am I defending the status quo. We will get to the visions and dreams by which, by the grace of God, our ministries can help transform the Church and help the Church transform the world. But we must be sure it is the Church that we are talking about: the Church in all its thus and so-ness, in all its contradictions and compromises, in its circus of superficiality and its moments of splendor. Although we may be offended by many of the messages, we should not pull the plug on the Times Square of American religiosity that is inseparably interlocked with the Church of Jesus Christ.

Thinking about the Church today is plagued by a mood of anti-institutionalism that pervades our culture. We too facilely posit form against reality, the institutional against the authentic. Institution is simply another word for social endurance. Even the most spontaneous and prophetic of movements cannot last unless they find institutional form. Witness the charismatic movement today with its dozens of publishing houses, television programs, national and regional organizations, and its controversies over the bureaucratic limits of "shepherding" and "discipling" its true believers. I admit I have never understood what people mean when they talk about "the institutional church." There is no other church of historical or social significance. It might be suggested that there is another church of theological significance. But the church we speak of theologically is not another church; it is *this* Church—in all its sweaty, smelly, concreteness—although viewed in a different and more comprehensive perspective.

The "true" Church of Jesus Christ is not to be posited against, is not an alternative to, this Church of empirical experience. The true Church is the Church truly seen; it is this Church transformed in the perspective of hope, based upon divine promise. I do not look for the collapse of this so-called institutional Church. It bears through history, however inadequately, the apostolic witness to the Risen Lord. It provides a modicum of meaning for the lives of millions. It provides the points of moral reference by which at least the potential exists for ordering this society more in accord with Judeo-Christian values. It provides both a platform and a community of discourse by which radical questions of personal and social judgment can be raised and pressed. What would Martin Luther King, Jr., or the Southern Christian Leadership Conference have been without the black churches and the institutional network of support within the white churches? In protesting the war in Vietnam, an organization like Clergy and Laity Concerned About Vietnam presupposed the Times Square from which and to which we could signal our message. The largest organization in America today addressing itself to questions of global hunger and development, Bread for the World, is premised upon a community of shared concern that reaches from the chancery office of Detroit to the revival tents of Tennessee.

This is the Church, and within its amazing and maddening diversity pastors and priests find their ministry. When we say in the creed, "I believe in one, holy, catholic and apostolic Church," we no doubt mean more than Methodist headquarters in Nashville or the Vatican in Rome, and so we should. *More* than, but not *other* than. "More than" in the ecumenical sense of comprehending the whole of the Christian community, far beyond the limits of nation or denomination. "More than" in the historic sense of acknowledging our place within and responsibility for two thousand years of Christian tragedy and triumph. And "more than" in the eschatological sense of hope, knowing that the "now" of the Church, as of the world, is to be fulfilled in the "not yet" of the coming Kingdom.

In the words of Wolfhart Pannenberg:

> The Church is true to its vocation only if it anticipates and represents the destiny of all mankind, the goal of history. . . . Any narrowing of the universal vocation of the Church, any deviation from its character as an eschatological community, results in depriving the Church of its social significance.[1]

Similarly, the Pastoral Constitution (Article 39) of Vatican Council II:

> To the extent that [earthly progress] can contribute to the better ordering of human society, it is of vital concern to the kingdom of God. For after we have obeyed the Lord, and in His Spirit nurtured on earth the values of human dignity, brotherhood, and freedom, and indeed all the good fruits of our nature and enterprise, we will find them again, but freed of stain, burnished and transfigured. This will be so when Christ hands over to the Father a kingdom eternal and universal: "a kingdom of truth and life, of holiness and grace, of justice, love, and peace." On this earth that kingdom is already present in mystery. When the Lord returns it will be brought into full flower.

Perhaps these passages imply too smooth a transition from things as they are to things as they will be. The biblical witness is that the transition will be anything but smooth: The seas will boil, the moon will turn to blood, the tares will be torn from the wheat, and there will be shocks of both pain and joy before the judgment seat of the Lamb, where it shall be revealed that the first are last and the last are first. As tumultuous as the transition is, however, it is still transition; that is, what will be will be what is—only what is will be fulfilled, transformed, consummated.

As all the Christian life is the life of hope, so also is the statement, "I believe in one, holy, catholic and apostolic Church." Its unity, its holiness, its catholicity, its apostolic fidelity—all these are present tasks, to be sure. But they are also promised reality and therefore, for people who live by that promise, they are *real* now. Only because of that reality can we, here and now, abandon ourselves to the ministry of that Church, in ministry to that Church. The Bride of Christ mentioned in Revelation 21 will be something quite new to our eyes, but she will be no stranger, for we will recognize her as the whore of Christendom transformed. It is only by trusting that promise that we dare now to call the whore of Christendom the Bride of Christ. We do so in hope, and that hope is the foundation of our ministry.

The theologies of all our churches all contain some distinctions between the doctrine of the Church and the Church of empirical reality. Some speak of the visible Church as distinct from the invisible Church, others of the corporal Church as distinct from the spiritual Church, others of the Church of ordinary history as distinct from the Church of salvation history, others of the Church of fact as distinct from the Church of faith. Some such distinction is obviously necessary. Apart from the promise, we could not surrender ourselves wholeheartedly to the ministry of the Church of empirical fact; to do so would be foolish; worse than that, to do so would be idolatry, giving ourselves to something less than the One who has ultimate claim upon us. But to surrender ourselves to the Body of Christ, as perceived in hope, is to surrender ourselves to Christ himself. In asking for such surrender, he asks nothing that he himself has not already done, for he has vested his future and vindication in the community he calls to his service.

The trouble with our distinctions between the Church of faith and the Church of fact, between the visible Church and the invisible Church, is that we permit distinctions to become separations. Thus we begin to speak as though there were two churches, rather than one Church that is "groaning inwardly as we wait for adoption as sons, the redemption of our bodies" (Rom. 8*). It is easy to think that we love an abstract, spiritualized, de-historicized Church, just as it is easy to love abstract, spiritualized, de-historicized people. In truth, to love abstractions is not to love at all; it is but a sentimental attachment to our own whimsies.

But, you say, you cannot love the real Church because it is so unspeakably unlovable. But what is the "real" Church? It is a great error, I believe, to think that only what now exists is real. To view the Church in terms of possibility and promise is not to depart from reality but to encompass the greater reality. The philosopher David L. Norton urges that we should be more careful in discussing reality or speaking of things as being "realized":

> To say that a possibility that assumes a working place in the existing world is thereby "realized" is to imply that it was unreal before. But pure possibilities are in and of themselves fully real—indeed, in respect of essence and identity they are supremely so. They are only nonexistent. And the belief that whatever is nonexistent is nothing is what George Santayana calls "a stupid positivism, like that of saying that the past is nothing, or the future nothing, or everything nothing of which I happen to be ignorant." . . . The propensity to this belief is widespread today.[2]

What is the Church of which we are ministers and for which we are to have love unbounded? It is the Church that "Christ loved . . . [he] gave himself up for her, that he might sanctify her, having cleansed her by the washing of water with the word, that he might present the Church to himself in splendor, without spot or wrinkle or any such thing, that she might be holy and without blemish" (Eph. 5). That is the *real* Church. And that real Church is in continuity with, inseparable from, this empirical, existing Church with which we are so deeply and so rightly dissatisfied. That possibility, affirmed in faith, is as real as the breath we draw. It is not simply a projection of a wish or of a worthy dream, but it is a possibility derived from the promise of God himself. The promise of the consummation has already been actualized by love in the life, death,

---

*Biblical quotations in this book are from the Revised Standard Version, unless otherwise noted.

and resurrection of our Lord Jesus Christ. "Love," says Norton, "is the relation between possibility and actuality in the integral life." Our God is a God of integrity; or, in more biblical language, our God is a faithful God.[3]

To love the Church, then, is to help it become what it is. The first axiom of classical Greek wisdom is, "Know yourself." The second is, "Become what you are." When St. Paul speaks of a Church without spot or wrinkle, therefore, he is not speaking of a different Church than the one with which we are so restlessly dissatisfied. No, he is speaking of this Church becoming what in reality it is. This does not mean that the whole of past and present Christianity will finally be vindicated and presented as the Bride of Christ, "holy and without blemish." We know there are tares among the wheat, but we are also warned by our Lord not to embark upon a premature and presumptuous effort to sort out the one from the other. That will be done in due time. For now, and until he comes in glory, our task is to love. And to love means to assist in the actualizing of possibilities perceived by faith.

WHOM WE WOULD CHANGE

I count it among the great graces of my life that I was for a time, until his death on April 4, 1968, permitted to work with Martin Luther King, Jr., as a kind of liaison between himself and the peace movement. Among the truths that he so powerfully declared and embodied was this: "Whom you would change you must first love." That means we must see more in other people than they see in themselves if we are to help them in becoming what they are. Wise parents know the truth of that, as does any good teacher, and as should every pastor. So often and so tragically we forget this truth.

Many of the radicalisms of the last decade forgot. Too often protest assumed a superior and sneering air; too often the voice of conscientious resistance was escalated into a screed of contempt. Never mind that there was sneering and violent contempt on "the other side"; when we stop loving we stop winning, no matter how many points we think are ours. Our task was not to burn the flag but to cleanse it; not to desecrate the ideals of America but to liberate them from their captivity to proudful arrogance and unjust war. Too often movements for change fail not for lack of analysis, nor for lack of commitment, but for lack of love. And when movements that are without love do succeed, their success is often a greater wrong than the wrong they set out to correct. Whom you would change—lastingly, and for the good—you must first love.

So also in pastoral ministry, it is precisely our passion for change that must stir up the gift of love. We all know how insidiously it happens that a pastor begins—perhaps at first unconsciously—to assume an adversary posture toward his people, to speak of "them" as the enemy. Then it is forgotten that prophecy is an office of love and not of contempt. Then it is forgotten that Amos, Hosea, and others spoke so straightforwardly precisely because they loved so recklessly, thinking so much more of the people of God than they thought of themselves. Then it is forgotten that the prophetic and priestly ministries are not antithetical but are forged together by the knowledge that whom we would change we must first love.

I know that our Lord told his disciples that there would be times when they should shake the dust from their feet and no longer cast their pearls before swine. Perhaps there are, after all, some sayings of our Lord that were meant to apply only to the earliest period of his Church's life. Be that as it may, we should hope to be spared the mandate of ever having to act upon those hard words, lest in the day of judgment they be turned against us. When as ministers we must sometimes acknowledge formally that a person has excluded himself from the fellowship, let it be done reluctantly, indeed with tears. It must be clear beyond doubt that we cannot exclude but can only respect the choice that that person has made and for which that person bears responsibility. Our model is the word of Paul to the ever-fractious and even swinish Corinthians: "For I wrote you out of much affliction and anguish of heart and with many tears, not to cause you pain but to let you know the abundant love that I have for you" (2 Cor. 2).

I started with the Times Square of American religion, with its garish lights that we can read all too well. Whether on the big billboards or in the alleys and sidestreets, we all have a place here. Priests and elders, charismatics and evangelists, healers and hustlers, Lutherans and Pentecostals, social activists and Businessmen for Jesus, millenarians and realists, Baptists, Arminians, and Enthusiasts of the Inner Light, it is all of a part; one circus, one Christ, one Church. "It is the only Church he got," and therefore the only Church we can have. As with Times Square, it is hard to separate the pornography from the playfulness, the truth from the deadly lies, the saved from the damned. And, as with Times Square, one wonders whether it might not be a "signal of transcendence." But no, with respect to the Church we know that that is the case. The lights of the Christian Church signal not simply our transcendent hope, but they are themselves a signal *from* transcendence in the form of a promise; and the promise is that, if we are faithful, if we have love enough, we will one day see that in reality these lights are part of "the city that has no need of sun or moon to shine upon it, for the glory of God is its light, and its lamp is the Lamb" (Rev. 21).

2.
Ministering by Hope Beyond Apology

Within the vast expanse of human experience, our placement is in the ministry of the Church in North America approaching the third millennium of Christian history. As I have suggested, this may not be the happiest of placements, but it is ours. Our thinking about Church and ministry should not begin "from above," so to speak, from revealed or authoritative truths, but "from below." This does not mean that we deny divine revelation. To the contrary, our understanding of Church and ministry, indeed our understanding of all reality, is based upon the truth of God revealed in Jesus Christ. But that truth is only meaningful (in the sense of not being non-sense) as it is related to the particularities of historical existence. There are lovers of paradox who disagree, but I do not think revealed truth can ever mean that A is non-A. It cannot mean that, because such a statement has no meaning. We are not standing in judgment upon revelation when we reject nonsensical interpretations of it; we are rather trusting that the revelation, as it claims, has integrity. If what purports to be revealed truth does not appear to be meaning-ful, the faithful response is not to submit oneself to patent nonsense but to search for fuller meaning. How we go about deciding what is "meaningful" must of course be open to meanings that far transcend the ordinary and often restrictive descriptions of "fact" in the modern world. A transcendent definition of reality, however, must always be related to the immanent and mundane which it presumes to define.

A PASSION FOR THE MUNDANE

I confess to a passion for the mundane. Only half-jokingly, we sometimes referred to St John the Evangelist, in Brooklyn, as "St. John the Mundane," in order to distinguish it from St. John the Divine up on Morningside Heights. Whatever scriptures and theology say about Church and ministry cannot define reality in a way that denies our experience of Church and ministry. Theology offers fuller definitions *beyond* existing fact, but it cannot legitimately offer definitions *contrary to* existing fact. The gospel of the Kingdom does not describe an alternative reality; it rather bestows meaning and dignity upon this reality that often seems so meaningless and unworthy.

Consider the images of the Church employed by Vatican II: the building raised up by Christ, the house of God, the temple and tabernacle of God, his people, his flock, his vine, his field, his city, the pillar of truth, and finally, the Bride of Christ, his Mystical Body. Obviously, such images do not consistently fit our experience of the Church. Yet we believe they are true descriptions of the Church we experience. We do not need to, we dare not, deny what is experienced in order to believe in the truth of these images. Indeed, to do so is a kind of perverse fideism, a submission to authoritative non-sense, an acceptance "on faith" of that which is devoid of meaning. Rather, these biblical images of the Church illuminate the reality of what we presently experience as Church. Here again, it is crucial to keep in mind that the real and the existent are not the same, that actuality does not exhaust reality. The ultimate reality that is to be established in the End Time, and that has already been revealed ahead of time in our Lord Jesus Christ, is the ultimate reality of this actualized and experienced Church. It is not simply that some day we will be able truly to say glorious things about the Church. We say them and say them truly *now*. Of course, we say these things in hope, which is simply faith's posture toward the future. If *then*, in the promised End Time, the things we say about the Church are manifested as true, then that means we are vindicated in saying such things *now*. The truth about anything is evident at the end of that thing—whether the "thing" in question be the meaning of a person's life, an era of history, or an experiment in a laboratory. What is true at the end is the truth along the way; the conclusion of the process makes evident the meaning of the process.

So the theologian says the Church is the People of God and the Mystical Body of Christ. The social scientist says it is the institutionalization of the historical forces and people claiming to be Christians. They are both right and each needs the other. Without the second, the theologian's statement is a meaningless abstraction. Without the first, the social scientist's statement is but an extremely limited definition of the reality it presumes to describe. One is not being more realistic or "hard-nosed" by settling for the social scientist's statement; one is simply confusing actuality with reality. Nor is one being more spiritual or faithful by taking the theologian's statement in isolation; one is simply ignoring the reality of which the statement is the fuller truth, and thereby depriving the statement of meaning.

All this may seem terribly theoretical, but it is closely related to how we understand our ministries. We have several languages about church and ministry, and we've gotten them terribly mixed up. What we learned in seminary, what we read in scripture, what we mostly preach on Sundays, seem dreadfully unrelated to what we experience in fact. Or, if they are related, they are related in a contradiction that we would sometimes just as soon not think about. The one language seems highly "theoretical" and "idealistic," the other "realistic" and down to earth. The one language is rather edifying, if imbibed during periods of what might be called the spiritual suspension of disbelief. The language of social and historical description tends to be somewhat discouraging. At least it does not present the Church as a fitting object of our unqualified devotion.

Freedom and responsibility—which is the exercise of freedom—are beyond crippling guilt. To put it in Reformation terms, we are justified by grace *in this situation;* we do not need to justify this situation. As Paul Tillich the preacher expressed it, we need to "accept our acceptance." And, accepting our acceptance, we are then freed to get on with the business at hand.

Many Christian ministries, however, have, by habit of thought and perhaps by vested interest, a crippling preoccupation with guilt. This preoccupation operates in a complicated way at the levels of theology, ethics, and piety. Especially among those who are the heirs of the Reformation, it is not uncommon that we do not feel good unless we feel bad. The alternative is not the banal gospel of "I'm OK, you're OK." One pastor friend gets closer to the heart of the matter when he proposes the formula, "I'm not OK, and you're not OK, and that's OK." But of course there is nothing flippant or facile about the liberating power of the new life of freedom that forgiveness makes possible. It is awesomely powerful both in its sense of freedom *from* and of freedom *for*—in this case, freedom for ministry.

It is liberating to know that we do not need to present an *apologia* for the Christian Church. We do not need to pretend that "real Christianity" hasn't been tried yet. We are not guilty of the gap between the Kingdom of God and the empirical Church. Indeed, it would be the height of presumption on our part to claim that we are responsible for, and therefore guilty of, that gap. We are not that important; our transgressions are not that consequential. This is not to deny that individually and corporately we have sins to confess, that we have in numerous ways resisted the coming of God's rule, beginning with his rule in our own lives. But the irony is that one of the ways the Church has resisted the coming of the rule of God is through its own preoccupation with guilt. Guilt is deadly entanglement with the past; forgiveness is the gracious opening to a genuinely new future.

We do not have to justify the Church. The magnitude of what is wrong with it does not mean, as some urge, that we should start saying what's right with the Church. That way lies self-righteousness, smugness, and fact-denying illusion. The ministry is not the Church's office of public relations, or it should not be. Our job is not to project a more positive "image" of the Church, as that term is used in the communications media. Our task is to take seriously the biblical images or models of the Church that illuminate the Church's full mission as the sign of humanity's future. As we take this biblical understanding of the Church seriously, there is ever so much in the empirical Church of which we must be relentlessly critical.

Whatever else we may be guilty of, we are not guilty of the fact that the Church is not the Kingdom of God. Far from our being embarrassed by the limitations of the existent Church, it is among our chief responsibilities to underscore the truth that the Church is not to be confused with the Kingdom of God. The Christian community points toward that Kingdom. In some important respects it anticipates that Kingdom. But the Church is as far in time from the Kingdom as is the whole creation of which the Kingdom is the universal future. The disappointment, discontent, and frustration that the world feels over its distance from perfection is also our disappointment, discontent, and frustration. In this sense, the Church is emphatically part of the world; indeed, as Paul describes it in Romans 8, the Church is the most restlessly yearning part of the whole yearning creation. The difference is that we know the reason for the hope of perfection that is within us (1 Pet. 3). That reason is the preview or proleptic appearance of our hope vindicated in the resurrection of Jesus the Christ. Living in communion with him, we not only share but articulate and intensify the world's discontent. Our gospel is not the gospel of optimism, which is, after all, simply a different way of looking at things. It is not simply an angle of vision but a new datum that we proclaim to the world. That datum, which is the message and life of Jesus, is the reason for the hope that is within us and, if only they knew it, the foundation and rationale of hope within all people. And so, because we do not pretend that the Church is the Kingdom of God, we offer no excuses for its not being the Kingdom of God. There will be no satisfactory

Church, no Church that can be embraced without ambiguity, until the world of which the Church is part is satisfactorily ordered in the consummation of God's rule. In short, we cannot get it all together until God has gotten it all together in the establishment of the Messianic Age.

AT THE EDGE OF THE THIRD MILLENNIUM

Whatever else we may be guilty of, we are not guilty of not being born into the first century. That may seem obvious, yet one suspects it is at the root of the bad conscience with which many minister. Perhaps when we were children in Sunday School or catechism class, the thought occurred to most of us how wonderful it would be to have been among the original disciples, to have walked with Jesus by the Sea of Galilee, to have heard the teachings from his own lips, and so forth. We perhaps felt cheated by being ushered into the wrong century. Many of the hymns and much of the devotional literature of our time still convey this sense of having "missed out." Sermons are preached that have about them the distinct air of "let's pretend"; they are pale imitations of the one-time television series, "You Are There." But we are not called to be disciples in the Palestine of the first century; we are called to discipleship in North America in the latter part of the twentieth century.

One does not wish to oversimplify a complex problem. There is a very real sense in which the "story" of God's People from the calling of Abraham through the apostolic era is *our* story. Especially as that story climaxes in the message and life of Jesus, we want to say to ourselves and others—to employ the title of another television show —"This is Your Life." But the biblical story does not invite us to project ourselves backwards in time. Such projection is illusory, it is fact-denying. And if we are not able to deny present fact, it results only in a vague discomfort, even a bad conscience, about being part of an inauthentic, derived, secondhand Christian experience. The biblical story is rather intended to illuminate our present and to open us to the future. That story is not about something that once was and is now gone except in pious memory. The story rather points toward what has not yet been, it points to the ultimate reality to which we are closer in time than were, for example, the first apostles. The renewal of the Church that we seek is not, finally, a renewal of "first-century Christianity" but a renewal of twentieth-century Christianity directed toward that End Time in which all the centuries find their meaning.

On the Lower East Side of Manhattan, I regularly walk past a small Hispanic storefront church. The sign outside declares in Spanish and English: "We found it! Pure life! Pure love! Pure doctrine! This is Galilee!" And that is to miss the wonder of it all, assuming that wonder there is. The occasion for thanksgiving is precisely that this is not Galilee but the Lower East Side—red-lined, drug afflicted, crowded, and oppressively shadowed by the signs of hopelessness. Grace is evident not in regression to an illusory purity but in courage to face the manifest impurities of Church and world on the Lower East Side of Manhattan.

Such misunderstandings arise not only among so-called fundamentalists but also among those who see themselves as the avant garde. A Roman Catholic sister says that in recent years her order has been entirely changed "in order to conform to the New Testament life-style." Apparently this "New Testament life-style" is a mix of de-institutionalizing of the order, communal experimentation along human potential lines, and "consciousness raising" for the liberation of the politically oppressed. We can be sure that nobody from the first century would have the foggiest understanding of such an amalgam of Freud, Marx, Erik Erikson, Paulo Freire, and this sister's idea of social democracy. Nor is there any reason why our first-century visitor should understand this phenomenon. It is not a New Testament life-style but one expression of twentieth-century Christian life-style in continuity with, but hardly in imitation of, the New Testament era. In fact, the apostles Paul, Peter, and James—if it had occurred to them that there might be a Church nineteen centuries after their time—would have been puzzled, even appalled, by the thought that we would be imitating the Church of that era. Imitating Christ, yes. Paul went so far as to suggest imitating him as he imitated Christ. But that we should imitate the church in Corinth, for example, is a very unappealing thought indeed.

While talk about a "New Testament life-style" can be radical, it can also eviscerate the deeper radicality of both our dilemma and our hope. That is, the false consciousness by which we project ourselves into the role of original members of the disciple band also distorts our understanding of Jesus the Lord. Because we are in fact products of the modern world, such false consciousness requires that we fashion for ourselves a Jesus with whom we can sympathetically identify. Thus Jesus becomes the Guerilla Fighter, or the Greatest Jock of Them All, or the Master Psychologist, or the Premier Organizer, or Broadway's superstar of the counterculture. A lord whom we fashion in our own image is no lord at all.

MINISTRY THAT IS APOSTOLIC

This touches on a dimension of pastoral ministry that is beset by powerful temptations. With the best of intentions we can easily compromise the lordship of the Christ. In our teaching and preaching we of course want people to sense a relationship to Jesus that is intimate, immediate, accessible, and pertinent to everyday life. Thus we tend to conform Jesus to what is already known and accessible. The result is that we tend to live not by reliance upon the promise of the gospel but by a myth of Jesus that is finally of our own construction. For example, parents try to explain to very little children who Jesus is. The child's mind, shaped by Bible stories and the sometimes winsome, usually saccharine art that accompanies such stories, envisions a Jesus who is a father figure or perhaps a big brother figure, maybe even an adult playmate and protector. The construction, like a character in a fictional story, may play a powerful role in the child's life, no less powerful for being fictional. Other children, or maybe even the same child, may experience a similar relationship with an imagined rabbit or with like companions that occupy a child's fantasies. This is not the place to explore the mysteries of a child's psychological development, and certainly we do not doubt the mysteries of God's ways of being present in Christ to that child, through all the confusions of such mythology. But in our proclamation of the Christian message we should not perpetuate into adulthood such childish patterns. That is, we should not substitute Jesus the protective playmate with Jesus the business partner, or Jesus the friendly confidant, or Jesus the whatever.

The question is commonly asked in moments of decision, "What would Jesus say if he walked into this room as a twentieth-century man?" It is homiletically attractive to speculate about answers to that question, but it is a grave disservice to the gospel. The harder task is to illuminate the misconception that is built into the question itself. Anyone who walked into the room as a twentieth-century man would not be the historical Jesus; and if Jesus were to walk into the room, it would not be as a twentieth-century man. If in our presentation of Jesus the Lord we are to move from a personality cult based on a myth to faith in the gospel promise, we must be prepared to help people understand the great cultural and historical gulf fixed between ourselves and the first century. This is contrary to our immediate pastoral instinct, which is to close that gulf, to demonstrate the immediacy and relevance of Jesus. But we should not be embarrassed by the fact that, were the first-century Jesus of Nazareth to show up among us today, we would have a very hard time communicating with him, and he with us. And if we were able to communicate, we might not like him very much at all.

The gospel does not consist in promulgating the myth of the loving and wise personality of Jesus. For many years in China people were taught to venerate Chairman Mao. Faced with decisions, cadres were instructed to ask, "What would Chairman Mao do in this situation?" And of course the Party kept the virtues and intentions of Chairman Mao always before the people and always up to date with current needs, as those needs were defined by the Party. In the lives of Christians, Jesus is not the "true" Chairman Mao, nor is the Church the equivalent of the Party, constantly refurbishing his relevance to the present moment. When in our preaching and teaching we present Jesus as that kind of Maximum Leader, we reduce the gospel to mythology, and the mythology is inevitably manipulated in the service of our purposes, and that is the very opposite of obedience to the Lord.

As scripture scholars persistently tell us, it is noteworthy that the gospel accounts are not biographies of Jesus. Unlike the heroic literature about the Maximum Leaders of the world, the New Testament does not present Jesus as a moral model on which our lives are to be fashioned. Especially is this apparent in the writings of Paul, where scarcely a reference to the personality and character of Jesus is to be found. The purpose of the New Testament, as of our ministries, is to assert the good news that in this Jesus, who remains emphatically distanced from us by two thousand years, God was fully present and acting on our behalf in victory over his enemies and ours. The victory was manifest in his being raised from the dead, in which event alone is the justification for calling him Lord. On that basis we assert his sovereignty over all things—a sovereignty that is now disputed but will finally, we believe, be vindicated in his coming again in glory.

The resurrection is the nexus between the Jesus of history and the Christ of faith. It is the good news that he is the Christ that has "carried" the Jesus of history through history, making him the contemporary of all peoples of all times. That contemporaneity is based not upon a constant updating of the person who was Jesus but upon the proclamation of God's decisive presence and action in him. To be sure, Christians of all times have envisioned Jesus through their own cultural perspectives. This we see in Christian art of the Orient, of Africa, of the Arctic, and of course of the Western European traditions. The proclamation of Jesus as the Christ means that Jesus cannot be separated from the Christ. The intimacy of communion between the believer and the believer's Lord requires concepts of similarity that make "identification" with the Lord possible. But our presentation of Jesus the Christ must always resist the "let's pretend" syndrome—let's pretend that our time is collapsed into the first century, or let's pretend that Jesus is among us as a twentieth-century man. The first "let's pretend" is a regression that denies historical responsibility for *this* moment; the second "let's pretend" reduces the Lord to a mythological figure who is put in service to our goals and ideals. Our message is never let's pretend; it is rather: Here is what is reported, here is the evidence for it, here are the reasons for acknowledging its truth, and here are the consequences for ourselves and the world of which we are a part.

It is tempting to present Jesus as a mythological figure of inspiration and moral guidance. Similarly, Jesus may be presented simply as the Great Teacher of a school of practical philosophy. In a similar way, a thoughtful person might claim Plato or John Dewey as his teacher. There is no embarrassment involved, for there is no extravagant claim about the Absolute revealed in such persons. There is of necessity, however, an embarrassment involved in our ministries and in the affirmation of all Christian believers. We declare not simply the superior wisdom or morality of Jesus but the sovereignty of Jesus as the Christ. The inescapable awkwardness of our ambassadorship on behalf of this disputed sovereign points both toward the future and toward the past. Toward the future, we must speak in hope of his claims being vindicated. Toward the past, we must speak of an event that is utterly singular and not susceptible to duplication or present proof. Therefore, the message that constitutes our whole being and life's work is vulnerable to the charge that we are proposing what might or might not happen in the future, based on what may or may not have happened in the past.

It does not relieve the awkwardness (nothing can do that short of the Kingdom come), but it places it into perspective to understand that this is the same saving awkwardness that marked the ministry from the earliest moments of the Church's life. The ministry of Jesus itself is outside the normal definitions and securities of a leadership role. That is, as Hans von Campenhausen notes, "Jesus comes on the scene neither as one demonstrably endowed with a particular charisma nor as the holder of an office within his nation."[1] Although some call him "prophet" and others address him as "rabbi," he has no rank or station or formal designation within his religious tradition. He comes before the people presenting himself and his own decision, and again and again we are told that the people are in awe of him, for he teaches "with authority." This authority *(exousia)* is either from God or it is mad pretension on Jesus' part, and on the part of those who attribute to him such extravagant authority. For the early Christian community the resurrection vindicated what they perceived—what they had hoped—Jesus would be. "In Jesus we see a freedom, a serenity, and a power of human nature which points to the future, and which before him had been unheard of. Jesus has no official status, but he has a mission; he is at the same time the one who is sent and the one who from the start and in his inmost self matches the demands of that mission."[2]

The very existence of the early Christian community, as of the Church today, is premised upon the "apostolic" witness to the resurrection. Indeed, as Paul's argumentation in 1 Corinthians 15 and elsewhere makes clear, being an apostle requires that one be an eyewitness to the Risen Lord. That apostolic witness is foundational for and, in an important sense, prior to the Church. Ministry, which is closely related to apostolicity, is not established by the possession of charisma but by an historical message about the Risen Christ. All Christian ministry is premised upon a nonrepeatable historical event that is valid for all time.

The word *apostle* derives from the Hebrew *shaliach,* which is a legal term for a representative or plenipotentiary who conducts business on behalf of another who has assigned him such powers. The apostles receive their plenipotentiary status from the Risen Christ himself ("and then he appeared to all the apostles," 1 Cor. 15). It is noteworthy that the bishops and others who were viewed as successors to the apostles did not claim to be apostles. They held "apostolic" office, but it is clear that their mission and authority rested upon a once-and-for-all relationship between the apostles and the Risen Christ. We are in the same tradition in which authentic ministry is apostolic ministry. We are related to that apostolic authority in our obedience to the New Testament canon which bears the apostolic witness. In some churches greater emphasis is placed upon an actual historical succession of ministries from the apostles. However historically dubious such tracings may be, they reflect a correct intention to anchor ministerial authority in the apostolic foundation. In seeing our placement in the apostolic tradition or *paradosis,* however, it is the message itself that constitutes our ministry. No succession of office, no charisma, no measure of spiritual effectiveness can substitute for that gospel. This is put very dramatically by Paul. He will take second place to no one in arguing for his qualifications as an apostle, but even his own authority is subject to the gospel: "Even if we, or an angel from heaven, should preach to you a gospel contrary to that which we preached to you, let him be accursed" (Gal. 1).

This brief excursus on apostolicity underscores the necessary awkwardness of our ministry. We cannot "authenticate" the lordship of Jesus by demonstrating his authority or utility as a contemporary leader. He is not a mythological figure for all seasons but most stubbornly Jesus of Nazareth of the first century. Nor do we "believe ourselves backwards" to that century, but we proclaim—by the grace of God, believingly and believably—in this moment the gospel promise of the abiding presence and power of Jesus the Christ. Unlike the storefront on the Lower East Side, the excitement and the awkwardness is precisely that this is *not* Galilee.

The distinction between the Jesus of history and the Christ of faith is necessary, and it is also necessarily elusive. It will not be clarified satisfactorily until he comes again in glory. Enough for now that that Jesus was revealed and will be revealed as the Christ. The Christ who is present to us now, according to his promise, is not a disembodied abstraction or principle that leaves the historical Jesus behind in the first century. We do not retrieve him from the past but rather anticipate him from the future. Jesus the Christ is one, and that unity prefigures the ultimate unity of God and his creation which will be manifest in the coming of the Rule of God. Christian ministry is faithful witness to that hope, founded upon faithful remembrance of the apostolic witness to the reason for that hope.

NO "FALL" OF THE CHURCH

It is, then, crucially important to our understanding of Church and ministry to recognize the singularity, the uniqueness, of historical events. We say that that very specific and problematic Jesus of first-century Palestine was revealed to be the Son of God, and in the power of the Spirit has been "taken up" into perfect unity with God who is the Power of the Future. As we anticipate that future in faith and hope, we have communion with him in whom the future of the first century, of the twentieth century, and, it may be, of the fortieth century has already been revealed. But, again, our calling is not to be the faithful Church of the first century but the faithful church of the twentieth century, in obedience to him in whom every century and every individual life finds its ultimate meaning.

Alfred Loisy, the nineteenth-century historian, was right in saying that Jesus came proclaiming the Kingdom of God but what appeared was the Church. The disappointment was, and continues to be, severe. But the great irony is that today we alleviate our disappointment with the contemporary Church by pointing back to the New Testament Church—which was the great disappointment to begin with! Our restless discontent should not be over the distance between ourselves and the first-century Church but over the distance between ourselves and the Kingdom of God, to which the Church, then and now, is the witness. To say that this is a great irony "today" does not imply that the temptation to revert to an earlier time in search of legitimacy is unique to our time. Already by the fourth century, Christian thinkers were pointing back to the apostolic era as representing the "pure" or "true" Church by which, in a vicarious or derivative way, the then-contemporary Church was made to seem more tolerable and authoritative.[3] The Church must explain its origins by reference to the apostolic era, and in the scriptures of that period it discovers what is normative for its faith and life. But the Church's existence today is not vindicated by reference to the first century. The Church is a community of hope, and hope can, by definition, only be vindicated by the future.

We should not, then, feel bad about not being the New Testament Church. That is not our possibility and therefore not our responsibility. Against the conventional wisdom, Church renewal in our time does not mean skipping back over the centuries to a different and presumably better time. So often we are told that the primitive Church was spontaneous in its passion, pure in its doctrine, courageous in its witness, world transforming in its influence. Then came the great "fall of the Church" as the Spirit was institutionalized and finally, under Constantine, settled down as the established religion of the empire. (Among my favorite New York subway graffiti is one at the 116th Street station. In big bold letters covering almost a whole wall, it proclaims: "CONSTANTINE LOVES CHRISTIANITY.") This stereotype of Christian history has demonstrated a remarkably perduring power, but it is filled with problems. The primitive Church may or may not have been all it is cracked up to have been. But the chief problem is with a view of history that inescapably relegates the subsequent history of the Church to a questionable status of "inauthenticity."

There is no doubt a great deal in the pre-Constantinian era that is exemplary, as there is in every period of the Church's life. From the past come many examples of courage, vision, imagination, and beauty. By reference to those examples we can criticize the Church today and stir it to renewal. But this process of renewal is not helped by idealizing or by demonizing any one part of the past. We can remember, and through remembrance be renewed, by the middle ages, the so-called dark ages, so often and so brightly lit by intensity of devotional life and hope in the face of death. We can remember, and through remembrance be renewed, by the extravagant labor of a tenth-century Church that built cathedrals of unparalleled beauty in order that, at the millennium, there might be on earth some places worthy of receiving the coming King. We remember St. Thomas and Abelard and the great doctors of the Church; the Catholic missionary enterprise of the fifteenth and sixteenth centuries, the Protestant of the nineteenth; the reformers of the sixteenth, both Protestant and Catholic, who did their work too well, designing patterns of church life in which we are still entangled long after the reasons for the separate designs have been overcome. And yes, we even remember people like Ambrose and Constantine and wonder whether our ways of relating Christian hope to public order give us any reason to be so disdainful of theirs. All this remembering and much more is to the end that, through remembrance, we may be renewed to be the Church in this time and place.

It is to this community that the Spirit is promised. The Spirit does not beckon us back to some prior time of his mighty works. He is mightily working now. The Spirit graciously lures us from guilt to freedom; he convinces us that this Church and this ministry, in all their inauthenticity, are authentic because, in the precise meaning of *authentikos,* they are the work of his own hand. And thus are we, the men and women of the Church's ministry, the stewards of the mysteries, freed to declare our time a new day in the two thousand years of apostolic witness. Thus are we empowered to view the

Church without illusion in all its appearances: the New Testament's virgin, Christendom's courtesan, post-Christendom's streetwalker —and to see in every appearance the Mystical Body, the Bride of Christ.

"The Spirit and the Bride say, 'Come.' And let him who hears say, 'Come.' . . . Amen. Come, Lord Jesus!"(Rev. 22).

3.
A Choice
of
Models

It is said that the decline of the Model T Ford began when rival General Motors started to offer models of different trim and color. Henry Ford stubbornly insisted that the Model T was the one best model and people could have it in any color they wanted, so long as they wanted black. Market metaphors are of limited usefulness in thinking about Church and ministry, yet they do have some application if we believe that the Church is for people. While we dare not pander to religious expectations by trying to accommodate every itch and fad (an impossible task, in any case), our thinking about Church and ministry should not be too far removed from responsive tension with the felt needs and hopes of the actual people of God. Tension requires both difference and similarity, distance and familiarity. If our notion of the Church is so different and distant from the community in which we minister, it may well result in interpersonal tensions of confusion and alienation, but it will not result in that creative tension which helps a community to become what it truly is.

But what is the Church—truly? The answer to that question will inform and shape the understanding of our ministry, remembering always that the ministry is not ours but the ministry of Christ and his Church. Almost twenty years ago, Paul Minear published *Images of the Church in the New Testament,* in which he analyzed nearly a hundred models and analogies of the Church that are used in the Bible.[1] We have already mentioned some of the images for the Church employed by Vatican Council II. More recently, Protestant theologian Robert McAfee Brown has explored different images of the Church, especially as they emerged from the ecumenical exchanges and social action movements of the 1960s.[2] On the Roman Catholic side, Father Avery Dulles's *Models of the Church*[3] offers a solid and comprehensive treatment of the options that command the attention of everyone who is seriously trying to think through the meaning of Church and ministry.

While the question is not new, the exploration of models is in fact always new. It is not an academic exercise but a day-by-day struggle to make sense of who we are and what we are doing. Models are crucial to this struggle because, in a very down-to-earth manner, we all live from models. That is, none of us lives a life of raw facts. We live in a world of interpreted fact, and models are controlling concepts in that interpretation. This is true of life considered in its most comprehensive reaches, and it is true of the particularities of our own everyday existence. Without such controlling concepts, life would be, as the cynic asserted, just one damned thing after another. The whole of the Christian enterprise can be seen as a defiance of that judgment. The Christian gospel is an interpretation of reality that bestows a saving and hopeful order upon our experience. Needless to say, we Christians believe the gospel is not just a human construct devised to "put things together" in order to hold chaos at bay. We believe the gospel is the revelation of the way things really are; that this interpretation of reality is not merely a human imposition but a divine disclosure. Powerful models that deal with the really significant engagements of our lives are, if they are true, always marked by this disclosive force.

In times when we are troubled and confused about what is happening in our lives, we may discuss our problems with a friend. In most cases the friend has no information about the problem that we did not already possess, but he may offer a new way of looking at it, a different model, if you will, by which the previously fragmented pieces begin to fit together. "Ah," we say, "I never looked at it that way before!" The sociologist of knowledge, Alfred Schutz, called these "Ah, ha!" experiences, and such experiences accompany most of the "breakthroughs" in our lives. Thus, far from being an academic exercise, reflection on models and controlling concepts has the most practical importance.

In our experience in marriage counseling, for example, we frequently discover that problems arise from a muddle of models. We find people trying to live out a marriage for which they have no model, and the models they do have are in ludicrous contradiction to what they are trying to be and do. In some instances a couple may be trying to pattern their life together along the lines of some other marriage which is for them a "model" of what married life should be. But by model here we mean something more conceptual, that may or may not be related to another particular marriage. It is the model, for example, of the popular media's suburban housewife who eagerly awaits the breadwinner's return to surprise him with his now wondrously clean shirt collars or a hamburger substitute that tastes as good as the real thing. The sexual and other stereotypes in this model have received blistering criticism in recent years and need no further comment here. My point is that the guilt and discontent felt by many who are trying to live out this model can only be resolved by addressing the model itself.

A skilled counselor offers people a choice of models. More precisely, he does not offer models so much as he illuminates possibilities that were there all along. Marriage may have a number of controlling concepts or metaphors: partnership in work, companionship on a life-long pilgrimage, love affair, building a household bridge across generations, contracting for mutually advantageous cooperation, or sacramental reenactment of Christ's union with his Church. Most marriages are, in fact, a mix of these and other models. Often marriage is a rich and complex process of shifting models, especially as people move through life phases of young adulthood, the middle years, and old age. Perhaps just as often and just as richly, marriage is a living out of one model that is constantly renewed in its disclosive and sustaining power, especially when that model is the mystical union that is described in the New Testament and supported by faithful participation in the Christian community.

TRADE-OFFS AND TENSIONS

As with marriage, so with other significant life engagements, and most certainly so with Christian ministry. When it comes to models of ministry, there is no shortage of choices. As noted in earlier chapters, American religion is marked by an amazing, some think maddening, variety. Among the 300,000 and more local churches in North America, almost anything in the line of ministry can be found. It would be arbitrary and not helpful at all to pick out one or more models and declare them the legitimate and authentic forms of ministry. Such variety can be splendid and liberating, and it can be terribly confusing. The ministry, like other occupations today, is much preoccupied with the discussion of "role models," "role expectations," "role conflicts," and such. The minister is expected to be preacher, leader of worship, counselor, teacher, scholar, helper of the needy, social critic, administrator, revivalist, fund raiser, and a host of other sometimes impossible things. Pastors harassed by these conflicting expectations and claims upon time and ability are tempted to embark upon an open-ended game of trade-offs. Today I'll be a little of this and a little of that; tomorrow I'll be a little of the other thing and something else. For the conscientious who are determined to keep the game going, it is a certain formula for confusion and collapse.

The inescapable fact is that a degree of such confusion is inescapable. It is little wonder that some ministers leave congregations in order to move on to some more "specialized" work where the expectations are neater and more clean-cut. But for those committed to communal ministry, the alternatives are not limited to moving "role pieces" around on the game board of the daily schedule. The better course is to ask what the game is about, or, in this case, to ask about the meaning of the community of which one's ministry is part. That is why the question about models of the Church is prior to the question about models of ministry.

As Dulles rightly observes, the very terms we use for ministry have built-in assumptions, both historical and operative, about the way the Church is conceived: "The various terms—such as minister, pastor, priest, and presbyter—are themselves biased toward one model or another." *Minister,* for example, connotes one who officiates at services of word and sacrament, or, sometimes, one who fulfills a diaconal role in meeting human needs. *Clergyman* has about it the idea of a clerical caste, set off by ordination in distinction from the laity. *Pastor* suggests the shepherding and governing of a parish. *Priest,* which derives from *presbyter* but is more commonly associated with the Latin *sacerdos,* underscores the mediating and cultic dimensions of ministry.

Today there is a great flexibility in the terminology used for ministry and in the manner in which ministers are addressed. *Pastor* is used by almost all Lutherans and by a growing number of Protestants, displacing the commonplace *Mister* and competing with the pretentious *Doctor. Father* is used by a few Lutherans, many "high" Anglicans, and most Roman Catholics, except where the last want to be called by their Christian names, thus countering what some view as the previously forbidding isolation of the Catholic priesthood. The terminology used for ministry may seem to be a subject more appropriate to etiquette than to theology, but "mere etiquette" is not merely etiquette. Reflected in such differences are quite different understandings of Church and ministry.

THE CHURCH'S BUSINESS AND OURS

Considerations of models of ministry touch on the ways we perceive ourselves and are perceived. And that of course assumes a good deal of self-consciousness in our doing of ministry. It seems possible that some people operate in a simpler and more straightforward manner. They are not "people of the third eye," aware of themselves being aware of themselves. We may sometimes envy what seems to be their innocence and guilelessness as they go about doing what seems to them perfectly self-evident. But others of us, perhaps most of us, are keenly aware of ourselves, ever puzzling about who we are and who we think we are and what might be the connection between the two. Of course we are cautioned against taking ourselves too seriously. It is said that we should be like the angels who can soar so high because they take themselves so lightly. There is wisdom as well as wit in that advice, but perhaps we have no choice but to take ourselves very seriously. And that not chiefly for psychological reasons but for reasons of vocation. Taking ourselves and our ministries seriously need not be a heavy and anxiety-laden business. There can be delight, whimsy, and surprise in our thinking about ourselves in ministry. "What on earth am I doing now?" "What on earth do I think I'm doing?" In responding to these questions of self-consciousness, we are thrown back into reflection not only upon ourselves but upon our understanding of the Church.

Perhaps every pastor has had the experience when visiting a parishioner that a child answers the door and excitedly announces to the parent that "God is here." The adults share a chuckle and observe that soon enough, maybe too soon, the child will realize the pastor isn't God. Yet the connection between the representative and the One represented is very strong, as is the connection between the Church and the ministry of the Church. All our talk about lay ministries and the ethos of democratization notwithstanding, the minister inescapably represents the Church. We are rightly disturbed when people speak of a local church as "Pastor Jones's church." Pastor Jones is first to protest that it is *Christ*'s church; and the more he insists on the point, the more people admire his modesty and give that as yet another reason for being a member of Pastor Jones's church. Similarly, the more a pastor affirms and celebrates the importance of lay ministries, the more is his own status and influence likely to increase. On the other hand, the pastor who "pulls rank" by citing his prerogatives and privileges is likely to find his position the more sharply challenged. The dynamics in all this are very curious. There is an unspoken understanding that the minister does in a very powerful way represent and embody the community's ministry. However, to say it or attempt to spell it out too clearly violates the democratic ethos of our culture and breaks the charm, as it were, of mutual trust between pastor and people.

As we go about our everyday tasks, our actions both shape and reflect our understanding of the models of the community's ministry. A lovely fourteen-year-old girl dies shortly after a tonsillectomy because of the criminal carelessness of an anesthetist. One rushes to the home to join relatives and neighbors in weeping and in raging at the wrongness of it all, and in offering up this outrage to him who judges justly and in mercy. One's being there is in a powerful sense the "presence" of the Church, and of Christ. Why is it so urgently, so pathetically, important that the pastor be there? Because he is the palpable sign of the supportive community and the community's Lord. Of course Christ has preceded the pastor. Of course Christ's presence is abidingly immediate to each believer. Of course, of course. But in such times of crisis these commonplaces are frighteningly distant and abstract. It is the personal character of The Presence in the person of the pastor that is believable and consoling. Is this superstition? Only the archetypal nineteenth-century German systematician would say so. It is human, part of that humanity subsumed by our Lord in his becoming flesh. In this ministerial task one signifies the Church, and the model of the Church signified is that of fellowsufferer, healer, consoler.

Similarly, it is by action that we articulate, for example, the model of the Church as advocate. Frequently we hear people ask why the Church doesn't speak up on this issue or that, just as we hear others complain that the Church speaks up altogether too much. Over the years, I have had the occasion to be very public in advocating courses of action on everything from community control of schools, to desegregating labor unions, to peace in Indochina, to alleviating world hunger, to protecting and helping pregnant teenagers. Hundreds of times people have said, "Thank God, the Church is finally speaking up on this." Many, many more times it has been, "What right do you have to speak for the Church on this?" To the latter I respond that I do not presume to speak *for* the Church but simply as one voice *within* and *from* the Church. But I know quite well that both the critics and the admirers have a point, that the ministry is of the Church, and, for better or for worse, with greater or lesser influence, that voice is perceived as representative. In order to justify such presumption, one reaches for the model of the Church as advocate—not a monolithic or univocal advocate, of course, but a community of advocacies regarding rights and wrongs only partially understood.

The model of advocate, especially in the inner-city ministry, engages one regularly and intensively in what can only be called political action. Political action not just on the public issues mentioned above but more commonly in exercising political influence on behalf of people in trouble. Many days are spent in courts or dealing with corrections officials on behalf of people, most usually young people, arrested or imprisoned. Here the relevant model of the Church, of which such ministry is part, is worthy of the most Constantinian notion of Christendom. The Church is quite frankly a power among the principalities and powers. Not a major power, perhaps, but major enough with respect to a particular slice of the city and a particular slice of the power structures to be of effective aid to people who, quite rightly, look to it for aid. Not only in courts and prisons but in problems related to schools, welfare, employment, and police practices, the inner-city church is in many ways a counterpart to the political clubhouses of the older city machines. One must have a model of the Church that accommodates this necessary function. For a period in the 1960s, during the brief ideological reign of "secular Christianity," some clergy in the inner city thought it the way of obedience to dismantle church structures and go into building community organizations. At St. John's we stubbornly stuck to building St. John's, in order that *St. John's* might continue to be the most effective community organization in that part of Brooklyn. Not only, not even chiefly, in what others would recognize as "social ministry," but in the ministry of worship, evangelism, prayer, and the sacramental lifting up of a piece of God's wounded world, there community is being built by the empowering vision of a transcendent community around the throne of the Lamb that far surpasses the designs and programs of what is ordinarily meant by community organization.

If our ministries are genuinely ministries of the Church, then we are not individual superstars or merely members of a "helping profession." If what we are doing is not the Church's business to do, then we ought not to be doing it. If, however, what we are doing is responsive to human need in articulated relationship to the gospel of Jesus the Christ, then it is the Church's business. Rather than viewing such ministry as extracurricular or, more precisely, extra-ecclesial, we should rethink the models of the Church by which we are operating.

MODELS AND ECUMENICAL PLURALISM

In thinking about models of ministry, none of us begins with a clean slate. Nor are we walking through a supermarket of possibilities, choosing this model and rejecting that one. In our own experience and in our own heads we are already the bearers of different, and sometimes conflicting, models. Some of these models we have inherited through denominational lines. Despite the commonplace assertion that denominations don't matter very much anymore, they show a perduring power when it comes to the churches people choose, and, more than we might want to admit, they shape the way the ministry of a particular church thinks of the Church itself. While many Protestant clergy receive their seminary training under "nondenominational" or "ecumenical" auspices, most denominations require some study of their particular "polity." In the view of some, polity involves little more than the details of pension systems and paperwork, plus the mechanics and stratagems of going along to get along. But, in truth, such apparently mundane stuff assumes certain understandings of the Church.

Implicit ecclesiology is probably much more formative of how we understand our ministries than is what we explicitly profess about the Church. Traditionally there is a great difference between the ecclesiologies of Southern Baptists and Roman Catholics. The conventional wisdom is that the latter have a "high" or "developed" ecclesiology, while the former have a "low," "undeveloped," or even nonexistent ecclesiology. It is more accurate, I believe, to say the ecclesiologies are quite different. The importance of ecclesiology in a particular tradition is not measured by the space it claims in theological textbooks nor by the frequency of homiletical references to the doctrine of the Church. We must rather ask what are the operative assumptions about the nature of the Church. In having such assumptions, we are all blessed and burdened by our denominational heritage. Our goal here is to bring such assumptions to light so that they are subject to examination and decision in trying to integrate the myriad "roles" of Christian ministry.

In addition to the denominational factor, we each have a placement within general "patterns" of religious life in America. These deal with communal expectations and behavior and may or may not follow denominational boundaries.[4] On the "map" of American religion, the usual territories demarcated are: mainline, evangelical, fundamentalist, pentecostal, charismatic, ethnic, and new, often synthetic, religions. There are other familiar categories, such as "liberal" and "conservative" (the meaning of those two has been wonderfully obscured in recent years), "confessional" and "ecumenical" (perhaps more pertinent to the European scene), and "protestant" and "catholic" (the most long-standing and comprehensive). We each live somewhere on this map of behavior, belief, and tradition. Our divided selves may not always be sure just where we live, but in general we know that we live more "here" than "there." Each place is marked by the models with which it asserts and maintains its identity. Wallace Stevens is right: "We live in the description of a place and not in the place itself." But he is only partly right. Through a comparative study of models we are liberated from complete captivity to one place. We should not want to be completely liberated, however. Complete liberation is a mirage, and the person who, through abstraction from particulars, thinks of himself as being universal has in fact only established another, and usually not very interesting, particular. Witness the fate of, for example, Unitarianism. Finally, Edmund Burke was right in saying that all true universalism is grounded in loyalty to one's own little platoon. One's own little platoon and its description of reality is not a resting place but the place from which and in which we effect significant change, including change in our understanding of Church and ministry.

The affirmation, indeed the celebration, of particularity should not be seen as the enemy of ecumenism. Except for the disinterested student of religion—which is not what the ministry of the Church is about—the discussion of Christian differences cannot pretend to be without bias. Bias is not a dirty word, although, to be sure, it is too often associated with bigotry. Bias, rather, is the angle of vision which is reflectively constructed from pieces of inheritance appropriated, and from personal discovery. The ecumenical cause is advanced as our biases are engaged; always remembering that bias is not the shield against, but our contribution to, the larger discussion.

In his admirable *The Purpose of the Church and Its Ministry*, H. Richard Niebuhr describes some of the tensions that must be kept in play, not in order to escape particularity but in order to enrich our own particularity and to contribute to the particularities of others. Niebuhr speaks of "polarities in the Church's existence":

> Among these are the complementary yet antithetical characteristics of unity and plurality, of locality and universality, of protestant and catholic. The Church is one, yet also many. It is a pluralism moving toward unity and a unity diversifying and specifying itself. It is, in the inescapable New Testament figure, a body with many members none of which is the whole in miniature but in each of which the whole is symbolized. Every national church, every denomination, every local church, every temporal church order, can call itself Church by virtue of its participation in the whole; yet every one is only a member needing all the others in order to be truly itself and in order to participate in the whole. Without the members there is no body; without the body no members.[5]

Niebuhr's words underscore the necessary caution that we are not to be looking for the perfect church. There is no "model church" in the sense that we might speak of a "model husband" or a "model university." All churches are exemplary in part, none is exemplary in whole. We are not considering the model church but models of the Church. To be sure, there are some individuals and also ministers who "church hop" from place to place in search of the spot where they can finally lay their burden down. They complain about not feeling at home here or there, forgetting that homelessness is the normal sensation of a pilgrim people. Their movement from tent to tent in the wilderness obscures for them the fact that the whole people are in movement toward the Promised Land. Of course the members of one tent may be more compatible, may be setting the pace and possessed of a surer sense of direction, and that is the tent where one might want to be. But one can travel with any tent, with any denominational household, so long as it does not separate itself from the larger pilgrimage.

We are not, then, speaking about the model church but about models of the Church. If that seems too ethereal and out of touch with reality, it is because we have once again confused the "real" with the "actual" or already existent. Any church claiming to be the model church is in danger of equating itself with the Kingdom of God. Models of the Church are to be affirmed for their evocative quality, for their power to evoke from the churches their capacity to be the Church that points toward the Kingdom.

Roman Catholicism has at times claimed to be the one, true, church. Other churches, notably the Lutheran Church–Missouri Synod, have claimed to be "the one, true, visible church on earth." In some cases the presumption is amusing, while in the case of Roman Catholicism it has seemed to others both threatening and condescending. In America, the threat has been handled by the constitutional nonestablishment of religion and by the Roman Catholic Church's theological legitimation of democratic pluralism, including religious pluralism. Vatican II said this about the one, holy, catholic, and apostolic Church that we profess in the Creed: "This Church, constituted and organized in the world as a society, subsists in the Catholic Church, which is governed by the successor of Peter and by the bishops in union with that successor, although many elements of sanctification and of truth can be found outside of her visible structure." Dulles observes: "The substitution of the term 'subsists in' *(subsistit in)* for the term 'is' *(est)* in previous drafts of the Constitution on the Church is one of the most significant steps taken by Vatican II."[6]

Increasingly it is recognized that the Church is composed of the churches. When we speak of models, therefore, we do not suggest that there is one model church which others should emulate, but neither should we deny that one church may more comprehensively symbolize the Church than does another. This understanding of

Christian pluralism did not come easily. In the West, the schism resulting from the Reformation of the sixteenth century threw the several communities into fevered competition for the title of being the true Church, since all assumed there could be only one true Church. Luther, for example, specified seven distinguishing marks *(nota)* of the Church that, at least to his satisfaction, secured the title for the churches on his side of the barricades. (One such sign, according to Luther, is "persecutions.") Not to be outdone, Roman Catholic writers multiplied signs of the true Church far beyond the four signs mentioned in the Creed ("one, holy, catholic and apostolic".) In 1591, the list totaled a full one hundred such signs. Ecclesiological arithmetic having proved inconclusive, the churches took to force of arms.

After many years of bloody warfare, Providence declined to render a decision acceptable to the several parties. Instead, God granted the secular Enlightenment, the American experiment, and two and a half centuries in which we were invited to reconsider the nature of Christian unity. Some critics argue that the affirmation of pluralism constitutes a compromise of truth for the sake of interreligious harmony. Getting along together may have something to do with love, and is therefore not a goal to be ashamed of. But at a most profound level, Christians who believe that God discloses his purposes through history have come to learn that pluralism is not merely the fact but is the necessary fact of the Church's existence. The great John Courtney Murray, whose work was so largely vindicated by Vatican II, was forced to conclude: "Religious pluralism is against the will of God. But it is the human condition; it is written into the script of history."[7] Today we might want to amend that and say that it was God who did the writing. Pluralism—with the contradictions inherent in it—is the necessary check to prevent any one church or the Church collectively from confusing itself with the Kingdom of God.

Models of the Church, then, are a subject quite different from the model church. And, as Niebuhr reminds us, no model or one set of models can be given a monopoly. Models are indeed controlling concepts, but the competition for control continues until it is brought to an end by the clarity of the Kingdom come. In their lively interaction, models sometimes confuse but they also correct one another. Some models are explanatory and some are exploratory, some are primarily disclosive and others primarily evocative. Yet finally these amount to the same thing, for what is disclosed is the Church in the process of becoming what it is, and in that disclosure the reality is, in part, actualized.

4.
Authority for Ministry

As prophetic is contrasted with priestly, as traditional is contrasted with radical, as piety is contrasted with action, so institutional is contrasted with authentic. There are tensions between each of these, but a tension is not an antithesis. Tension is not aimed at the negation of one by the other but a working out of interdependence. True prophecy is in and for the priestly community, the tradition in its fullness is the font of radical witness, action that is not empowered by piety is empty and imitative, and institution is the social reality of the Church in all its authenticity and inauthenticity. The Church defined sociologically and the Church defined theologically are not two churches but two descriptions of the one Christian people.

Institution should not be equated with organization. It is accurate to say that sports is an institution in America, or that the family is a basic social institution, yet neither sports nor the family is comprehended by any organization. Much of the animus toward the institution derives from its confusion with the organization. At the same time, the institution cannot be abstracted from the organizations that are part of it. The institution of sports cannot be understood apart from the National Football League, and an understanding of the Church in this country must come to terms with the Southern Baptist Convention.

The equation of the Church as institution with the Church as organization is always a temptation. Roman Catholicism perhaps went farthest in "theologizing" a particular polity or organization. But Anglicans in their understanding of episcopal succession, Presbyterians, at least originally, in their distinctive notions of church governance, and Baptists in their insistence upon local autonomy have, along with others, sometimes tended to tie the Church as institution very closely to a particular form of organization. Although few of us would seriously claim that our organization—whether a denomination or a local church—is *the* Church, many of us act as though that were the case. We even go farther and aspire to being the Kingdom of God, as witness the ways in which organizational aggrandizement is described as "kingdom building." The organizations of the Church, we need to be reminded, are in the service of the institution that is the Church, and the Church, in turn, is to point beyond itself to the coming rule of God.

THE WORK OF CHRIST AND THE WORK OF THE CHURCH

The Jesuit Robert Bellarmine (d. 1621) defined the Church this way: "The one and true Church is the community of men brought together by the profession of the same Christian faith and conjoined in the communion of the same sacraments, under the government of the legitimate pastors and especially the one vicar of Christ on earth, the Roman pontiff." That standard definition served Roman Catholics for a very long time. It had a number of advantages: It provided a remarkable organizational cohesiveness, a stabilizing sense of continuity, and a powerful corporate identity. As Bishop Emile De Smedt argued at the start of Vatican II, that way of thinking also has major drawbacks. It encourages, he said, clericalism, juridicism, and triumphalism. Clericalism tended to make the ministries of the people of God mere appendages to the "official" ministry of the Church. Juridicism nurtured a top-down governance that squelched innovation and renewal. Triumphalism invited the hubris of making the organization a "total institution" of control, blurred the line between Church and Kingdom, and, of course, doomed ecumenism by its dominant metaphors of battle and victory. As observed earlier, Vatican II and subsequent developments have moved Roman Catholicism a long way from Bellarmine's tight and exclusive definition of the Church. In the nature of historical swings, some of the most virulent expressions of the anti-institutional mood are today found among Roman Catholics.[1]

The work of the Church and the work of Christ are not coterminous. The Church is a particular institution in history, while Christ is the Lord of history. The Church's mission is to proclaim and manifest his lordship. Augustine wrote, "Many whom God has the Church does not have; and many whom the Church has God does not have." It is undoubtedly true, but it is the kind of statement that some Protestants tend to like too much. It lends itself to an easy misreading in which the Church is not only relativized, which is necessary, but is made almost incidental to God's purposes, which is disastrous for those whose ministries are inescapably ministries of the Church.

Nonetheless, it is important to emphasize that the work of Christ is not limited to the work of the Church. The finite can contain the infinite, but it cannot exhaust the infinite. The aspect by which the Christianly finite contains Christ the infinite is sometimes called "the catholic substance"; the protest against the notion that the finite exhausts the infinite is then called "the protestant principle." But principle and substance are hardly mutually exclusive. As Richard Niebuhr observes, "Protest has no meaning apart from what is protested against. The Church cannot be protestant without being catholic."[2] Protest and substance, the notions of incarnation and universality, are mutually interdependent in a relationship of tension. And, of course, today the protestant principle is by no means advanced only by Protestants, nor is catholic substance the peculiar emphasis of Roman Catholics or Eastern Orthodox. We are more aware of this fact since Vatican II, but in truth the protestant principle/catholic substance distinction has never been a clear line between Roman Catholics and others in the Western church. Roman Catholics have had their share of protestors, although, to be sure, they are always tolerated short of breaking communion with the bishop of Rome. And Protestants, especially Lutherans and Anglicans, have historically insisted that their movements are within and for the historic and universal substance of the whole Church. Baptists too, who might be considered the more "radical protestants," have traditionally asserted their continuity through the ages back to the apostolic community.

This historical consciousness of the real, *empirical* Church is crucial to our understanding of the limits and possibilities when it comes to the model of the Church as institution. We are reminded of the limits by contrasting the work of the Church, a particular and identifiable community, with the work of Christ who is the empowering rationale, or *Logos,* of all reality. We are reminded of the possibilities—and the breathtaking responsibilities—in view of Christ's extravagant promises to this community and his command that the community be the articulator in the world of his purposes for the world. That articulation is, quite simply, the gospel which we are to carry to the ends of the earth under the authority of the One who promised to be with us to the end of the age.

THE CHURCH OUTSIDE THE CHURCH?

The keen awareness that God's purposes are greater than the institution of the Church can, however, lead to some very confusing ecclesiology. One theologian, for example, takes his cue from Hebrews 13 ("Therefore let us go forth to him outside the camp, bearing abuse for him") and suggests that "the camp" is the Church. "The Christian does indeed go inside the church . . . but what he learns 'inside' is that God is 'outside' in the midst of the brutality and brokenness of life."[3] The problem with this otherwise admirable way of thinking is in the next step, which suggests that real Christians, and therefore the "true Church," are to be found outside the institution that is the Church. The proposition that the Church is to be discovered outside the Church has a certain dramatic and homiletical appeal, but it is likely to be puzzling to most people and, if acted upon seriously, leads to an abandonment of the community in which our ministries receive their meaning. This was in large part the confusion at the heart of much talk about "secular Christianity" and "religionless Christianity" only a few years ago.

The churchly can indeed degenerate into the churchy, true religion into religiosity, piety into pietism, and action into activism; but to abandon the first of any of these polarities is too high a price to pay for avoiding their distortion. Devotion to the institution cannot become institutional*ism* so long as we remember the limits of the institution. Institutionalism arises from the equation of the institution with the Absolute. The only Absolute to which we can be absolutely devoted is God and the coming of his rule—that is, the Kingdom of God. Anything else is idolatry. Yet we devote ourselves wholeheartedly, although always critically, to the anticipation of that Kingdom in the Church. The choice is not between the idolatry of institutionalism or un-Churched Christianity (even if the latter were possible and not the de-historicized abstraction that it in fact is). One reason that makes that false choice seem attractive is that conscientious people, abhorring the danger of idolatry, refuse to commit themselves to anything other than the Absolute. But if we are not able to commit ourselves to the Absolute that is in the process of becoming, we may well be incapable of recognizing the Absolute in its consummation. Profound commitment in marriage, in friendship, in creative work, is not a compromise of our pledge to "seek first the Kingdom of God." Not, that is, if it is precisely the preliminary, or proleptic, presence of the Kingdom in these enterprises that we commit ourselves to. It is in this faithful anticipation of the Kingdom that commitment to a marriage partner, for instance, can be most surely "for the Kingdom's sake." And so it is in our devotion to the institution that is the Church.

The model of Church as institution contains another aspect that is troubling for many Christians. The discomfort is vaguely connected with the ancient maxim, *extra ecclesiam nulla salus* ("Outside the Church there is no salvation"). Since it is obvious that the great majority of humankind—in the past, present, and likely in the future—is outside the empirical Church, it would seem that the *extra ecclesiam* formula means that most people are not saved. That unhappy prospect (and one wonders about the heart of anyone who is not saddened by it) can evoke a number of responses. One can multiply evangelistic efforts in order to bring everyone, or at least many more, into the fold. One can simply deny the proposition, in the belief that a loving God is not capable of such a "monstrous" exclusion. Or one can redefine "Church" in a way that stretches the boundaries far beyond the institution that is the historically identifiable Christian community.

The first response has probably always been a motivating part of Christian evangelism, even among Protestants who have little use for the *extra ecclesiam* formula. The second response, denying the truth of the formula altogether, is not made lightly by those who have a decent respect for history, remembering that the formula originated with Origen and St. Cyprian and has been more or less consistently reaffirmed in the mainstream of the community. The third response, redefining what is meant by "Church," is the most popular.

Roman Catholic theology traditionally has allowed that saving grace is not limited to the Church, although in the Church alone such grace is tangible in the elements of scripture, teaching authority, sacraments, and the life of sanctification. Thus the apparent contradiction between the universal salvific will of God and the *extra ecclesiam* formula was softened in part by an acknowledgment that those outside the Church could be saved by "baptism of desire." More recently, such theology has gone farther toward turning *extra ecclesiam* into a complete tautology. In short, all who are saved are, by definition, not *extra ecclesiam,* since the *ecclesiam* is composed of all who are saved. A corollary of this approach is to declare that all who act upon the grace of God are in fact Christians, albeit in many cases they are "anonymous Christians." One can understand and sympathize with the purpose behind such formulations, but they do tend to play havoc with what is meant by the term "Church." Some have suggested, perhaps unkindly, that talk about "anonymous Christians" is really an evasion of the problems inherent in Christianity's being in such a minority position in the world. The concept of anonymous Christianity is, they say, a kind of evangelization by redefinition. It is much easier to redefine the world than to convert the world.

Extra ecclesiam nulla salus is, on its face, a hard saying that has often been applied harshly. The understandable desire to soften its import is misdirected, however, if it ends up by employing tautology that empties the concept of Church of any specific or historical reference. It is important to underscore the preliminary and limited nature of the Church. We are not asked to devote ourselves simply to a grand idea, but to a very particular community, to a historical institution that, we believe, anticipates even now the future of the whole world, indeed of all reality. With respect to the existent institution called the Church, it is surely appropriate and necessary to say that there is salvation outside the Church. One must at the same time emphasize, however, that there is no salvation outside Christ. To say there is salvation outside Christ would, of course, implicitly deny the cosmic and universal nature of the victory won in his cross and resurrection. In the End Time, when all things are consummated in him and all creation acknowledges him as Lord, then all the saved will be in the company called "Church."

SECULAR CHRISTIANITY AND THE GRAND INQUISITOR

There are few questions as important to the young pastor as this relationship between Christian essence and Christian institution, between gospel and Church. The question can hardly be avoided. Just as the adolescent is shocked by the gap between what parents and other authority figures say and what they do, so any normally thoughtful person is forced to come to terms with the difference between the Christianity he is taught and the church that is supposed to exemplify that teaching. Recognizing the difference—even the contradiction—one can respond in the profound manner associated with some forms of Christian existentialism. In that way of thinking, "true Christianity" and historical Christianity are viewed almost as enemies; one must choose one or the other. The same theme occurs, at a more superficial level, many times in popular culture. We all know people who claim they are too serious about Christianity to belong to the Church. The grubby and compromised Church is unworthy of their high Christian commitment.

The very opposite of this approach is represented by the Legend of the Grand Inquisitor in Dostoevsky's *The Brothers Karamazov*.

Here, it will be remembered, the Grand Inquisitor equates Christianity with the institutional Church absolutely. When Jesus appears in the Spanish town square, the Grand Inquisitor has him put in jail and spends all night explaining to the silent Jesus why he has no right to come back and interfere with the Church's operation. After this eloquent defense of the Church's mandate and authority, the Cardinal Inquisitor declares to Jesus, "Go, and come no more. Come not at all—never, never!"

The awesome brilliance of the Legend of the Grand Inquisitor is in its recognition that Christ and Church, movement and institution, cannot be neatly meshed. It resolves the tension on the side of Church as institution, against the Christ. In tragic truth, the Grand Inquisitor is just more explicit and self-conscious in his handling of the inescapable dilemma than are many clergy who have in fact "resolved" the dilemma in a similar way. It is tempting to say that the Grand Inquisitor represents one "extreme" and the idea of unchurched Christianity represents the other. The solution, therefore, is to find the middle of the road between extremes. But, as someone has remarked, the middle of the road is where we find dead skunks and a yellow line that goes on and on. A middle-of-the-road ministry is not the answer.

Both alternatives, I believe, must be rejected in favor of a third. Secular or churchless Christianity must be rejected because in fact there is no Christianity apart from the historical community that bears its truth, however inadequately. And it must be rejected because the ministry is inevitably preoccupied with the building and sustaining of the Church. The minister who goes through life working for the Church, while all the time claiming to be devoted to some abstract Christianity divorced from the institution that embodies the abstraction, will never really be able to believe in what he or she is doing.

At the same time, the Grand Inquisitor's "resolution" must be rejected because, without any point of reference beyond the institution itself, it destroys the critical perspective by which the institution must always be kept under judgment. Not to put too fine a point on it, it results in idolatry. The alternative to both of these false resolutions is commitment to the Church "for the sake of the Kingdom." Such a commitment includes the candid acknowledgment of the scandal of historical Christianity in the lively hope that the grand things we affirm about the Church will be vindicated in the coming of the Kingdom. Like the Grand Inquisitor, we recognize that the real work of Christ has been committed to human efforts and human institutions. In opposition to the Grand Inquisitor, we know that these efforts and institutions do not warrant our whole-hearted commitment unless the promise to which they point is actualized in history. And therefore we pray urgently and always, "Maranatha! Come, Lord Jesus!"

BY WHAT AUTHORITY?

Another aspect of the Church as institution is related to the question of authority. When I was a boy, the automatic response to any moral or doctrinal problem raised was, "What does our church say about that?" The assumption was that "our church" had the answer—and it almost always did have *an* answer. We have already noted the ways in which the apotheosis of the organization also served Roman Catholics in maintaining a strong sense of coherence and continuity. But one need not have been Missouri Lutheran or Roman Catholic to know the force with which institutions can supply a sense of authority. The dynamic is present in every denomination, no matter what its formal ecclesiology. A Methodist pastor friend, momentarily depressed about his ministry, remarked one day, "I don't know if God wants me to be here, but the bishop sure does." A decent respect for organizational judgment may sometimes get one over temporary humps of uncertainty, but it is a very shaky foundation for ministry. As churches take on more of the jargon and methods of secular corporations—systems analysis, efficiency studies, and such—local pastors view themselves as branch managers of the business. This neatly answers the question, "By what authority do you presume to be a minister of Christ and his Church?" All one has to do is produce a corporation document, much as someone else might prove that he is authorized to run a franchise of McDonald's hamburgers.

The claims attached to the ministry are truly audacious. These claims cannot be justified by appeal to a document from corporate headquarters, whether corporate headquarters be Rome or New York City or Grand Rapids, Michigan. Having outgrown this very limited idea of where their authority comes from, many ministers today are casting about for some other source of authority. And many have seized on the idea of professionalism. Just as the medical doctor or the lawyer are *authorized* by virtue of training and certification to do some specialized thing, so ministers hang diplomas in their offices in order to reassure themselves and others that somebody gave them the right to do what they are doing.

The idea of profession has, of course, a charming, even inspiring, history. It has to do with openly declaring or avowing one's beliefs and commitments. Thus in religious communities it is said that a member is "professed." But today the idea of profession has undergone significant change. It has more to do with specialization, competence, and certification. Certification, in turn, is chiefly, and often self-servingly, aimed at keeping the function in question (medicine, social service, teaching, and so forth) under the control of the peer group from which professionals receive their authority.

In 1972, the Carnegie Commission on Higher Education issued a study, *Professional Education,* which listed ten marks of the professional. They merit examination and should be compared with our understanding of Christian ministry:

1. A professional is involved in a full-time occupation that provides one's principal source of income.
2. A professional has a strong motivation or calling to a field of endeavor.
3. A professional possesses a specialized body of knowledge and skills acquired over a prolonged period of education and training.
4. A professional makes particular decisions concerning clients in terms of general principles, theories, or propositions.
5. A professional is assumed to have a service orientation.
6. A professional's service is based on the objective needs of the client. Hence there must be frankness and confidentiality between client and professional.

7. A professional is assumed to know more accurately than the client what is best for the client. In short, the professional demands autonomy of judgment in the performance of professional duties. This attitude, of course, places the client in a potentially vulnerable position, which in part explains the need for ethical codes.

8. A professional associates with professionals in the same field, establishing standards, licensing, and other formal entry examinations. The professional association's function is primarily to protect the autonomy and integrity of the profession.

9. A professional's knowledge is assumed to be limited to a particular professional field. It does not give a license to be an expert in every area.

10. A professional makes services available but normally is not allowed to advertise or to seek out clients.

That list is fairly typical of what is meant by a professional in our world. While the Christian ministry is compatible with some of the characteristics mentioned, the list as a whole should give us great pause in describing the ministry as a profession. The professional has clients, the minister serves a community. While the minister helps people with individual needs, the very essence of his work is to bring people into the community of worship and mutual support. The minister does not assume that he knows what is best for the client. (Neither should teachers, for that matter, but that is another story.) To the contrary, he is engaged with sisters and brothers in seeking together the will of God for their lives. Far from refusing to advertise or seek out clients, the ministry is one of bold proclamation and relentless search for the lost and ignored. And what is the "particular professional field" to which the ministry is limited? Religion? But the Christian faith encompasses the whole of life and reality. But enough. It is obvious that any ministry that finds its authority in contemporary notions of professionalism is on perilous ground indeed.

Yet the walls of many clergy offices are littered by diplomas and certificates from academic institutions and professional associations. It is a pitiable imitation of the doctor's office, where diplomas are designed both to intimidate patients into accepting doctor's orders and to assure them that they are in good hands. One should not try to intimidate the people of God, especially with something that is finally so trivial as academic diplomas. Perhaps the pastor might hang up a piece of paper certifying that he has achieved a certain level of holiness and spiritual discernment, but the institution that could issue such certification has yet to be found. It is bad enough that one should try to intimidate or impress parishioners with such shoddy evidence of authorization. What is much worse is that the minister himself might derive his sense of authority from such evidence. The appeal to the appurtenances of professionalism is a poignant confession of vocational bankruptcy.

"Let him who boasts, boast of the Lord," writes St. Paul. "For it is not the man who commends himself that is accepted, but the man whom the Lord commends" (Rom. 10). If the wall of the pastor's office is to make a declaration worthy of the calling, let it display a simple cross or crucifix. That, finally, is all we have to say for ourselves. Upon that cross and the community of resurrection faith gathered around that cross our commitment stands or falls. That is the insecurity that is at the very heart of our freedom. That insecurity cannot be relieved—we should not want it to be relieved—by a letter from corporate headquarters or certification from a professional association.

In *The Minister and the Care of Souls,* the late Daniel Day Williams wrote: "Real personal authority arises out of the concrete incarnation of the spirit of loving service which by God's help becomes present in the care of souls. And this means that ministerial authority can be lost as well as won."[4] Such authority, if it is to be effective, must be demonstrated more than it is asserted. Indeed, when one has to explicitly assert authority it is usually a sign that the authority has already been lost.

One hastens to add that the authority for ministry, while it is personal, is not individualistic. Again, the ministry is the ministry of the Church, and therefore there must be means by which the "inner call" to ministry is ratified and celebrated by the "external call" of the community. I dare say that in every pastor's life there are times when the inner call seems frighteningly uncertain and one just muddles through for a while on the strength of the community's assertion that one is indeed called to the ministry. In *Brother to a Dragonfly,* Will Campbell describes a very successful Baptist minister who privately admitted that he thought his whole ministry a sham. Why, then, asked Campbell, do you go on with it? "Because I was called, you damn fool!" retorted his tormented friend.

So it is that in moments of vocational anguish we kneel in prayer and argue with the God who called us. A premise of the argument is that he has promised his Spirit to the Church and that the Church, praying the Spirit's guidance, called us to ministry. While that objective or external call can help carry us through periods of self-doubt, it too finally depends upon our personal belief about God's relationship to the Church of which our ministry is part. And authority—in the sense of the confidence that we and others have in our calling—always comes back to what Williams describes as "the concrete incarnation of the spirit of loving service which by God's help becomes present in the care of souls." Not only can ministerial authority be lost as well as won, but if it is not always being won, it is surely in the process of being lost. Fortunately, the process is reversible.

Ministerial authority is never really secured against the threat of loss. Religious organizations with their certification systems and titles and dignities can provide extra safety locks on our professional doors. These might inhibit the skeptical from breaking in and challenging our authority. But like extra locks on a New York City apartment door, their chief effect is to encourage the honest to remain honest. They provide little deterrence to the determined. The most determined challenger of our ministerial authority is within ourselves. Those who are ordained into established churches may have other people challenge them on their authority to do this particular thing or that, but their authority to exercise the ministry of Christ and his Church *as such* is readily conceded, at least within the boundaries of the authorizing community. The doubts from within ourselves are not so easily silenced by reference to a diploma of vocation, a contract, or a bishop's appointment.

By what authority do you do what you are doing and say what you are saying? The question was persistently put to our Lord. He obviously could produce no certification from the temple authorities. He spoke rather of the sign of Jonah and of a temple that would be destroyed only to be raised again in three days. The future would reveal that he is indeed the one he claimed to be. And he was vindicated. In short, he did not finally ground his authority in any existent authority, for all existing authorities were themselves in question. One questioned authority cannot be validated by appeal to other authorities equally in question. We said earlier that the loss of ministerial authority can be reversed. It must be reversed daily, for it is daily thrown into question from within. Whether or not it is reversed depends upon our taking the risk that marked the ministry of Jesus. As paradoxical as it may seem, our authority derives from the risk we take.

The authority of ministry is most uncertainly grounded when it seems most certainly grounded in existent reality. There are pastors who derive their confidence from their competence. That is, their ministries "work," sometimes spectacularly so, in organizational growth and, so far as it can be measured, in lives changed. But the calculations of success are precarious proof of authority. The ledgers of history's conflicts offer small comfort to those who would make success the insignia of the divinely approved. To yearn for such comfort is unbecoming in those who proclaim the cross as the sign of ultimate consolation. To rely upon such comfort is betrayal of the risk that is Christian ministry.

Our own competence is not, then, proof of our authority; nor does our proven incompetence withdraw the warrant from what we so inadequately try to do and be. Our certifications and diplomas are as doubtful as are the authorities that issued them. Nor will the determined invader of our peace who challenges us from within be contented by our appeal to the Church or to the Church's scriptures, for these are as much subject to challenge as is the particular ministry that we try to cloak in their dignity. We are right to be impressed by the longevity, the diversity, the achievements, and the grandeur of the Church Catholic, but all that does not finally prove the truth of the message it bears.

Despairing of such proof, ministers are tempted to settle for an authority and legitimation that derives from the approval of peers, or from occasional expressions of gratitude from those who are helped in one way or another. A hospital chaplain may, pathetically, be sustained by the assurance of the medical doctor that his ministry is useful in the healing process. More pitiably, a minister confesses to feeling legitimate when he marries people by the authority vested in him by the state. One is surely scraping the bottom of the barrel of securities when he feels elevated by playing the role of Caesar's minor clerk.

DISPUTED SOVEREIGNTY

Questioned from within and from without, should not our answer be as prompt and as forthright as St. Paul's? "So then we are ambassadors for Christ, God making his appeal through us" (2 Cor. 5). Surely, we think, this and this alone is our authority. And we are right, but it is not so simple as it may seem. This authority is quite different from the authorities, warrants, and legitimations we have been discussing. The warrants derived from ecclesiastical organization, from professionalism, and from competence are derived from existing reality. They quiet our uncertainty, decrease our doubt, diminish our sense of risk. In all these respects, they are quite different from the authority that derives from the ministry of Christ.

To live by the authority of Christ is to abandon the search for authority as authority is understood in other vocations. Compared with other members of the diplomatic corps at the courts of the world, an ambassador for Christ is in an awkward position. Most ambassadors bear the authority of and are legitimated by the sovereignties that they represent. But the sovereignty of the one we claim to represent is itself in question. The claim is under the shadow of a history shadowed by powerful evidence against his sovereignty. The shadow will not be dispelled, the question will not be answered, until he returns in glory.

In the times, then, when we his ministers feel useless, uncertain, and devoid of authority, we can seek several remedies. We can find dignity in representing to the world two thousand years of a formidably impressive tradition, and that is no little thing. We can find worth in the good done for clients, even if the community is misguided in its ultimate hope. We can find satisfaction in competencies exercised, even if the voice that we once heard call us to the work now seems to have been an illusion. There are many justifications for ministry in which we can find dignity, worth, and satisfaction, but finally the justification for Christian ministry is derived from him who forbids us to seek our authority from any existent reality short of the reality of his Kingdom come.

At the courts of the principalities and powers that rule this present time, other ambassadors can strut and preen themselves in the dignities bestowed by existing sovereignties, however paltry. With Paul we could say that, if we wished to boast, we as ministers of the Church have reason to boast more mightily than all of them. It is a powerful thing to be the formally designated representative of the institution of Christianity; by comparison with that, other institutions are of rather lesser impressiveness. But presiding over that style of power and importance is the ghost of the Grand Inquisitor. A very lively ghost still today, to be sure.

We will not play that game, however. We will not boast nor compete in the rivalry among sovereignties of the present time. We are the ambassadors of a sovereign who is to come; who, until he comes, is enthroned on a cross, exhibiting his majesty in love that suffers with a world that suffers because its defiance delays his rule. Around that cross and the hope of his coming a community has gathered. It is the institution called the Church, gathered, we believe, by the Spirit, in continuity with the apostolic witness. We are to minister to its nurture, its endurance, and its growth. We are responsible for that institution, although our authority is not finally derived from it. Our authority is derived from the promise around which the community has been gathered.

We draw strength and confidence from the gathering itself. "Therefore we are surrounded by so great a cloud of witnesses . . . looking to Jesus the pioneer and perfecter of our faith, who for the joy that was set before him endured the cross, despising the shame, and is seated at the right hand of the throne of God" (Heb. 12). The passage might better be translated: He made light of the shame, or even, he flaunted the shame. So also with the institution of the Church and our ministries in it—the embarrassment of it, the absurd ambiguities, the seeming uselessness of it—all this we despise, indeed all this we flaunt, for the joy that is set before us.

We are premature ambassadors, having arrived at court before the sovereignty of our king has been recognized. It is awkward, of course, and our authority is very much in question. We must resist the temptation to relieve the awkwardness by accepting a lesser authority from another kingdom.

5.
Reconciliation Against Resignation

Among the favored ways of thinking about the Christian community, few meet with such ready approval as the idea of healing and reconciliation. In the biblical passage which describes us as ambassadors of a disputed sovereignty, reconciliation is the key point: "So we are ambassadors for Christ, God making his appeal through us. We beseech you on behalf of Christ, be reconciled to God. For our sake he made him to be sin who knew no sin, so that in him we might become the righteousness of God" (2 Cor. 5). Closely connected to this biblical view of the ministry of reconciliation is the understanding that, in Christ, God offers the gift of peace. In both the Hebrew Bible and the New Testament, peace—the *shalom* of God—is tantamount to salvation. It means the bringing together of what was separated, the picking up of the pieces, the healing of the wounds, the fulfillment of the incomplete, the overcoming of the forces of fragmentation by forgiving love. In short, *shalom* is the content of the rule of God, the promised goal of pilgrim hope.

Little wonder, then, that clergy take so enthusiastically to the concept of themselves as peacemakers, reconcilers, and healers. The Church itself can be understood as an outpost of *shalom* in a distinctly unpeaceful world. This is an extension of the Jewish understanding of the Sabbath as *shalom*'s outpost and anticipation in time. For the observant Jew, the Sabbath is a foretaste of the Messianic Age, the promised order of eternity played out and thereby briefly actualized ahead of time. In contemporary Protestant thinking there is still a tattered remnant of this eschatological understanding of the Sabbath Peace. It appears in residual "Sabbath laws" banning certain forms of commerce and play and is today limply supported by utilitarian arguments about the need for recreation and a day of rest. In its historical roots, however, this view of the Lord's Day, like the Jewish understanding of the Sabbath, is not connected with the need for relaxation but with the need for intensification, of heightened awareness, that anticipates the hope of cosmic healing.

The view of the Church as a healing community, as a preview of the great *shalom* of eternal salvation, emphasizes the "priestly" dimension of ministry. Once again, however, the priestly is not the antithesis of the prophetic. To the contrary, it is only the prophetic invocation of the coming new order that gives content to the priestly anticipation of that order. Without that prophetic and eschatological vision, the priestly function would degenerate into the bland business of trying to "make do" with the world as it is. In that case, the ministry of reconciliation becomes little more than the superficial business of trying to hold things together, to contain profound conflict under the veneer of harmony, to make the intolerable tolerable, to substitute an accommodation for the consummation we are to seek.

It is the sorriest comment on the Church today that an observer viewing its myriad activities and ministries might not recognize it as an eschatological community, a community pledged to the *shalom* of God's rule. That is, it is not immediately apparent that this is a community premised upon a promise of what is to be. Especially when we speak of the ministry of reconciliation and healing, the tone is too often one of adjustment to present reality, of restoring old relationships, of patching up. Thus, to the eschatologically restless Christian, the language of reconciliation seems pale by comparison with the prophetic word of expectation.

Reconciliation becomes mere accommodationism when we forget to ask: Reconciliation to what? The answer should be obvious: "We beseech you on behalf of Christ, be reconciled to God." Since in biblical thought the being of God cannot be separated from the rule of God, reconciliation means to be at peace, to be at one, with the promised new order. "Your Kingdom come!" is a prayer that the reality of God be actualized in empirical fact. It is a prayer of reconciliation, although at first it may seem to be quite the opposite. On the face of it, "Your Kingdom come!" accentuates the disjunction between the way things are and the way things are to be, between God and our present moment. In truth, the radical and prophetic nature of the ministry of reconciliation becomes evident in that the *shalom* of God, to which we are to be reconciled, means trouble for our relationship to the world that is short of that *shalom.* It is in this light that we understand our Lord's words about having come not to bring peace but a sword. The more we are engaged in the priestly ministry of reconciliation, the more must we be attuned to the prophetic vision of that to which we are to be reconciled. Only in this way can the idea of the ministry of reconciliation, now in bad repute among those determined to settle for nothing less than the Kingdom, be rehabilitated.

One reason the ministry of reconciliation is in bad repute is that it has sometimes been confused with the ministry of resignation. Being reconciled to the rule of God is quite the opposite of being resigned to things as they are. The rule of God means earthshaking and heavenshaking change, transformation both cosmic and personal. The Kingdom has not yet been consummated. That is why we continue to pray, "Your Kingdom come!" It has been said that Christians can be divided between those who see the faith in terms of changing and those who see it in terms of coping. The first see the gospel as promise and power for the changing of the present order in obedience to the will of God. The second see the gospel as a guide and consolation that helps them cope with things as they are. Coping can easily degenerate into the techniques of resignation.

The change-oriented can easily slide into rhetorical evasion of everyday facts that so stubbornly resist the coming of God's rule. The distinction between coping and changing is useful but limited. The ministry of reconciliation does indeed help one to cope—not by resignation to the present but by lively hope that the promised future is already, here and now, making all things new.

Immediately prior to our passage about being ambassadors of a disputed sovereignty, we read: "Therefore, if any one is in Christ, he is a new creation; the old has passed away, behold, the new has come. All this is from God, who through Christ reconciled us to himself and gave us the ministry of reconciliation . . ." (2 Cor. 5). The concept of reconciliation, then, must be rescued from notions of passivity and mere adjustment. Reconciliation means transformation. In New Testament thinking, God reconciles us and the world to himself. God is not reconciled to the world. He has not resigned himself to accepting this botched creation as it is. He has not accepted a more "realistic" perspective and adjusted his original expectations to fit the limits of human nature and history. If that is what is meant by reconciliation, then reconciliation would be no more than the acknowledgment of defeat. The Christian language of reconciliation speaks not of defeat but of triumph and hope. The defeat of the cross is, in the light of the resurrection, the triumph of love.

Reconciliation, then, is not an adjustment to limitations, nor is it a negotiated settlement. It is not reciprocal in the sense that man and God were enemies and have now worked out terms of settlement by which they can live as friends. The supremacy of God and the priority of God's initiative in Christ are key to understanding reconciliation. He is not resigning himself to us, he is reconciling us to himself (Rom. 5). This transformation is dynamic and lifelong. True, the foundation that makes reconciliation possible has been laid "once and for all" in the death and resurrection of Jesus. The foundation, however, is not an end in itself but precisely that, a foundation upon which the transformation of ourselves and the world can be constructed. Here the distinction between justification and reconciliation is very important. Justification is accomplished fact, reconciliation is the continuing process. We proclaim justification, we appeal for reconciliation. "We beseech you on behalf of Christ, be reconciled to God." This is not to say that justification is God's work and reconciliation is our work. It is God who justifies and it is God who invites and engages us in the living out of the justified life.

Reconciliation is walking by the Spirit, in Pauline language, and the Spirit, it should be remembered, is always the Spirit of God. "For God has done what the law, weakened by the flesh, could not do: sending his own Son in the likeness of sinful flesh and for sin, he condemned sin in the flesh, in order that the just requirement of the law might be fulfilled in us, who walk not according to the flesh but according to the Spirit" (Rom. 8). The law was not accommodated to our weakness but is being fulfilled in us by the power of the Spirit, as it has been fulfilled in Christ. What is being actualized in our lives is the reality already established in the life, death, and resurrection of Jesus the Christ. Since we are already now "in Christ," the reality of our lives is accurately described as one in which "the old has passed away, behold, the new has come."

In the first chapter, we spoke of the "actual church" and the "real church" and reminded ourselves that reality should not be confused with what is already existent. So the distinction between the actual and the real helps us to understand reconciliation as the actualization of God's work in Christ. We are the ministers, or the servants, of that reconciliation.

CONFORMING AND TRANSFORMING

Admittedly, this scriptural and theological excursus may seem far removed from the everyday tasks of Christian ministry. The fact is, however, that reconciliation is a dominant metaphor for ministry. Others expect us to be, and we likely expect ourselves to be, reconcilers. Unless our understanding of reconciliation flows from this biblical understanding of a life-transforming process, the idea of being a minister of reconciliation is, frankly, not very exciting. Without this theological vision that points us toward the coming Kingdom, reconciliation is little more than helping people to adjust. Ministers of reconciliation then become brokers of other people's problems, negotiating temporary settlements between sins in conflict. The danger is that reconciliation is perverted into conformation. "Do not be conformed to this world but be transformed by the renewal of your mind, that you may prove what is the will of God, what is good and acceptable and perfect" (Rom. 12). When we are helping people to cope by conforming rather than to change by transforming, when we make smooth the way of accommodation, when we relieve the tension between the actual and the real, then we have become reconcilers who have betrayed Christ's ministry of reconciliation.

The minister today is surrounded by such temptations to betrayal. In pastoral counseling, in personal and group therapy, in the social therapy of political action, we are tempted to aid and abet the forces of conformity. The glittering prizes of ministerial "success" are in large part reserved for the most skilled practitioners of the techniques of adjustment. It is bold and, by some standards, absurd to lay claim to the ministry of reconciliation. As we saw in our discussion of ministerial authority, we are embarrassed to be representing a disputed sovereignty and are therefore tempted to accept our license from some lesser but more widely recognized sovereignty.

The metaphors of healing and reconciliation have been so dominant in thinking about Christian ministry that John T. McNeill could write a classic history of Christian ministry with almost exclusive reference to these metaphors. In his *History of the Cure of Souls,* [1] McNeill notes that the Socratic idea of the philosopher as the physician of the soul *(iatros tes psyches)* was largely taken over into Christian ministry, especially as ministry was focused on the penitential functions of confession and forgiveness. In the modern world the status of "physician of the soul" has migrated to the professions of psychiatry and psychology. It is touchingly ironic that many ministers now hope to be recognized as "useful" by borrowing from psychology the function which psychology borrowed (or stole, as the case may be) from the ministry, and which had been taken from Greek philosophy in the first place. Admittedly, that is an oversimplification of the history involved, but there can be no doubt that there is still today a debilitating deference which the ministry shows to the psychological enterprise. In trying to resolve their uncertainties about themselves and their place in the world, ministers are especially vulnerable to seeking license and legitimation from the kingdom of psychology. Unlike the disputed sovereignty of the Christ, psychology is securely ensconced at the court of modern culture.

Some years ago, the brilliant Freudian, Philip Rieff, described the cultural hegemony of psychology in *The Triumph of the Therapeutic.* The triumph, it must be confessed, is also evident in much current thinking about ministry. The key assumption of the therapeutic is that self-actualization and mental health are the highest goods, that the purpose of church and ministry is not to mediate salvation, not to appeal for reconciliation to God but for reconciliation to self. In fact, it is not uncommon to find Christian writers today who challenge the very distinction between being reconciled to God and being reconciled to self. The mark of being reconciled to God, we are told, is precisely the knowledge and acceptance of self as that is measured by the criteria of psychological health. The logic behind this assumption is not entirely unpersuasive. After all, there is a sense in which God is the destiny of each person, and therefore to be at peace with oneself may have the appearance of being a kind of psychological version of the Sabbath Peace that anticipates the promised future. A major problem in this way of thinking, however, is that a very large proportion of those whom we call the saints of the Church were anything but models of mental health. Paul, Jerome, Luther, Joan of Arc, and Mother Teresa of Calcutta—all thought and behaved in ways that would readily get them certified as psychotic in a reputable mental health clinic today.

Twenty years ago and more, the triumph of the therapeutic became manifest in the enthusiasm that seminaries showed for pastoral counseling. Then it was largely a Protestant phenomenon. Now it is to be feared that many Roman Catholics are embracing with a sense of fresh discovery the possibilities of making the same mistakes. In 1961, Daniel Day Williams wrote, "It is true to say that contemporary psychology has helped theology recover the significance of . . . radical personalism. Psychologists have given us fresh cause to realize that the meaning of all our theological symbols comes to us in relation to the struggle to become mature persons, capable of handling the threats and creative opportunities of life."[2] That theological symbols "come to us" in the midst of our human struggle cannot be doubted. Unfortunately, Williams invited the reader to infer that the truth of the symbols is to be measured by their contribution to our becoming "mature persons." What Williams left to inference in his theory of "linkage" between psychology and theology, many others have since made explicit. The claim is that theological assertions have no "meaning" apart from their utility in advancing our therapeutic agenda—whether the goal of therapy be social justice, economic well-being, or mental health.[3]

Candidates for ministry are urged to seek clarification of motive, to discover the integrity of self, so that they may give themselves, in Williams's words, "without pretense in the service of God and neighbor."[4] Self-examination has of course a venerable place within the tradition of Christian spirituality. But the point of self-examination is not the assured establishment of one's sincerity or authenticity but the abandonment of self in reliance upon God's forgiving love. The New Testament scholar Krister Stendahl has written perceptively about the misuses of Pauline theology in legitimating "the introspective conscience of the West."[5] Paul did not, says Stendahl, engage in endless and anguished introspection in order to discover the integrity of self but celebrated the integrity that was his by virtue of God's gift in Christ. Far from wallowing in the ambiguities of his existence, Paul was confident that, according to the law, he was a righteous man. The observance of the law could not, however, "justify" him before God. Justification is a gift external to the self, bestowed at God's loving initiative. If the law revealed by God could not justify, how much less are we justified by the dicta of the modern contrivance that is psychology.

NURTURING A ROBUST SKEPTICISM

The ministry should not be scornful of psychology. A robust skepticism, however, is very much in order. Whatever techniques and insights may help people to cope with their unfulfilled lives in an unfulfilled universe should be welcomed, as long as they are not deceived into thinking that complete integrity is available short of the integration of all things in the final rule of God. There is an inevitable disjointedness, if not "pretense," in our ministries; we are positing a possibility that has not been proven, holding forth a promise not yet vindicated. We are not, Paul writes, servants of the "flesh" but of the Spirit. It does not yet appear what we will be. "Maturity" is not a present option to be achieved through therapy but a promise to be embraced by faith. "Now hope that is seen is not hope. For who hopes for what he sees? But if we hope for what we do not see, we wait for it with patience" (Rom. 8).

This patience is not to be confused with resignation. It is the patience of God who suffers with his defiant creation (1 Pet. 3:20). In the Christian view, health—mental, spiritual, and physical—is to enter into God's *pathos*. In light of the cross, Christians proclaim the triumph not of the therapeutic but of the pathetic. Thus what the New Testament calls patience must appear to the nonbeliever as impatience, as a refusal to accommodate ourselves to things as they are or as we could make them to be now. Christian courage is the refusal to sell out to the pleasures of an undisputed sovereignty; it is holding out for the vindication of the disputed sovereignty to which we are pledged. At times, perhaps most of the time, the dispute rages within our own hearts, but we choose to take the side of the argument that declares: "For I am sure that neither death, nor life, nor angels, nor principalities . . . will be able to separate us from the love of God in Christ Jesus our Lord" (Rom. 8).

We refuse to be intimidated by those who deride our hope as "pie in the sky." If pie is one's metaphor for the fulfillment we seek, and if "the sky" means that it is beyond our present contriving and grasping, then, yes, most certainly, we stake our hope on pie in the sky. The maturity of modern psychology's autonomous person who is adjusted to "reality" without the aid of religion's props and crutches is the sickness for which the gospel of reconciliation is the cure. The older Freud of *Civilization and Its Discontents* recognized the limitations of the present and in this respect was far in advance of many practitioners who today lay claim to some piece of his mantle. The Christian proposition is that the discontents, the feeling of alienation, the inability to be "at home" with existent reality, are all signs of health to be celebrated. The fatal disease is the premature "resolution" of that which cannot be and must not be resolved except by the resolution of all things in the consummated lordship of the Christ.

Today there are encouraging signs of skepticism, if not of robust skepticism, toward the psychologizing of the ministry of reconciliation. The bloom is off the rose of pastoral counseling—in part, perhaps, because many who saw therapy as the chief rationale and legitimation of their ministries have made a clean breast of it by hanging out their shingles as full-time and frequently well paid counselors; and also, perhaps, because some pastors recognized that counseling was consuming a disproportionate amount of time taken from evangelism, study, preaching, and other dimensions of ministry. At the same time, it is worth noting that some surveys have shown that many parish clergy devote no more than two hours a week to counseling. Thus it may be that the new skepticism toward the excessive emphasis upon counseling is in part due to the awareness that a disproportionate amount of seminary training and ministerial identity had been given over to a function that, at least in many cases, occupies a relatively small part of day-by-day ministry.

A robust skepticism toward the imperium of psychology can be helped along by personal experiences. Here I have some confessions to make. I remember that when I was a very small boy, perhaps no more than age four or five, my parents were talking about an older person I knew and saying that he would likely "have to be sent to Kingston." (Kingston, Ontario, was the site of the insane asylum, as it was then called.) I was utterly intrigued by this possibility of drawing a line between the sane and the "crazy," and after some reflection on the subject, I proudly declared to my mother that I thought I could be crazy if I really tried. Her reaction was strong and immediate: "Don't you ever say that! Don't you ever decide to be crazy!" The interesting thing, and this made a lasting impression, is that she assumed I was quite capable of it. It was understood that there was a thin line between sanity and insanity, that there was something arbitrary about the distinction itself, and that crossing that line was somehow related to choice and character.

The point of the story is not that the "mentally ill" choose to be that way. Obviously there are compulsions, traumas, and environmental pressures that produce derangements, and it is often impossible to trace their complicated interrelationships to anything that we would recognize as choice. At the same time, however, we live by what the sociologists of knowledge call "constructions of reality," and, for the person whose consciousness is capable of entertaining the possibility of different constructions, there is an inescapable element of choice. Some constructions we call health and others we call sickness. It is toward these labels that we ought to exercise the most robust skepticism.

The debunking of psychological and psychiatric deceits has already begun in our society. One thinks of the work of Ivan Illich and of Thomas Szasz, who has written persuasively about "the manufacture of madness" and about the ways in which government power strips people of the dignity of being responsible for their actions by categorizing them as mentally incompetent, and frequently depriving them of liberty far more severe than if they had stood trial for their alleged offenses. Laws and professional practices have made it possible for thousands of families to get rid of the Uncle Charlies and Grandma Smiths for whom they no longer care to care. Then, of course, we are today more keenly aware of the abuses of psychiatry in totalitarian societies, such as the Soviet Union, where dissidents can be discredited and confined by assignment to psychiatric custody. One does not wish to adopt the view of R. D. Laing and others who propose that mental illness may be the only true sanity, but neither can one agree with those who dismiss all challenges to therapeutic orthodoxy as a defense of "irrationality." The point is not to defend irrationality but to plead for a rationality that is capable of criticizing the confining rationalism of a professional mindset that imposes a cramped and truncated construction on reality.

THE TRUTH IS IN THE WHOLE

The therapeutic mind set must be challenged in a Christian community that calls people to believe that they are the instruments of divine purpose, that fulfillment is to be discovered in loss, that life at its highest is devotion to the lowest, that the air we breathe is shared by angels and archangels, that pure joy is to be identified with a convicted criminal on Calvary's continuing road to life through death. As Christians we must discover again the apparent preposterousness of our faith. The New Testament calls it a scandal, and the shame of the churches is that the world is not scandalized. As ministers we might worry when a good church member claims that she saw three angels last night and describes their appearance in detail. But we should be much more worried about the member who denies the very possibility of that having happened. In sad truth, a good many ministers are referring the first kind of Christian to therapeutic functionaries who have a professional vested interest in persuading their clients that the far reaches of human experience must be denied as illusory.

Recently I attended a funeral, and the pastor of the family involved had shared with them his knowledge about the stages of grief which he had culled from Kübler-Ross and others. Family members discussed with one another which stages they had passed through and where they now were on the spectrum. It was clinical. It was awful. Like patients in a doctor's office exchanging observations about their diseases. Much better an old-fashioned wake, with much food and drink and nostalgia and raging at the unfairness of it all, and reaffirming the fragile bonds between the living, and discovering again that through it all and in it all there is the quiet knowledge of a triumph that is somehow connected with a distant Easter morning in which all the threats to the present and the future were swallowed up in victory.

Why do we Christians succumb to the dismal notion that the truth of a thing is to be found in the parts of a thing? It is urged that, if we analyze and deconstruct and separate the pieces, we will understand the whole. As though we could better understand the genius of the Sistine Chapel if we studied the chemical components of Michelangelo's paint and plaster. The whole is infinitely more than the parts, and Christians, who live from a divinely revealed story that encompasses the whole of reality, should be defiant of every reductionism that claims to "explain" the elephant by reference to the precise description of its parts.

The dominance of counseling theory and technique in many

seminaries and many ministries reflects a massive failure of nerve, perhaps even the idolatry of wanting, like the children of Israel in the wilderness, a more palpable god. A recent article in a professional journal argued that the pastoral counselor must himself be in therapy and, presumably, be certifiably healthy if he is to help others. Seminarians are encouraged to probe the intestines of their psyches in order to determine that their motives are unqualified and their intentions pure. After all, how can you help others if you yourself are in need of help? "Doubtless you will quote to me this proverb, 'Physician, heal yourself.' . . . And they rose up and put him out of the city, and led him to the brow of the hill on which their city was built, that they might throw him down headlong" (Luke 4). He did not accommodate them; he was not the model they wanted.

Seventy-five years ago, and still today in some circles, Jesus was depicted as the world's best salesman, a holy hustler. Others have depicted him as the great social planner and reformer, or even as the revolutionary guerilla fighter. More commonly he is declared the paragon of mental health and human fulfillment. In some literature it seems the image of Jesus is stuck somewhere between Carl Rogers and Che Guevera. But he cannot be contained in any of these conceptual boxes, and most certainly not in the box of therapeutic orthodoxy. What is the psychological term for holiness?

Robert Coles, the distinguished psychiatrist and author, expresses his puzzlement at bishops, seminaries, and placement boards that want candidates to have a clean psychological bill of health. Church agencies want "modern scientific knowledge" to be brought to bear upon the "selection process." Sometimes, says Coles, a psychiatric evaluation may be helpful, "but there are many psychiatrists who have no real understanding of what a religious vocation is about; and some of us are narrow-minded, smug, possessed of our own sectarian, ideological faith—hence the last persons in the world who ought to be writing letters of 'evaluation' to bishops." "A psychology of 'adjustment' and 'adaptation' is so often an acquiescence to the most banal and crude, if not blasphemous, in a given society." Not so incidentally, Coles notes, the psychological notions of "normal" and "deviant" are frequently veiled value judgments designed to conform to the desires of the "principalities and powers." Coles himself has been asked by bishops and agencies to participate in this evaluation process: "No one has ever asked me what qualifications—what understanding of the spiritual life—I have to fill out these various forms. All I need do is affix the letters M.D. after my name, indicate my psychiatric affiliation, and my words are accepted as thoughtful and helpful."[6]

It is not as though the Christian tradition is bereft of the ideas and terminology by which human life can be described. The cardinal virtues of prudence, justice, fortitude, and temperance; the sins of pride, envy, sloth, despair—are not these ever so much more textured and rich and comprehensive than is the jargon of our therapeutic society? It is no advance to "explain" the meaning of love by translating 1 Corinthians 13 into the professional prattle of the clinic.

It is at least unbecoming and probably blasphemous to norm the Christian life by the criteria of the therapeutic. The quest for purity of intention in one's ministry is futile, and those who think they have achieved such purity simply have not asked the hard questions. If we rummage through what Yeats called "the rag and bone shop" of the human heart, the discoveries are ghastly. Nobody ministers "without pretense," and the demand that we should is paralyzing. We are *not* paralyzed because, after our bouts with scrupulosity that drag us through labrynthine explorations of motives within motives, we emerge defeated and therefore triumphant. Like Will Campbell's preacher, we declare, "Dammit, I'm called." Or, better yet, like Paul: "For necessity is laid upon me. Woe to me if I do not preach the gospel! For if I do this of my own will, I have a reward; but if not of my own will, I am entrusted with a commission" (1 Cor. 9).

Just so.

CHARACTER AND GRACE

Pastoral counseling will be more closely related to reconciliation when its emphasis shifts away from the "meeting of human needs" to the formation of character. Of course it is a good thing to meet human needs, but the language of need-meeting is today too much in the service of need-production. More and more people today are engaged in professional or paraprofessional enterprises that do not produce things but produce services. If the services are to be bought, there must be a market. Those who peddle the services manufacture the market of needs which the services supposedly meet. Some years ago, a group of psychologists proclaimed, presumably on the basis of rather elusive survey research, that thirty-five percent of the population of New York City was mentally disturbed enough to be in need of treatment. If that figure is accepted, therapists should be kept in business for quite some time to come. (Lest the uncultured despisers of New York jump to conclusions, the implication was that the rate of disease was representative of the American population as a whole.)

Ministers used to be accused of manufacturing guilt feelings because their profession claimed to have a corner on forgiveness. After years of training in counseling, it is to be feared that some of us ministers are in the business of manufacturing needs—including, ironically, the need to be free of guilt feelings—so that we can be useful in facilitating their relief. From forgiveness to facilitation is quite a comedown. For a less demeaning and more distinctive ministry, we need to shift the metaphor from the meeting of human needs to the formation and sustaining of Christian character. Character implies the courage and grace to live the good life in a world where needs go largely unmet.

The language of character has fallen into disuse in our culture. It sounds almost archaic. We still speak of someone being "a real character," but that has a different and very limited connotation. The concept of character has a venerable place in the Christian tradition, however, and is closely associated with notions such as virtue, responsibility, honor, and obligation. In current understandings, character has little to do with pastoral counseling, and that is a measure of how thoroughly counseling has become captive to secular ideology.

Psychotherapy has a great deal to say about the *characteristics* of thought and behavior but is little concerned with the *character* of the person. Especially in the more popularized versions of therapy (and that is often the level at which churches and ministers are involved), man is seen as a bundle of needs to be discovered, expressed, examined, and met. Such therapy keeps the person in perpetual dependency as he alternately whines and exults in the exploration of new needs. And it sustains the illusion that such needs are problems to be resolved, problems that *can* be resolved. In their more fatuous forms, psychotherapies suggest that problems discovered *are* problems resolved, that self-knowledge is self-healing. Christian faith, too, affirms the axiom, "Know thyself." But the discovery of our real selves is not through internal probings but external promise; becoming our true selves is not a therapeutic project but a vocation.

Character is fidelity to that vocation. The ministry of reconciliation is to help reorder the characteristics of a life into the character of a life. As Jesus noted that grapes are not gathered from thorns, or figs from thistles, so much Christian moral thought is focused too much on context or situation or principles rather than on the self as agent. The "perduring self" is, in Christ, the new being whose character must be ever more transformed in tune with the destiny that is one's vocation as a Christian.[7] Some Protestants who are very strong on "justification by grace through faith" are nervous about stressing character because it seems to border on "works righteousness." Certain traditions in Roman Catholicism also emphasize a sacramentally transmitted grace in a way that neglects the changed life. Similarly, "crisis theologies" and some forms of Christian existentialism concentrate almost exclusively on the discontinuous, spontaneous, moment-by-moment demand of obedient decision. There are, for example, surprising parallels between Rudolf Bultmann and evangelistic fundamentalism in that, although employing different language, both call for foundation-shaking confrontation and conversion but slight the tasks of transformation in which the new being becomes manifest in new ways of being and acting.

All Christians have in their traditions the resources for conceptualizing this transformation. They are usually to be found in the doctrinal textbooks under the heading of sanctification. The ministry of reconciliation is closely connected to the gift and task of sanctification. In ministering to Christian people we do not call for conversion as though they had never heard the gospel. Even less should we give the impression that the existence of real and stubborn problems somehow throws into question whether they have really made the decision for Christ. It is to the perduring self that we must attend. That we are new beings in Christ is God's sheer gift; the construction of character is the actualization of that gift. It is a painstaking process of becoming who, in Christ, we already are. It requires respect for the everyday experiences, the quotidian aspects, of the Christian's pilgrimage. Thus the ministry of reconciliation is not only a shattering ministry, destroying the illusions of lives falsely constructed, but also a sustaining ministry. The ministry is one of both judgment and of nurture, and to know how these differ and when which word is required is a pastoral gift of spiritual discernment.

THE GIFT OF DISCERNMENT

When counseling is subservient to psychotherapeutic orthodoxies, it becomes vacuous and imitative and is a betrayal of the gospel of reconciliation. When counseling is controlled by a theology of crisis and conversion, it undermines the nurturing and sustaining dimensions of the cure of souls. "I therefore, a prisoner for the Lord, beg you to lead a life worthy of the calling to which you have been called" (Eph. 4). Character is fidelity to that vocation. Paul assumed, and we should have no difficulty in understanding that there is a difference between the more worthy and the less worthy life. Many Christians today, unfortunately, are made very nervous by the idea of the worthy or good life. The idea of the good life smacks too much of pagan classicism or of the smug self-righteousness that Jesus condemned in some of his contemporaries. Then, too, we sometimes prefer the excitement of escalated existentialist rhetoric and conversionary now-or-never appeals over the more demanding and patient care of day-by-day pilgrims, of people who have discovered their true selves in the End Time but must live out that truth one day at a time. In pastoral care and preaching we must rehabilitate the concept of the good and honorable person, always remembering that the worth involved is derived exclusively from the sheer gift of the calling to which we have been called.

This involves no compromise of the unqualified grace by which God accepts us as we are. It is sometimes said that the Old Testament was the religion of law while the New Testament is the religion of gospel—indeed, some go farther and say Christianity is not religion at all but liberation from the bonds of religion. The psalmists and prophets understood better than we that the grace and mercy of God are manifested precisely in his giving of the law to Israel. Grace is in the calling, the promised destiny is in the covenant, and of that calling and covenant the law was the sign. For Christians that call and covenant have been signed and sealed, declared and vindicated, in the cross of the risen Lord. The law, as Jesus said, has not been abolished but fulfilled, and we are actualizing that fulfillment as we live lives worthy of the calling to which we have been called. The ministry of reconciliation intensifies the wrestling between present fact and promised destiny, and character is the product of that contest.

There is no getting around the fact that the notion of character implies judgment. And this runs up against the popular assumption that counseling should be "nonjudgmental." When people say counseling should be nonjudgmental, one suspects that they mean it should be noncondemnatory. Judgment is of the very essence of spiritual discernment. Still today in Orthodox Jewish circles there are religious courts in which the faithful bring their disputes to be adjudicated by a rabbi or group of rabbis. Of course there are major differences between the ways that Orthodox Jews and Christians understand the role of the law. But whether our theologies accommodate the fact or not, the truth is that Christians too assume that religion has something to do with normative morality. Not infrequently people want a judgment about whether they did right or wrong, and that is not necessarily wrong. They should not be dismissed as moralistic, uptight, inhibited folk who need to be "freed up." They may not be helped by the pastor who turns the question back on them with: "Whether it's right or wrong isn't the question. The question is how do *you* feel about it?" These good people came for informed counsel, not simply to be thrown back upon their own confusions. They assume, perhaps wrongly, that their pastor, by virtue either of training or of character, possesses a discernment that is worth taking into account in what will, after all, finally be their decision about the matter.

The word *religion* comes from the Latin *religare,* which means to bind or tie together. We may protest all we wish that Christianity is not religion. People will receive our protest with mild amusement at first, but if we persist in it, they are likely to become irritated. If they cannot count on the Church for some kind of binding or normative ethic, and if the Christian faith does not help tie together the disparate pieces of a confused universe, they will begin to wonder what is the point of it all. Obviously, many who wondered have now wandered away from the folk altogether.

To say that there is a normative ethic does not mean that most people are eager to submit to it. In many cases they merely want to get some bearing on their moral behavior by knowing which precepts they are violating. Many years ago I served an internship under a Midwestern pastor who was famed as a counselor in marital crises. Beyond his own large parish, people would come from great distances to seek his help. Once, over a drink at the end of a long day, he remarked that thirty years of experience had taught him that most people who came for counseling really came to have him agree with their side of the dispute. "Seventy percent of counseling," he said, "is just listening and trying to get people to talk to one another. Twenty percent is explaining as simply as you can Christian teaching as it applies to this case. And ten percent is offering your opinion. They came for your opinion and you've no right to deny them that. What they do with it is their business, and you have little control over that." One might quibble over the percentage breakdown, but my own experience suggests that the basic approach is sound enough.

In centuries past, clergy had recourse to large tomes which listed almost every conceivable action and gave the moral judgment appropriate to it. The discipline was called casuistry and is today much scorned as mechanistic and depersonalizing. No doubt it often was that way—about as mechanistic and depersonalizing as today's stages of grief, marital bliss by manuals, and primal screams. The reappropriation of the concept of character requires a new appreciation of the minister as spiritual director. A director is not a dictator

—we could not be that even if we wanted to—but a guide. The amazing Father Dudko, the Russian Orthodox priest who has since been silenced by the Soviet regime, was asked at one of his Saturday night conversations, "What is a confessor?" "Your confessor," answered Dudko, "is someone who worries about your salvation." What a marvelously simple answer, and how alien it seems to current talk about pastoral counseling.

THE TRIUMPH OF LOVE

Those who make a fetish of being nonjudgmental are often unreflectively and destructively the most judgmental. It is destructively depersonalizing to suggest that there is no right or wrong for which people are responsible. This is not to say that right and wrong are always clear and unambiguous, but it is to say that the most elementary respect for another person requires an acknowledgment of that person as a responsible agent. We do that person no favors by reducing him or her to a bundle of compulsions and social and psychological conditionings. We are all "determined" to a large degree, no doubt, but the Church's ministry must resist rather than abet the forces of determinism. We should have no illusions about being value-free professionals, nor should we think that others who make that claim are in fact value-free. In therapy and even in public education there is today a new emphasis upon dealing with values. It is proposed, however, that we can address value questions in a value-free way. The practitioners of this approach say their task is not to propose, and certainly not to impose, values but simply to engage people in "values clarification."[8] Concealed in this approach is the base value that what one feels is right for oneself *is* right. That base value judgment is antithetical to any Christian understanding of calling, of covenant, of salvation. It leaves no room for any substantive statement about the nature of Christian character, about what it means to live the life worthy of the calling to which we are called. Salvation cannot be equated with self-actualization or self-expression. Being true to oneself, in Christian perspective, means to be true to the self one is called to be. Our appeal is not that people be reconciled to themselves. Rather, "We beseech you on behalf of Christ, be reconciled to God."

This should not be understood as but another critique of modern "permissiveness" or "situational ethics." There is no defense here of legalism, nor of authoritarianism, nor of a rigid mindset that is incapable of reverencing the diversity and mystery of human feelings and action. To the contrary, the argument is against a rigid psycho-orthodoxy that imposes a demand for self-realization that cannot truly be realized short of the Kingdom come. It is against the perversion of the notion of reconciliation into resignation. In a larger view of therapy and healing, it is a terrible thing to deprive people of the direction that points beyond self. This, then, is an argument for love, for that greater love which liberates us from compulsive and dead-ended introspection. "By this we shall know that we are of the truth, and reassure our hearts before him, whenever our hearts condemn us; for God is greater than our hearts, and he knows everything." And, knowing everything, he loves us, "for God is love" (1 John 3 and 4).

If it seems to us too general and even vacuous to say that the ministry of reconciliation is the ministry of love, the judgment is upon us. Many years ago now, Richard Niebuhr pondered the purpose of the Church and its ministry and he finally came to the conclusion that that purpose is "the increase of the love of God and neighbor." Lest that was thought too obvious, he told us what he meant by love, and his telling of it is a fitting conclusion to this chapter:

> By love we mean at least these attitudes and actions: rejoicing in the presence of the beloved, gratitude, reverence and loyalty toward him. Love is rejoicing over the existence of the beloved one; it is the desire that he be rather than not be; it is longing for his presence when he is absent; it is happiness in the thought of him; it is profound satisfaction over everything that makes him great and glorious. Love is gratitude: it is thankfulness for the existence of the beloved; it is the happy acceptance of everything that he gives without the jealous feeling that the self ought to be able to do as much; it is a gratitude that does not seek equality; it is wonder over the other's gift of himself in companionship.

Love is reverence: it keeps its distance even as it draws near; it does not seek to absorb the other in the self or want to be absorbed by it; it rejoices in the otherness of the other; it desires the beloved to be what he is and does not seek to refashion him into a replica of the self or to make him a means to the self's advancement. As reverence love is and seeks knowledge of the other, not by way of curiosity nor for the sake of gaining power but in rejoicing and in wonder. In all such love there is an element of that "holy fear" which is not a form of flight but rather deep respect for the otherness of the beloved and the profound unwillingness to violate his integrity. Love is loyalty; it is the willingness to let the self be destroyed rather than that the other cease to be; it is the commitment of the self by self-binding will to make the other great. It is loyalty, too, to the other's cause—to his loyalty. As there is no patriotism where only the country is loved and not the country's cause—that for the sake of which the nation exists—so there is no love of God where God's cause is not loved, that which God loves and to which he has bound himself in sovereign freedom.[9]

6.
Sacrament
and
Success

Talk about the Church as "sacrament" can open an ugly can of worms. In few areas are disputes between Christians and between different traditions so heated as in the debate over the nature and number of sacraments—or indeed over whether we ought to talk about sacraments at all. (Some Protestants find all talk about sacraments impossibly "papist" and prefer to speak of the "ordinances" of Baptism and the Lord's Supper.) My purpose in this section is not to address, and certainly not to resolve, the hoary squabbles over how many sacraments we should count or what makes a sacrament "valid." It is rather to look at the idea of sacrament itself and to see how it can illuminate our understanding of Christian community and our ministries in that community.

Since the idea of sacrament has been such a point of controversy among Christians, one might question the wisdom of using it as a major metaphor for Church and ministry. The answer is that, despite the history of misunderstanding that the idea bears, the sacramental concept is deeply rooted in the biblical and historical faith of the Christian community. And in large sectors of the Church it has in recent years been ecumenically reconstructed in a way that makes a former point of division a new point of convergence among Christians. In this reconstructed sacramentality, it is no longer adequate to say that some churches are sacramental and some are nonsacramental. It might be countered that groups such as the Salvation Army and the Quakers repudiate the notion of sacrament altogether. But even the Salvation Army's understanding of the preaching of the gospel contains a distinctly sacramental element, and the Quaker meeting is closely related to "the consolation of the brethren," which Martin Luther, for one, was not unwilling to call a sacrament.

THE PLEDGE AND THE MYSTERY

The Latin word *sacramentum* originally referred to an oath or a pledge, especially a soldier's oath of allegiance. Although it has sometimes been used in this sense by Christians, especially in connection with confirmation or rites of personal dedication, this has not been the primary usage. Yet today we should perhaps reconsider the rich resources implicit in this meaning of sacrament. The Church, whatever else it may be, is a pledged community. The earliest Christian confession, "Jesus Christ is Lord," is not only an assertion of fact but a pledge of personal and communal allegiance. The acknowledgment of Jesus Christ as God and Savior is the core confession of the twentieth-century ecumenical movement. Every local church has some rite for the reception of members that makes explicit such a pledge of allegiance. Thus the revival meeting's invitation to come forward and accept Jesus as personal Lord and Savior is, far from being nonsacramental, premised upon and a celebration of this *sacramentum*.

In recent years there has been among all Christians a revived sense of Christianity as an eschatological faith. We are ambassadors of a disputed sovereignty that will one day be vindicated in the Kingdom come. Another way of saying this is that we are a covenanted community. Thus The Baptist Faith and Message, adopted by the Southern Baptist Convention in 1963, speaks of the local congregation as covenanted "in the faith and fellowship of the gospel, observing the two ordinances of Christ, [and] committed to His teachings." The covenant is established, of course, by God's initiative. The *sacramentum* is first of all God's humbling of himself in love, pledging allegiance to us in Christ, and then our faithful response of allegiance to his love. In biblical perspective, we can speak of different "covenanting moments," such as the covenant with Noah, with Abraham, with Jesus, and with the Church; but there is finally only one covenant—namely, that God is keeping faith with his creation and will consummate what he has begun. In the resurrection of Jesus from the dead, that consummation has already been anticipated, the *sacramentum* has been vindicated and assured. In living out that assurance in faith, we are already now the "new beings" whose true nature will, according to Romans 8, be revealed in the End Time.

Some Christians emphasize that God's gracious covenant *(sacramentum)* is first to the Church and then to individuals as they are incorporated into the Church. Others insist that it is persons who are first "saved" individually and then associate with other saved persons to bring the Church into being. The end result in either case is a community that is marked by its pledge of allegiance (its *sacramentum*) to God in Christ. Today, few would dispute the assertion that there is no person other than the person in community. That is, even the most rugged individualist is, as the social scientists say, "socially constructed." Beginning with the most elementary "givens" of language and family nurture, each individual is a communal phenomenon. Even the weapons we use to resist or change our social milieu are supplied us by that milieu. Of the many communities of which we are part, and of the many other communities of which we may choose to be part, the Church is the community whose *sacramentum* we affirm with ultimate allegiance.

Even the legendary person who comes to Christian faith without having any contact with other Christians but only with the Bible or an evangelistic tract is in fact joined to the community. The Bible is the book of the community's experience, reflection, and inspired faith. It is no less God's book for its being the Church's book. Thus we can and should transcend the sterile dispute about whether Bible or Church is supreme. That dispute only made sense when the Bible was de-historicized and de-communalized and when those on the other side of the question posited the Church as the "true Church" of a specific ecclesial organization. The understanding advanced here of Church as sacrament encompasses all the communities which comprise the historical community that is marked by its *sacramentum* of faith in response to God's *sacramentum* in Christ.

Scholars note the difference between the Latin use of "sacrament" and its use in Christian thought, where it is the word employed to translate the Greek *mysterion* (mystery). But if we understand the sacrament of God's gracious covenant in Christ and our Spirit-inspired response to that covenant, the Latin *sacramentum* is indeed a very apt translation of *mysterion*. Speaking of the allegiance that constitutes marriage, Paul writes, "This is a great mystery, and I take it to mean Christ and the church" (Eph. 5:32). Here sacrament as mystery and sacrament as pledge of allegiance come together. Most churches, perhaps all, recognize that marriage is finally constituted not by the pronouncement of the Church, and certainly not by the licensing of the state, but by the mutual pledge of allegiance by the man and woman involved. The covenanting word, also in marriage, is a creative word. It partakes in the biblical understanding of the mystery of the *logos*, the very Word of God. The word of promise is not a *mere* word but, when rooted in the covenanting Word of God, it is an effectual word that creates what it declares. Here, then, is the convergence between the "secular" Latin *sacramentum* and the "spiritual" New Testament *mysterion*. At this place of meeting, all Christians—whether or not they are in a "sacramental" tradition—can explore together Augustine's classic formula that a sacrament is "the visible form of invisible grace." Or we might say that it is the promised future in present fact. Or the prolepsis of the hoped-for consummation. Or the partial actualization of the real. There are many ways of saying it, but each way is related to the *mysterion*, the mystery of grace, and to *sacramentum*, the gift of fidelity to that mystery. However it is said, the core confidence is that this world is encompassed and shrouded by other worlds, that reality is so much more than reductionist "realists" contend, and that the whole of all that is and will be has been subjected to God in Christ.

WHAT DIFFERENCE DOES IT MAKE?

Every day the thoughtful Christian minister is challenged by the question as to whether his work really makes any difference. But how do we measure making a difference? By the number of lives transformed? Well, yes, we do see that occasionally—very occasionally. One does encounter ministers, often of an evangelical or charismatic persuasion, who hold forth ebulliently about the "miracles" to which they have been party. The sick are healed, the sad are happy, the gossips are overcome by charity, and the greedy are generous to the point of inviting bankruptcy. In my limited experience, such claims do not bear close examination. What one usually has in such cases is a group of excitable people exciting one another by confusing the fantastic with fidelity. It is the familiar story of the disciples' enthusiasm when there were many, many disciples in the heyday of Jesus' ministry, before "he turned his face toward Jerusalem."

If we are honest with ourselves, such signs of really making a difference are very ambiguous. So also with the signs of institutional growth, although, sorry to say, this seems to provide a basis of confidence—or, conversely, a cause for despair—in many ministries. Institutional growth is the last refuge of ministries that are spiritually sterile. Anniversary sermons regularly point to statistical growth or to the new educational wing as evidence that "God has richly blessed this ministry." But the question that keeps erupting within us, as to whether our ministry *really* makes any difference, cannot be answered by reference to a debt-free "church plant"—to use the ugly term of the managerially minded.

Some years ago, and still today in some quarters, the question was addressed in a different way. The proposition was advanced that every significant question is finally a political question. From this it was concluded that really making a difference means bringing about concrete change in terms of political oppression, hunger, urban decay, and a host of similar problems afflicting humankind. A long time ago, the now venerable Karl Marx said that for centuries philosophers had been trying to understand the world and now the time had come to change the world. But being at his best a reflective man, it is doubtful that Marx today would be confident that he and those who have seized his mantle have really made a difference—or if they have, that it is a difference for the better. In any case, it was and is demeaning to Christian ministry to measure the worth of what we do by our impact on the slice of reality that is political and social change.

Posted on my wall is this portion of wisdom from Ralph Waldo Emerson. I have frequent reason to reflect on it.

> How do you measure success? To laugh often and much; To win the respect of intelligent people and the affection of children; To earn the appreciation of honest critics and endure the betrayal of false friends; To appreciate beauty; To find the best in others; To leave the world a bit better, whether by a healthy child, a redeemed social condition, or a job well done; To know even one other life has breathed because you lived —this is to have succeeded.

It is a beautiful and humane statement, but for Christians there is a yet deeper grace. If we understand the radically liberating significance of sacrament, we live by grace beyond all criteria of effectiveness. In his tome on the history and theology of Christian ministry, Bernard Cooke runs through a number of ways in which we might understand the "purpose" of the Church. "Yet," he writes, "one cannot avoid the impression that the principal ministry of the community is exercised by *being,* precisely by being a community of faith and love, and as such bearing witness to the presence of God's saving action in Christ and the Spirit."[2] Paul pleaded with the Corinthians "not to accept the grace of God in vain." At the same time, he was surely responding to his own deepest questions about his ministry. The Sunday School booklets depict his missionary journeys as a triumphal march through the known world. Two thousand years later, we are awed by the consequences of a ministry that then, more often than not, seemed a shambles. Paul's response to his own uncertainties appealed to a sharp awareness of the sacramental, of the interplay between visible and invisible, known and unknown, present fact and promised future: "We are treated as impostors, and yet are true; as unknown, and yet well known; as dying, and behold we live; as punished, and yet not killed; as sorrowful, yet always rejoicing; as poor, yet making many rich; as having nothing, and yet possessing everything" (2 Cor. 6).

Here is that perfect conjunction of the sacramental: sacrament as *mysterion,* the mystery of grace, and sacrament as *sacramentum,* the pledged allegiance that knows that it is by fidelity and not by success that it will be judged whether we have received God's grace in vain. Our ministries are not liberated, and we cannot be signs of liberation to others, as long as we are captive to the criterion of effectiveness by which the world would bind us. By "the world" we mean in this instance what Paul describes as "the flesh." The conflict is not, in the first place, between us who are the saved and others who are the unsaved. If the conflict implicit in our faithful living out of the Christian *sacramentum* is seen primarily as a conflict between the Church and the world, we are in danger of missing the whole point of the Pauline picture of the Christian struggle. The conflict is within ourselves; it is a conflict between living according to the flesh and living according to the Spirit. Nor is the struggle aimed at our achieving some decisive spiritual victory, although that military metaphor is frequently used in biblical and classical literature. The achievement involved, however, takes on a meaning quite different from our usual talk about achievements. It is always a matter of living out the gift already given. This is the heart of liberated and liberating ministry: to know that our ministry and the goal of our ministry are gifts. We do not need to sniff around the secular criterion of effectiveness in order to be assured that our ministries are legitimated. We and the work we have been given to do are already legitimated and justified by the grace of God. This is God's *sacramentum* in Christ and the community he has called into being; it is the premise and the promise on which alone we can act in confidence.

THE GIFT THAT IS GIVEN

The angels over the fields of Bethlehem did not call the shepherds to the task of peacemaking or peacekeeping; they declared the gift of peace. The greeting of peace which the disciples give on entering a house is not a wish, nor is it a command. It is a gift which is either accepted or rejected as a gift. It is a present reality so real that, if it is rejected, it returns to the disciples (Luke 10:5). In Pauline thought that peace is equivalent to salvation. To view that peace as something which we must establish is to think according to "the flesh," and the sure consequence of that is death. To act upon the peace that is given is to live according to the Spirit and thus to know life. In Romans 8, *thanatos* and *zoe* are juxtaposed in a way that is parallel to what we today might mean by oppression and liberation. The understanding of our ministries as sacramental and of the Church as sacrament is the way to liberation from the imperiously oppressive demands that our work be legitimated by the criterion of effectiveness.

As is evident by now, this sacramental view depends upon a very lively sense of the *transcendent.* For understandable reasons, such a view runs into stiff opposition from many Christians who care deeply about the "worldly tasks" to which God calls us. These Christians are repulsed by a transcendence-directed piety that seems to operate on the level of mystical experience and eternal truths that are untouched by the messy, smelly stuff of human history. Against such a transcendent view, they posit an understanding of Christianity that stresses the *immanent.* In some current versions of "liberation theology," this alternative goes so far as to insist that "God *is* society"; that the utility of prayer is to be found only in its contribution to revolutionary "consciousness raising"; anything else is escapist "magic."[3] This form of liberationism, I have suggested, is in fact an old and dreadful form of captivity. Yet it can also be seen as an understandable reaction to types of piety that seem indifferent to the problems of the actual world of God's own reckless loving.

In unhappy truth, so many ministries today are caught in the false choice between transcendence and immanence. False though it is, the choice is powerfully and persistently posed. We feel the pulls and pushes of it within ourselves, for we have internalized this false way of thinking. On the one hand are the "spiritual" dimensions of Christian existence, on the other the "secular" tasks. It is not uncommon today to find ministers who were some years ago actively engaged in civil rights, community organization, and antiwar activities. Now they say they are in a period of reflection and consolidation, exploring the spiritual dimensions. At the same time, especially among "evangelicals," one finds an awakening of social consciousness that is somewhat nervous about not losing its ties to the transcendent. As it comes out in conversation and writing, it seems that there are two ways of being Christian—the Christianity of immanence and the Christianity of transcendence. In truth, there are many ways of being Christian, but none of them is built upon choosing between immanence and transcendence. Nor is it a matter of "striking a balance" between the two, for the two are not in opposition. They are not even in tension. Each is the necessary consequence of the other.

If we really take seriously the world and ourselves in it, we are driven to the transcendent. This is the wisdom of Luther's insight that even the ungodly have their gods in what they care most about. More recently, that insight has been updated by Paul Tillich's emphasis upon religion as "ultimate concern." Peter Berger makes a similar point from the perspective of sociology of knowledge, emphasizing "the signals of transcendence" that we encounter in everyday life. Language about the transcendent—about God, the Spirit, the Kingdom, and so forth—is not merely a heightened way of describing our own experience. Rather, such language refers primarily to the reality beyond our experience which we intuit within our experience. God is the reality beyond ourselves to whom we are converted.

A DOUBLE CONVERSION

To speak of conversion touches upon the experience of being "born again." "Born-again Christianity" admittedly has a bad reputation for perpetuating the false choice between transcendence and immanence, with immanence coming out the clear loser. The new birth is seen as a movement *away* from the world and *toward* God. In important respects, this view of the movement involved in religious conversion is inevitable. That is, it is inescapably a movement away from any definition of "the world" that excludes the transcendent reality we call God. Christians should not hesitate to admit, but rather should be emphatic in declaring, that such definitions are truncated and contrary to our experience. It is a great service to the world, and to the world within ourselves, to expose its pretensions, to note that it and its problems and proposals are not so important as they are made out to be. In this respect, "otherworldly" Christianity, which often takes a conservative social and political form, makes an important contribution. But the contribution is chiefly in pointing out by contrast the alternative error of an equally "worldly" Christianity. Fortunately, we do not have to choose between the proposition that "God is society" and "God is unrelated to society." What is required of the born again is to be born again. That is, a synthesis of immanence and transcendence calls for a double conversion.

The first conversion happens when, against all the truncated and oppressive definitions of reality and achievement, there breaks upon us the truth of God in Christ. Such breakthroughs are so liberating, and the accompanying experience can be so spiritually intense, that we are sorely tempted to despise what we previously thought to be reality. The "world" becomes a word of opprobrium; it is unworthy of attention from those who have their minds on higher things; it is of no final consequence; perhaps it is even illusory. But this is a one-dimensional spirituality that misses the doubling nature of Christian conversion. It is possible for those who have been converted to the religious experience itself. It is possible for those who fall in love with transcendent reality in an abstract way. It should not be possible, however, for those who have encountered the God who reveals himself in Jesus the Christ. To be converted away from the world toward this God is immediately to be converted back to the world. In other words, if we are truly converted to God in Christ, then we participate in *his* conversion to the world. We cannot love him if we do not share his love for his creation.

But it should be clear that the religious commitment to the immanent is finally for the sake of the transcendent. Some years ago, when "secular Christianity" held sway in some quarters, a Roman Catholic missionary sister wrote that the time had come for Christians to love the poor not for Christ's sake but for their own sake. She worked in Mexico and demonstrated an expansive and apparently inexhaustible caring for "the wretched of the earth." No doubt the juices of caring flow more naturally and strongly in some people than in others. But the proof of love is in loving the unlovable, in affection that is not sustained by affinity. Unless each human life is the mirror and bearer of transcendent reality, it seems neither likely nor logical that we should relate to that life with the reverence that love implies. The Mexican peasant girl, the senile old man in the nursing home, the insufferable parish gossip—these are not loved for their own sake, because we do not encounter them on their own but within the sacramental bonding of a double and doubling conversion; conversion to the transcendent God who in Christ has made himself vulnerable to our loving and our hurting in the immanent.

"MATTHEW 25"

Ministry in the inner city has taught me what little I know about the connection between spirituality and success, between sacrament and satisfaction. It was a heady thing at age twenty-four to move into the heart (some would say the core) of the Big Apple and discover how quickly one can become "an important person" who "makes a difference." I confess there were too many times when I believed the advertisements for myself issued by myself and others. In the kingdom of the disheartened, the optimist is king. And Brooklyn was disheartened and disheartening. But optimism about the difference one can make is of course a feeble premise for ministry; it cannot be sustained without delusion of self and others. I had already in seminary intuited that a sustained commitment to service required something more, an intense engagement in the sacramental mystery of The Presence. I doubt if I understood the connection very well then, and I am far from understanding it fully now, but all my experience has reinforced that intuition.

And not my experience only. I have observed over the years many ministries in the inner cities of America, and I have witnessed many burned-out cases. Young men and women, and some not so young, who came with admirable devotion and determination to make a difference, but finally the evidences of futility exhausted that devotion and broke that determination. Brooklyn and the South Bronx, and their counterparts in Cleveland, St. Louis, Chicago, and Los Angeles, do not deal kindly with those who would change the world for the better. There have been tragic instances of people abandoning ministries, shattered by a sense of guilt and betrayal; of people accepting positions in suburbia as an admission of defeat; even of suicide.

Generalizations must be made with care, but I venture this: Where the most difficult ministries are sustained, where ministries are least likely to be accompanied by the criterion of success, endurance is empowered by the sacramental anticipation of transcendent hope. Many times people have remarked the frequency with which vital inner-city ministry is joined by a lively emphasis upon liturgy and sacrament. It is no accident. And not in inner-city ministry only. The same joining of devotion and transcendence, of *sacramentum* and *mysterion,* is evident among those who work with the dying in, for example, the hospice movement. Or consider a pediatrician in a hospital here in New York. She works exclusively with extreme cases, with children suffering from the most bizarre deformities, with children battered, neglected, and starved, children on whom others have given up. By any utilitarian criterion of reducing unpleasantness and strengthening the racial stock, many of them should be killed or left to die. Such preoccupation with the world's expendable ones is, in the view of the dominant culture, morbid, if not mad. Asked why she does it, this vivid and vivifying woman answers quite simply, "Matthew 25": "Lord when did we see you . . . ?"

And so Georges Bernanos's country priest saw in his parish the face of Christ. And so we must pray for that vision if we are to be free from the illusions of success, if we are to endure. One is reminded of the words of Jesus about the poor who are always with us. The words have often been twisted into an excuse for ignoring human need. In fact they are an invitation to open-ended commitment, to endurance. The spikenard of celebration is not antithetical to, it is essential to, that commitment. Only Judas protested the waste. Our call is to lavish devotion, knowing perfectly well that others, and sometimes we ourselves, will think such devotion a waste. And when we run out of devotion to lavish, we do not try to force an enthusiasm that is not there but turn again to the word, the water, the bread and wine that bear his inexhaustible devotion to us.

The sacramental source and shape of ministerial endurance is most evident in work among the poor and expendable. But such work only throws into sharp relief what must be true of all ministry. Indeed, those who work effectively among the effective people and importantly among the important people are in far greater danger of forgetting this truth, and thus of keeping ministries alive by daily transfusions of lies. The lies of success and satisfaction are seductive and mortal enemies of ministry that is grounded in the sacramental perception of The Presence that can alone give meaning to our work. None of us is immune to these seductions, most particularly when others assure us of our success. Flattery, provided that it be disguised as something other than flattery, is infinitely sweet. So Decius Brutus says of Caesar: "But when I tell him he hates flatterers, he says he does, being then most flattered." Like politicians and entertainers, the clergy are peculiarly susceptible to flattery. It is a professional aphrodisiac. To accept flattery for being powerful or talented is a moral flaw, to accept flattery for being holy is to steal from God. We should not sustain our ministries by stealing.

The alternative to the lies of success, however, is not the mystique of failure that confuses incompetence or ineffectiveness with the way of the cross. The Christian is freed to strive with joy and succeed with thanksgiving. Success—whether in its presence or its absence —holds no terrors for those who have received their approval and invested their hope elsewhere. Christians are freed for high-spirited engagement in politics, in social change, in the arts, in business, in every worthy enterprise. As ministers we can care, and care deeply, about achieving the many things that are to be achieved; about playing a therapeutic part in the healing of the emotionally distressed, about building churches where more and more people encounter one another more and more significantly, about preaching effectively to human needs, even about writing a book on ministry. All these enterprises are worthy for the sake of God in Christ. Having been doubly converted, we can embrace these tasks freely, without the terrible fear that their success or failure is the final measure of our ministry. The gift is already given. Part of the gift is the task. While the gift is fulfilled, the task remains incomplete until the Kingdom is consummated. The task is God's. While it encompasses the whole creation, it is in the Church that the task is recognized and celebrated as God's task. Simply by recognizing and celebrating that fact, the Church becomes a *sacramentum* to the world, a communal pledge of allegiance that history's travail is not in vain.

7.
The Search for Community

Along the way the Church makes its witness in different and often ambiguous ways. The impulse to impose *the* Christian life-style or *the* model of ministry is wrongheaded. Unless it is restrained, it inevitably results in the "unchurching" of Christians who are shaped by other impulses that have equal claim to being inspired by the same Spirit. Within this community the celebration of ambiguity does not preclude contestation over differences. The choice is not between schism for the sake of truth or superficiality for the sake of unity. One serves the community poorly if one does not contribute to it the most vigorous advocacy of what one believes to be right. Disagreement is not to be tolerated but to be nurtured. As John Courtney Murray was fond of remarking, disagreement is an achievement. When we say we disagree, according to Murray, we usually mean we are confused. It takes clarity, integrity, and hard work to arrive at real disagreement. But in all our disagreements and confused agreements the unshakable confidence is that our unity—like the peace the angels announced to the shepherds—is a given. That confidence rests on our *sacramentum,* our mutual pledge of allegiance, to reverence one another within the mystery of our being a people led by God toward that time in which we shall "know even as we are known." Only then will the wheat be separated from the chaff and our disagreements illuminated as diverse perceptions of the landscape through which we pass on our pilgrim way.

Of course not all Christians subscribe to this sacramental understanding of Church and ministry, even as it is redefined here. Observers of the Christian scene have noted with alarm the growth of the "electronic church." Thousands of pulpit entrepreneurs and multimillion dollar "Christian networks" thrive on the selling of a Christianity that is divorced from, even posited against, Christian community. A few years ago, there was a ruckus in Denmark when a TV pastor proposed mailing the bread and wine of Holy Communion to his viewers. Such bizarre developments, however, almost despite themselves, underscore the inherently communal nature of Christianity. The same point is underscored by radio evangelists who offer their listeners "blessed scarves" and other religious trinkets. People want something palpable, something they can touch and feel. Thus even these most vulgar gimmicks are, no doubt unknowingly, responsive to a sacramental impulse. The "spiritual" is not hostile to the palpable, but the palpability that God wills for his Christians is chiefly other people. Hell may not be other people, but Christianity would no doubt be easier without them. Of course, then it would not be Christianity; for Christianity is the articulation in history of the truth that God is love. And love, alas, is impossible without other people.

Solid-state spirituality that centers on TV tube and cassette is in a very fragile state indeed. But we should not panic in the face of a "communications revolution" leading to the electronic church. As with most revolutions, its impact is probably greatly exaggerated. Forty and fifty years ago, when religious broadcasting was just getting under way, many of the same fears were expressed. When the late Walter A. Maier began "The Lutheran Hour," which was for many years the largest gospel broadcast in the world, it was alleged that people would stop coming to church because they could "get the Word of God at home." The people who expressed this fear seemed to think—or at least to worry that most Christians would think—that the Church could be displaced by a cosmic public address system. But most Christians in fact seem to have more sense than that. They know that that is not God's way. To be sure, God made some announcements from above, as with the angels at Christmas and the voice from heaven at our Lord's baptism and transfiguration. But these were exceptions and even then the transmission was jammed, getting through only to the very few for whom the message was intended. God's way is to enter from below in the form of living out the ambiguities and the terrors of the human condition. In the mangers and crosses of history, in the disappointments of friendship, and in the heroism of pledged allegiances kept, his presence is sacramentally signaled and secured.

Most Christians seem to understand, perhaps intuitively more than as a matter of logical deduction, this communal character of Christian existence. The simplest proof of this is that the serious ones do keep coming together. Whether when they talk about the Church they mean the broad reaches of the one, holy, catholic and apostolic Church or the little meeting house down the road, they act on the intuition that their relationship to God has something to do with their relationship to the community. The best understanding, of course, is that which holds in one thought the majesty of the Church catholic and the troublesome little band of people at Third Methodist. The communal intuition on which they act may not be legitimated by the Christian teaching they hear. As mentioned before, in that teaching the Church may be accidental or even hostile to the process of "being saved." But the people, thank God, know better than they are taught. The whole Christian message affirms the majesty of the merely human.

BEING A SACRAMENT

Ministry that understands itself as ministry of the Church, then, is uninhibited in teaching, preaching, and celebrating the Christian life together. Such ministers understand that the Church *has* sacraments (whether two, or three, or seven, or, as Hugh of St. Victor counted them in the twelfth century, thirty) and that the Church *is* a sacrament. *Life Together*, the title of Dietrich Bonhoeffer's classic and most winsome work, is an appropriate and urgent focus of our ministries. This is not to disparage those dimensions of Christians' piety that are exercised in solitude. But even the shut-in grandmother who lives alone reading her Bible is in fact, through that very Bible, in communion with the Church. "I don't see the point of visiting Mr. Watson any more," a theological intern who didn't care much for visiting the sick to begin with, once told me. "He's over ninety and senile and just babbles on or goes into deep silence, no matter what you say." The intern sinned the sin of presumption in thinking his was the only voice of the Church in that sickroom. To dismiss someone as senile is an easy way to relieve ourselves of the responsibility of reverence for those who have entered into languages and communications that we do not understand.

No doubt Mr. Watson lived in communion and communication with the Church—with parents and pastors of decades ago, with his children long dead, with the characters of Sunday School lessons lately retrieved. It is no accident that Christians involved in the growing hospice movement that offers loving care for the dying are empowered by a keen awareness that we live in a world within worlds. The same is true of perhaps the most dramatic parable of the Church as sacrament in our time—the sisters who work with Mother Teresa in sacrificial reverence toward the forsaken and dying of Calcutta. Only this overwhelming sense of the transcendent empowers one to undertake the most mundanely immanent tasks of cleaning the putrid sores and hearing out the babbled wisdom of people who, by most existing definitions of reality, are not worth the trouble. Because the Christian understands God's *sacramentum* with his creation, we must stand supportively with the most vulnerable—at the entrance and exit gates of life, and all along the way—defying those who view the most vulnerable as the most expendable. The immanent obligations of this transcendent truth apply as much to our engagement in political change as in personal care.

This transcendent confidence is our ministerial charter of liberation from all the truncated utilitarianisms to which we are otherwise captive and by which the worth of what we do is destroyed. We must never hesitate to insist that it is not sentimental poesy but a statement of fact that "no man is an island," that we are each diminished by the loss of the least. Cosmic interdependence is not the discovery of recently faddish ecological and economic theories, but has been understood by Christians of all centuries and was well expressed by Francis Thompson in the last: "Thou canst not stir a flower / Without troubling of a star."

The Christian understanding of cosmic sacramentality is in crucial ways different from current economic and ecological notions of interdependence. It has little in common with the wilderness romance of those who "find God" in unpeopled places, or who discover it is easier to love animals because we can impose our meanings upon their barks and grunts. Recently, a missionary in Asia lamented the grotesquely distorted values of our culture. The "boat people" from Indochina were fleeing their new tyrannies and were being turned back by the ships they hailed for help. Japan and other Asian nations refused them haven. "Ten thousand or more refugees," said the missionary, "lie on the bottom of the sea, and American singers cancel engagements in Japan to protest the Japanese killing of porpoises." Between people and porpoises our priorities should be clear. Only as we enhance the centrality of people in the sacramental economy of creation can human beings be held accountable for all things bright and beautiful, all things great and small. Humankind is the crown and the cantor of creation. Our dignity is manifest in the exercise of our responsibility, and our chief responsibility is to be the cantor, the sayer and the singer of the praises of him in whom all creation finds its meaning.

One is bemused and appalled by Christians who come to an understanding of cosmic interdependence through political, ecological, or economic theories. None of these theories can, in a satisfying and sustaining way, answer the brutal but inescapable question, "Why should we give a damn?" Why, for example, give a damn about the hungry of the world? Because otherwise the revolutionary hordes will overrun us by force? Not bloody likely, and any attempt would likely be very bloody. Because it is to our benefit that the poor be integrated into a world economy? The proponents of "triage" and of "lifeboat ethics" make a plausible case for ridding ourselves of the wretched of the earth. No, finally we care because it is not poetry but revealed truth (although, to be sure, a revealed truth sometimes best expressed in poetry) that the human community is one. Because God is One, all who are God's are one. The Church is a communal articulation of that truth.

THE PRIVATE AND THE COMMUNAL

It is the purpose of the Church to *sight*, to *signal*, to *support*, and to *celebrate* the future of all humankind. This is what it means to say the Church is a sacrament. It is the partial actualization of the reality of the Kingdom. Within this mystical communion even the most solitary act of devotion is a communal event. As we must minister against the notion of privatized salvation, so we must try to overcome the ideas implicit in, for example, the distinction between "private prayer" and communal prayer. There is no such thing as private prayer, there is only prayer in private. And even prayer in the appearance of privacy is, in wondrous truth, communal prayer. If it is prayer through Christ, as all Christian prayer must be, then it is prayer in communion with all who are in communion with Christ.

A priest of my acquaintance is a theologically sophisticated soul, well aware of the corporate and communal emphases in modern eucharistic thought. Yet, when his work prevents him from taking part in his community's liturgy, he regularly goes into the chapel and offers mass alone. It is all very pre-Vatican II. It is even more (or less) than that, since not even a server is present. "I do not quarrel with the corporate emphasis of contemporary liturgical thought," says he, "and I know some would think my practice highly questionable. But to me it is clear beyond doubt that this is a communal liturgy offered with the whole Church on behalf of the world." Such practice is alien to most Western Christians today, whether Roman Catholic or other, but we should all be very much at home with the intention. If to stir a flower is to trouble a star, how much greater is the communal presence and how much greater the cosmic consequences in our acts of devotion. To stir the mysteries of Bible, of water and bread and wine, to name the Name that is above every name, is to call the universe to attention.

How petty, then, are the fears and how contemptible the criteria by which we permit our ministries to be called into question. Possessed of this transcendent truth, we cannot be intimidated by those who deride as "magic" what does not fit the procrustean bed of their blindness. Those who dwell in what Plato described as the cave of the shadows may not abide the witness of others who have stood up and seen the reality of which the shadows are but a reflection. For those who see only the shadows, their religion is at best their own projection from what they think the shadows might imply. But for those who are persuaded of the reality that has appeared in Christ, the shadows are the present of what is to be. Their faith, and the community in which that faith is shared and sustained, becomes the *sacramentum,* the pledge and promise, that the shadows will be superseded by the reality to which they point.

The purpose of the Church is to sight, signal, support, and celebrate the coming of the Kingdom. Having sighted that coming in the Christ, the Church is to signal it in word and life. As a sacrament, the Church symbolizes the future of the whole of humankind. This understanding of the Church is firmly grounded in the documents of Vatican II, is frequently alluded to in the statements of the World Council of Churches and other ecumenical agencies, and has a long and venerable tradition both in Catholic religious orders and in the "intentional communities" of Quakers, Brethren, Mennonites, and others. Surely this is one of the most exciting hopes of Christian ministry: to be an instrument of the Spirit's upbuilding of a community that, by the very quality of its life together, signals ultimate hope to the world.

One suspects there is not a preacher in Christendom who has not at one time or another, or at many times, exhorted the flock to emulate the early Church. It is alleged that the pagan world looked at that community and declared, "Behold, how they love one another!" But those who said that must not have been looking at the Church in Corinth, if Paul's accounts are to be credited, nor, if the Book of Revelation is to be believed, at the churches in Ephesus, Pergamum, Thyatira, and several other places. The pagan historian Ammianus Marcellinus, writing in the fourth century, wrote that the emperor Julian "quite rightly admonished the quarrelling bishops of the Christians who had been introduced into the palace along with their divided people. He urged that each man should freely serve his own religion, forbidden by no one. . . . For he had learned that the hatred of wild beasts for man is less than the ferocity of most Christians toward one another."[1]

It is probably fair to say that, as often as not, the communal life of Christians has obscured rather than signaled the love of God. Not infrequently, life together is mainly strife together. This commonly comes as a shock to young men and women entering the ministry. Among those who later leave to go into professional counseling or to take holy orders in the church of Health, Education, and Welfare, a frequent reason given is disillusionment with sheep who turned out to be wolves. It is easy to say that such ministers should have known better, that their idealized view of the Church was naive and immature, and what did they expect from a Church that is, after all, made up of people.[2] But it must be admitted that there is no adequate preparation for the virulence of sheer nastiness that so often erupts in the life of the Christian community. It is a special sort of nastiness, perhaps because proximity to the sacred multiplies the force of the demonic. Envy, resentment, and unalloyed hatred can make their appearance in any human association, but they seem so ghastly in the Church because they so flagrantly contradict the stated purpose of the association.

CONFLICT RESOLVED AND RESTRAINED

A pastor must have the highest expectations of his people, a vision of them grander than their vision of themselves, but that does not mean that one plays innocent about the forms of maliciousness that can infest Christian community. Paul knew all about the ways in which Christians "bite and devour one another" (Gal. 5), are overbearing and constantly feuding (1 Cor. 1), are lacking in humility and knowledge (1 Cor. 8), and otherwise betray their high calling. On all these occasions, Paul "recalls" them to be who they are (Rom. 15). And so we are in the business of constantly recalling the community to community. Today many clergy take courses in "conflict resolution," and there are no doubt values in that. But there is also the danger of giving evil dynamics a kind of legitimacy in the life of the Church. We are counseled, "Let's all get together and work out our hostilities, suspicions, and resentments toward one another." But some evils are not to be worked out and some conflicts are not to be managed—they are simply not to be admitted into the community's life at all. Does this drive conflicts underground? Perhaps so, but some things must be suppressed. The answer to many of the evils that arise in the life of the Church is not resolution but repentance, and, short of repentance, restraint.

There is scarcely a ministry that is not marred by the gossip, jealousies, and petty ambitions of parish life. The wise pastor will, I believe, work intensively with people on a private basis, but in communal settings he will permit not an iota of legitimacy to such expressions. For example, at a vestry or parish council meeting, Henry makes a derogatory remark about another member of the council whose leadership he resents. Let the minister respond immediately, "I'm sorry, Henry, that is not the way we speak of brothers and sisters in Christ." Let him "recall" the community to its formal definition as a fellowship of love. No matter that the pastor may be thought slightly too "homiletical" or excessively sensitive. If he is not able to recall the meeting to its proper purpose and tone, better he should leave the room than that he should enter upon acrimonious exchanges. The fear of "hurting the pastor" may not be the best reason for people to be kind to one another, but it will do in a pinch.

The discipline of salutary suppression is essential when people bring the minister bits of dirt about other members, as some inevitably do. We must tell them that, unless they have first talked it over face to face with the other person, we do not want to hear a word about it. (The alert pastor will likely have picked up the bit of dirt before the arrival of the gossip's retailer, in any case.) But these procedures are already spelled out in Matthew 18; and were they observed more closely, the Church today would more believably signal the love of God. Especially is this true in churches where there is more than one pastor or other potential ambiguities in leadership roles. It seems to be very much the exception when in multi-pastor churches leadership is marked by wholehearted and mutual trust and support. The Absolom syndrome is as virulent today as in King David's court. In one parish I know of, a younger pastor, steeped in the techniques of the human potential movement and of conflict management, nurtured a nest of discontent against the senior pastor for many months. He protested, perhaps he even believed, that he was "resolving" these hostilities when in fact he was encouraging them; he was encouraging them from the first day they were admitted as a legitimate part of congregational discourse. Given a toehold, all such hostilities, suspicions, and jealousies tend to compound themselves.

Of course there are unpleasantnesses that cannot and should not be suppressed. Pastors are sometimes tyrannical and guilty of flagrant neglect of duty. Members do act in mean ways to one another, and differences must be resolved. With respect to conflicts between pastors, a good word must be said for what is usually called "professional ethics." That means working things out between the pastors involved and, if that is not enough, calling in whatever outside pastoral help is available. It is a foolish pastor who undermines his colleague among the people; the more he wins the more he loses, for he only sets himself up to be undermined. Above all, personal animosities and party squabbling must not be permitted to infect the life of the congregation as such. Every parish has a certain number of troublemakers—that seems to be an eminently safe generalization. We do not mean the people who raise troubling but necessary questions but the people who, it must finally be concluded, just enjoy making trouble, or, if they don't enjoy it, at least they cannot help it. They must be lovingly restrained or, failing that, simply bypassed in the communal life and work. No church officer or volunteer is so valuable that his or her services are worth draining the fellowship of its joy or distracting it from its purpose.

Of course this counsel goes against the view that all conflicts are resolvable, that all interests can be harmonized, if only we are prepared to work them out with patience, candor, and rationality. It is a winsome dogma. The harder truth is that, in this far from the best of all possible worlds, there are vices and resulting tensions that cannot be resolved—certainly not in the romper room of pop psychology—but can only be offered up at the altar of God. The peace we make with our brothers and sisters before going to the altar is often a very partial peace; it is sometimes more of a truce and a pledge to be decent to one another, in the hope of one day more fully actualizing God's promised *shalom*. Community as God's gift in Christ is as unshakable as the rock of salvation; the living out of it is always fragile and tentative. The wise pastor knows that by persistence of word and consistency of action he will always be "recalling" the congregation to the gift by which we are defined as the Church of Christ.

Then too, the Church deals in ultimates, thus creating a climate in which vices, as well as virtues, can be carried to their limit. In other associations that do not purport to specialize in the virtues of love, it is assumed that the purpose of the association is limited and that hurts inflicted can be healed elsewhere—in a community of healing love such as the Church, for example. It is especially depressing when the place of healing inflicts new hurts. There is no hate so hateful as the hate that is exercised in the name of Christian love. There is no appeal from it because it has incorporated into itself the point of appeal. The poison has co-opted the antidote. Today there is much discussion of "iatrogenic" disease, meaning diseases caused by medical treatment itself. Similarly, in the community of love and hope, the experienced minister learns the force of ecclesiogenic hostility and despair.

Ministry must focus on the quality of the community's life, but it must never rely on it. One recalls the legend of John, the evangelist and apostle, when he was a very, very old man. Carried into the church for his final sermon, he said, "Little children, love one another." And then he said it again, and again, and again. In fact, that was all he said. And some of the people thought it a shame that the silliness of a senile old man should be exhibited in such a fashion; but others understood that John's sermon summed up a long life's reflection on the meaning of the gospel. Like John, we must never weary of the simple exhortation to love. Such inexhaustible perserverance is derived not from the response of the people but from the inexhaustible love of God in Christ. With respect to the ministry of love, the proof of the pudding is not in the people but in the promise.

COMMUNITIES OF SPECIALIZED INTENT

Martin Luther King, Jr., spoke of the vision of "the beloved community," and that is finally an eschatological vision. But its promise is to be anticipated now, and it is the Church's mission to signal that anticipation to the world. That signal is sent when Christians are, as they sometimes indeed are, a loving community, but it is sent most surely when the Church proclaims that the Church and the whole creation are beloved by God. Particular intentional communities of Christians may by the quality of their life together signal the love of God. This is the intention of classic religious orders such as the Franciscans or Benedictines. Recent years have witnessed the growth of communities of intensive sharing among charismatics, and there are several lively communities of "evangelicals" brought together around Christian commitment to an agenda of social witness and change. Those who participate in such communities soon learn—as Benedict well knew in the sixth century—that there is no simple equation between intensity of interaction and the quality of love.

For a number of years in the inner city of Brooklyn, about a dozen of us—men and women, teachers, social workers, and pastors—shared a form of communal life and work. While it is not true that familiarity breeds contempt, intensity does give rise to contention. The clearer the intention and the greater the intensity, the harder one must work at sustaining community. Anyone who wishes to avoid the ambiguity of more ordinary church life by entering intentional community is likely to be badly disappointed. The ambiguities are magnified, not diminished. This will come as no surprise to the millions who live in that most common form of Christian community, the family.

The impulse to form communities of particular intention has almost always been part of the Church's life. Following World War II, there was an upsurge of interest in community life among Protestants, inspired by the examples of the Iona community in Scotland and the Taizé community in France. One fervently hopes that interest will continue and grow in the years ahead. But such communities should not be viewed as an alternative to the larger Church as a sacramental signal to the world. Even in the strongest community, the chief signal is not in the quality of the life together. The signal is in what is proclaimed. That proclamation is made in word and in the work to which the community devotes itself—whether that work be perpetual adoration of the reserved sacrament or caring for Calcutta's street people. Only as a consequence, in a way that is not to be the chief focus of attention but is almost, one might say, incidental, only in this way is the quality of shared life itself the signal of the promise. Bonhoeffer wrote in *Life Together:* "In true Christian love, one speaks more to Christ about the beloved than to the beloved about Christ." Only in drawing upon the transcendent presence and promise is the immanent project of community empowered.

As with so many of the most important things in life, community eludes those who seek it too earnestly. Similarly, it is hard to love the person who so insistently demands to be loved. Indeed, Jesus suggests that it is not by grasping but by surrender to something greater that life itself is gained. In seeking life beyond our lives we find our lives. It was a hard saying then and it is a hard saying now. We seem to feel that we have a "right" to love, acceptance, and the experience of community. If the life of the Church does not provide this, then the Church has failed and we have been cheated. Certainly such a failing Church cannot be a sacrament signaling anything of significance. Every pastor knows the wayward member who absents himself or herself because "the Church doesn't meet my needs." It is the skilled and sensitive pastor who is able to engage such persons in a critical examination of how needs are to be defined. Such examination can lead to liberation from the chains of narcissism by which we are bound.

Augustine, Luther, and a host of others who have thought about it have declared the essence of sin to be "man turned in upon himself." Over the human condition and tightly woven throughout it is the legend *incurvatus est.* So virulent and insidious is this self-centeredness that it is even able to seize upon the dynamics of community. That is, on the face of it, it would seem that the yearning for community is a movement from oneself toward others, but that is not necessarily the case. What caters to *my need* for community is only a small part of what should be meant by community. It may be quite the opposite of community. The conventional wisdom in current writing on community, as also on sexuality, is that authentic relationships are joyful, creative, integrative, and self-enhancing. Such are the buzzwords of a banality that dares not risk the loving community of shared sorrow, of confusion and disintegration, of forgetfulness of self.

The Christian Church does not *and should not* signal to the world the possibility of community in which alienation is overcome, loneliness is banished, disagreements are harmonized, and people are perfectly integrated into a common consciousness and cause. Such a group reflects not the terrible love of God but the self-indulgent mush of conformity and false consciousness. The Church should not strive for such community—not because it cannot be attained, but because it is attained all too easily. Although people who go in for this form of community frequently claim to be the avant garde, it is in fact regressive. One has only to let oneself slide back into adolescent hungers for acceptance, for belonging, for at-oneness. Real community is not homogeneity. It is the discipline and devotion of disparate people bearing with one another in the hard tasks of love.

Community clutched is community lost. Our *sacramentum,* our pledge of allegiance, is not to our self-fulfillment in community but to the beloved community of God's promised Kingdom in which alone we will find fulfillment. Paul is emphatic in his assertion that it does not yet appear what we shall be. Therefore, any community conforming to what we now define as our authentic selves must be inauthentic. Such community is not a provocation to pilgrim venture but an act of closure. Community that is defined in terms of meeting our present needs suffocates in its very success. It does not breathe the air of promise. It denies our ultimate need to subject our needs to Christ. *Incurvatus est.*

LETTING DISILLUSIONMENT DO ITS WORK

The third curate who labors under a tyrannical pastor in a Boston parish of ten thousand souls casts an envious eye at the failed experiments he reads about in the *National Catholic Reporter* (a publication which, his pastor makes clear, he ought not to be reading in the first place). At age thirty-two, our Father O'Connell finds his days crammed with mechanized routines of weddings, funerals, hospital visits, confessions, masses, and dreary dinners with a boozy superior whose intellectual interests are bounded by roof repairs and the success of the Boston Celtics this season. The syndrome is ecumenical. The director of Christian education in a large Methodist church in Fort Worth groans under the bureaucratized grind of lesson plans, recruiting half-hearted volunteers for programs of uncertain purpose, and churning out mimeographed assurances that everything is just dandy at "the friendly church."

Of the more than 300,000 local churches in America, it is hard to say what is the normal or typical situation. But circumstances like those in the Boston Catholic and Fort Worth Methodist churches make up a very large part of the religious scene. Young people coming through the seminaries today must brace themselves for the possibility of years of ministry in these and similar situations. They, like those who have gone before them, will lament the absence of community. They will resent being viewed as junior engineers of mass religiosity and will wonder what all this has to do with the high vision of the Church as sacrament. Nor is such disillusionment and frustration limited to those who are slotted to be minor cogs in the machinery of large urban and suburban parishes. Ministerial expectations can be even more confining in the small town or rural parish in Illinois or North Carolina. The young pastor is quickly put on notice that he is there to service the religious habits of those who pay the bills, and indeed is expected to recruit others to this institution of predetermined purpose. He or she is a prophet, to be sure, and prophetic posturing that does not call for change is welcomed; a teacher, to be sure, provided the teaching does not call for rethinking of first principles; a priest, to be sure, as long as the point isn't pushed too far—for in an individualistic and voluntaristic culture where alternative media compete in offering instant salvation, nobody's ministrations are indispensable.

We have said that aspirants to the ministry must brace themselves for these situations of disillusionment. Of course there are alternatives. One may elect to join up with a more intentional community, and that can be a promising or dismal alternative, depending on what one intends. If one intends to commit oneself, in company with others, to a work that is generally neglected and despised and that requires individual and communal discipline that challenges the flabbiness of more conventional church life, then such a decision is in the venerable tradition of radical vocation. Such decisions deserve to be encouraged much more than they are in most churches today. Such radical Christian vocations will always, God willing, be a part of the Church's sacramental signal and challenge to the world.

If, however, one intends to seek out like-minded people who are in search of the experience of community as such, the enterprise is more doubtful. Even if it is unfair, it is understandable that some others will view such a decision as an evasion or as self-indulgent. Kinder folk might simply be tolerant of it as another instance of a group doing its own thing. The track record of such communal quests is, at best, ambiguous. In the past decade or more, many hundreds of "communes" were begun in order to demonstrate "alternative life-styles." Those that have lasted have generally been built upon deeply religious motivation. And, of the religious communities, staying power has been most marked among those that have developed a well-understood discipline tuned to a clear communal task. In short, for all our modern pretensions, the basics of community in the latter part of the twentieth century are not all that different from what they were when Benedict wrote his Rule in the first part of the sixth century.

In fact, however, most ministers are not going to elect membership in an intentional community of the type we have been discussing. If community is to be found and signaled, it will be in connection with institutions such as First Methodist, Grand Boulevard

Baptist, St. Bonaventure's Catholic, and All Saints Lutheran. But here too it is both possible and tempting to evade the bracing challenge of dealing with the Church as sacrament. In any local church with more than one or two hundred members, it is possible to cultivate communities within the community. In truth it is desirable that this should happen, for the interests and the levels of commitment to diverse interests are not uniform within any group. It becomes a problem when the result is the building of "a church (or churches) within the Church." It becomes a problem when, as one Lutheran pastor recently remarked of a group in his parish devoted to social action, "This is the only group that keeps me going here; without them, I have a hard time thinking of this congregation as the Church." Other pastors in other places might say the same thing about groups devoted to liturgical renewal, Bible study, or charismatic prayer. Here, to the extent that it is to be found at all, is that "community" for which we yearn.

Yet our ministries are of and to the Church, not just to the sectors of the Church that we select. The local pastor is called to the Church in that place as it forms and identifies itself. Real community, community that signals something new, is community that crosses the lines of race, class, and natural affinity. The compositions of most local churches already reflect a selection process—whether conscious or not—along racial, class, and ethnic lines. Yet even a congregation made up ninety percent of middle-class Italian Catholics or German Lutherans or WASP Episcopalians or black Baptists contains within it the great divides which genuine community must bridge: divides of personal hostility, of likes and dislikes, of conflicting ambitions, of different political orientations, and, most important, of quite different ways of understanding what it means to be a Christian. Frequently such "normal" congregations are put down as bland or uninteresting. Those who specialize in the presumably prophetic have an armory of rhetoric by which to expose the fatuities and hypocrisies of conventional church life. Such people are the experts in the teaching of contempt, and countless clergy have learned their lessons all too well.

Again, true prophecy is the opposite of contempt; it is an office of love. It takes little effort to depict congregational life as dull, vapid, and devoid of anything meriting our devotion. So much depends upon the interpretation. Family life can be dismissed as mindless, sex as dirty, and politics as absurd—if one is minded to interpret them in these ways. When powers of interpretation fail, cynicism, disguised as sophistication, is a ready substitute. Its corrosive power can soon empty any entity of meaning. The notion of the Church as sacrament—as signal of the beloved community—is easy prey.

We have said the minister in search of community must be braced for disillusionment. But it is more than a matter of gritting one's teeth inwardly and bearing with the disappointment. The disillusionment must be permitted to do its work of challenging our thinking about community itself. After disillusionment comes the work of reconstruction, of re-envisioning our view of the Church and re-impassioning our commitment to the ministry of the Church.

8.
To Celebrate
the
Mystery

In declaring the sovereignty of Christ, now disputed, we declare the future of the whole world. Critics of what is called the theology of hope frequently complain that it does not address the needs and hungers of *here and now.* And no doubt some theological statements about the Kingdom and about hope reflect that failure. But it is precisely in speaking of the future that we address the here and now; for the needs and hungers of the moment cannot be understood except by reference to that healing and filling which is the promised future.

The good news is that the future is already present in Jesus the Christ. In the 1920s and 1930s, some Americans and other Western sympathizers returned from revolutionary Russia to declare, "We have seen the future, and it works." As we know in retrospect of the Gulag Archipelago, and as they probably should have known then, they saw only what the regime wanted them to see. Since then other political pilgrims have visited other presumably noble social experiments and proclaimed other futures that work. Almost without exception, later evidence of massive hunger, political executions, and concentration camps has discredited such proclamations. Such perennial disillusionment with political utopias has led Jacques Ellul, for one, to condemn "the political illusion." What should be condemned is not the illusion of politics as such, but the illusion that politics can satisfy the deepest yearnings of the human condition.

Yet in contending for the disputed sovereignty of the Christ, we too are proposing some kind of political solution. Politics has to do with the right ordering of the city, the *polis,* and the Kingdom of God is the promised right ordering of the city of God and the city of man. This is the radically new politics that makes everything else that claims to be the "New Politics" dismally dated by comparison. What is genuinely good and noble in our political strivings is taken up and fulfilled in the consummation of the Kingdom. What is base—although often disguised as good and noble—is purged by fire. In sighting the Kingdom we have made a political sighting, and from it we make a political statement; but it is so thoroughly superior to what presently passes as politics that it is only with great caution that we should describe ours as a political vision. Against those who would capture the vision to support the American Way of Life or to reinforce the struggle for scientific socialism, we must insist upon the uncapturably restless singularity of the Kingdom promise. In making possible a loyalty to a vision that is not captive to the illusions of the present—whether political, economic, or therapeutic—the Christian gospel addresses the most urgent need of the here and now, the need for liberated openness to the future.

Although the vision, properly understood, is political, modern ideas about politics have become so debased and tyrannical that they must be "debunked" by those who contend for the new politics of the Kingdom. In sorry truth, many well-meaning Christians intensify rather than resist the tyranny of what is meant by politics. Thus a diocesan official in Brooklyn bemoans the fact that some inner-city pastors chose as their year's focus of effort "liturgical renewal." "Here you are surrounded by bombed-out housing, a school system that is a criminal exercise in diseducation, youth unemployment of forty percent, and children's lives devastated by drugs, and you're going to escape into 'liturgical renewal'?" he remarked with disdain. "Why don't you do something that makes a difference in the real world?"

AFFIRMING THE "REAL WORLD"

Ah, the real world. How very compelling, how tyrannical in its insistence, is that phrase. The "real world" is regularly invoked in service of the imperiousness of politics. The English novelist E. M. Forster used to bridle when others urged him to "face reality." He would go through the motions of turning around in a circle. "Which way should I face," he would ask, "since it seems that reality is all around me?" And so it is when we are urged to attend to the business of the "real world." To be sure, there is among Christians a kind of latent Hinduism that denies the reality of experienced fact. We must always oppose those forms of spirituality that are linked to notions of divine truth so sublime that they cannot be demeaned by contact with the thus and so-ness of ordinary life. The possibility of embracing that kind of spirituality was closed to us by the incarnation. Yet it is precisely in liturgy that, with exquisite lucidity, we come to terms with the thus and so-ness of everyday experience. The real world is the world of which Christ is King. In signaling that truth, the Church makes its most important and most distinctive contribution to the here and now.

We are to sight, signal, support, and celebrate the coming of the Kingdom. Having sighted the Kingdom in Jesus the Christ, we signal his presence in our proclamation and, however ambiguously, in our life together. Part of that signal is our support for the works of love and struggle for justice. Thus it is true to say that social engagement is "constitutive of gospel proclamation," as papal statements and much recent theology assert. But such engagement is never the total substance of, never the substitute for, such proclamation. Most important, social or political effectiveness is not the norm of all we do or say in our ministries. Our proclamation can no more be held hostage to politics than it can be hostage to psychological notions of the therapeutic. A recent study from the National Council of Churches dealt with the alleged oversupply of clergy and proposed some possible remedies for the problem. It concluded on the limp note that more survey research was needed "in order to determine whether there might not be spiritual needs among the American people that might be met by the Christian gospel." Of course this is ludicrously wrongheaded. As though the Christian gospel is limited to whatever "spiritual needs" might be turned up by survey research. As though our mission is not to the whole person —spiritual, physical, intellectual, social. As though we are not to be calling radically into question what people define as their "needs." As though the Church were in the business of market research, sniffing around for little things to do that might make it seem useful again.[1]

To sight, to signal, to support, to celebrate—in each of these dimensions of mission we must pray for greater nerve to risk everything on the coming of the Kingdom. Specifically, we must assert the ultimate "worthwhileness" of worshiping God, quite apart from, if necessary, any benefit that gives worth to an activity. In the words of the 1975 Hartford Appeal, "We worship God because God is to be worshiped." I say quite apart from any benefit *if necessary.* In fact it is not usually necessary to separate the benefits. That is, one can enumerate an impressive list of "benefits" to be discovered in the activity we call worship. Participating in the liturgy, the *leitourgia,* of the People of God can heighten consciousness, build social solidarity, enhance personal identity, advance the appreciation of the beautiful, relieve anxieties, and a number of other good things. But the worthwhileness of worship must never be premised upon anything other than the unsurpassable worthiness of God. *For the very sake of the world* we must assert the sovereignty of God; *for the very sake of the present* we must assert the priority of the future. Not only is it true that liturgy *should not* be vindicated by reference to any present utility; it *cannot* be. Our worship of God can only be vindicated by the consummation of the rule of God. Only in the coming of the Kingdom will it be obvious that we were not worshiping an illusion.

But God raised him high
and gave him the name
which is above all other names
so that all beings
in the heavens, on earth and in the underworld,
should bend the knee at the name of Jesus
and that every tongue should acclaim
Jesus Christ as Lord,
to the glory of God the Father.

(Phil. 2, NEB)

That purpose has not yet been accomplished. All beings do not now bend the knee, nor does every tongue acclaim. We do. What all should acknowledge and one day will acknowledge (with joy or with regret) we now acknowledge. It is that acknowledgment—that bending and acclaiming, that worship—that finally and alone makes us the Church, a people ahead of time.

SPECIFYING THE MYSTERY

It must be admitted that for many ministers their role as leader of worship does not have high priority. There are many reasons for this, and we touch on some of them in this chapter. For some, worship is a routinized activity of simply "following the book." In many congregations, other activities, usually organizational or related to personal crises, make overweening demands, whereas there is no popular clamor for rethinking the liturgy. Then too, some ministers are put off by experiences with "liturgical renewal" that suggest there is something precious or effete about such interests. Finally, however, interest in worship suffers from the fact that it often seems "irrelevant to the real world." Although few would state it so bluntly, prayer seems to be a distraction from so much that needs doing. Prayer is closely related to piety, and when was the last time you heard someone referred to as pious when it was not meant as a put-down? When one says, for example, that a statement was pious, it is usually implied, if not said, that it was a pious platitude. In the real world of relevance, piety has acquired a very bad name.

Yet piety, devotion, and reverence are the attitudes integral to true worship. It is a grievous fault in our thinking when we set reverence against relevance. It is debilitating to true worship when the expression of reverence is tailored to conventional notions of relevance. Were one to indulge in paradox, it is not too much to say that the most relevant thing about worship is its irrelevance. True worship is an act of liberation because it defies every criterion of utility by which our lives are too much bound.

This does not mean we should strive for irrelevance as an end in itself. Antiquarians who defend the use of esoteric language and obscure ceremony frequently emphasize the need for "a sense of mystery" in worship. But we should not mistake obfuscation for the Christian mystery. *The* Christian mystery is the presence of Christ among his people, the reality of the Kingdom's presence because the King is present where two or three are gathered in his name. Whether in a rural Methodist chapel or in a cathedral's solemn high mass, everything done and said in Christian worship should be a manifestation of, a clear response to and a clear pointing toward, this mystery of Jesus the Christ encountering and accompanying his people on the way to the Kingdom. Incense, vestments, chanting, tambourines, testimonials, dancing, and "Amen corners"—all are appropriate to the extent that they illuminate *the* mystery. The best form becomes perverse when it is merely a contrivance to create a "worshipful atmosphere" or to run tingly sensations up and down our spiritual spines.

Every form of worship is relevant, if you will, to the purpose of worship when it makes clear the fact that here is a community doing an utterly singular thing. It is something that is not done—or should not be done—at political rallies; that is not—or should not be—experienced in sexual ecstasy; that is not—or should not be— characteristic of our daily labors. The utterly singular thing about worship is that it is the communal response of unqualified encounter with the Absolute. The activity called worship is not true worship if it can be done legitimately in any other context. That is, worship, if done in response to anything other than the mystery of God in Christ, is idolatry.

Thus the risk of idolatry is integral to the meaning of true worship. It is frightening in that, if the mystery proclaimed turns out not to be true, one has surrendered oneself to a false god, and therefore to death. This is the inescapable risk of an unqualified act. Worship that has a purpose beyond itself is much safer. That is, if one participates in liturgy because it is aesthetically uplifting or psychically soothing, the benefits are secured quite apart from the truth of the mystery. But then one has not engaged in true worship. Even in that case the language one has affirmed speaks of the Absolute. But if one did not really mean what one said, then one is just a superficial person guilty of blasphemy at worst. One has to be much more serious about worship to run the risk of idolatry. Unhappily, many of the reasons given for "going to church" are invitations to blasphemy.

The sign on the front of a Presbyterian church in Indianapolis reads: "Join Us For Worship. You Will Feel Better For It!" It is far from obvious that worship will make one feel better. To be sure, in a very ultimate sense, surrendering oneself to God in thankful trust will make one *be* better. But along the way to being better the Christian is sure to go through times of *feeling* worse. Repentance, after all, involves a painful loss of self, an abandonment of false securities, and the travail of new birth. It is also true with respect to what happens on Sunday mornings: Woe to you when they say it feels so good.

One of the troubling things about the ebullient testimonials of the "born again" is that the birth seems to have been without pain, without scars, without sacrifice. Neo-Pentecostals in particular, but not Neo-Pentecostals alone, make the new birth sound more like winning the lottery than walking the way of cross and resurrection. The payoff, we are told, is family harmony, business success, sexual fulfillment, and a host of other goodies. One hears little about the gifts of the Spirit that have to do with suffering. "We rejoice in our sufferings, knowing that suffering produces endurance, and endurance produces character, and character produces hope" (Rom. 5:3). "Blessed be the God and Father of our Lord Jesus Christ. . . . For as we share abundantly in Christ's sufferings, so through Christ we share abundantly in comfort too" (2 Cor. 1). "But rejoice in so far as you share Christ's sufferings, that you may also rejoice and be glad when his glory is revealed" (1 Pet. 4).

The scriptures are emphatic that there can be no new birth without death. Luther caught the idea in explaining the meaning of baptism in his *Small Catechism:* "What does such baptizing with water signify? It signifies that the Old Adam in us should, by daily contrition and repentance, be drowned and die with all sins and evil lusts and, again, a new man daily come forth and arise, who shall live before God in righteousness and purity forever." True worship is radically countercultural in a culture that, as Ernest Becker has analyzed it so devastatingly, is set upon "the denial of death."[2] The poet J. V. Casserly has devised an epitaph that might be applied to the lives and deaths of many: "An old dissembler who lived out his lie / Lies here as if he did not fear to die."

Many Christians, notably the martyrs of all times, have given convincing witness to their transcendence of the fear of death. If we do not fear death, however, it is because we have had so much experience with dying. "We are buried with Christ by baptism into death, that, like as he was raised up from the dead by the glory of the Father, even so we also should walk in newness of life" (Rom. 6). And not only at the moment of baptism, but in every act of worship there is a dying. In most churches today there is much talk about worship as the celebration of life, and that is good. But it must be asked whether we are celebrating life in the defeat of death or in the denial of death.

When we say that we celebrate the coming of the Kingdom, the celebration we have in mind is more a passion than a party. The passion is the pathos of God in Christ, leading his creation with suffering love toward the fulfillment of his promise. A recent Latin American book on political theology ended on the subject of worship, declaring that "we celebrate our hope, our solidarity, and our commitment to justice." The suggestion is that our celebration is the celebration of ourselves. It makes little difference whether the proposition is advanced by the revolutionary priest in Guatemala or by the born-again car dealer in Houston, whether it is offered in service of dialectical materialism or blatantly self-indulgent materialism; the proposition is perverse. The truth is, "We worship God because God is to be worshiped."

It is common today (maybe it has itself become a cheap shot) to quote Bonhoeffer's warnings about "cheap grace." Certainly the invocation of such prophetic rumblings is not very helpful if it simply makes people feel guilty about having missed out on moments of heroic confrontation with evil incarnate, as in the Third Reich. The connection between worship and the risk of self-surrender is more obvious where one can be jailed or executed by a regime that tolerates no allegiance to higher sovereignty. The connection is more tenuous in a situation such as ours in North America where, at least in many places, one is more likely to be censured for *not* gathering with the worshiping community. Yet here too, or here especially, true worship should stimulate the exercise of heroic virtue. Is there surrender, is there a daring and a dying, for the thirty-five-year-old homemaker of St. Paul's Church, Massena, New York, and for J. C. Penney's regional sales manager who is a member of Gospel Tabernacle in Los Angeles? Surely the daily dyings and abandonments of self are no less heroic for these people than for Bonhoeffer and his friends, although they may be less dramatic and public.

Worship is the perilous enactment of God's *sacramentum* with us, and ours with him. When we speak of worship as "celebration," we must know that we are not celebrating our securities and satisfactions. We are celebrating the perilous business of love—of that supreme love that did not and does not turn back from the cross. Casserly speaks of the old dissembler who lived out his lie. One day the undertaker will get his chance, and with his painted smiles try to make dissemblers of us all. We should not do the undertaker's work for him. Sunday mornings that are designed to make people feel good and to accept all that is unacceptable short of the Kingdom's coming are peddling the painted smiles of the denial of death.

There is a fixed smile that seems to go with a certain style of Christian piety. It is depressing in its fixedness, as though it were kept in place by the fear that a moment's suspension of obligatory happiness would constitute a denial of the joy of salvation. "Smile, God loves you!" exhorts a little yellow button on a million Christian breasts. Tremble, God loves you! Weep, God loves you! Persevere, God loves you! Repent, God loves you! As Dorothy Day of *Catholic Worker* notoriety keeps saying, "God's is a harsh and dreadful love." The celebration that we call worship has less to do with the satisfaction of the pursuit of happiness than with the abandonment of the pursuit of happiness. The Christian proposition is that only as we enter into the pathos and promise of God's love do we discover the peace that surpasses what is understood by happiness.

There is no prescribed emotion or psychic "set" for true worship. Yet we witness ministers—worship leaders, they are called—standing before the assembled people and saying things like, "And now let's all be happy, celebrating the beauty of this day and affirming each other in the creative bond of caring that is God's presence among us. . . ." And so on, and so on. Such ministers are not celebrants but cheerleaders. Ministers ask, "And now shall we pray?" As though they were going to put it to a vote. And once I heard this, "And now shall we pray with happy hearts, thanking God for all his goodness?" And I imagined someone in the third row from the back responding, "No, I'm sorry. My wife is dying of cancer. My heart is not happy but broken. I do not want to give thanks but to rage against the unfairness of it all." He asks for peace and is offered a painted smile.

In the liturgy, the celebrant invites, "Lift up your hearts!" And the people respond, "We lift them to the Lord!" Nothing is said about the state of hearts so lifted, only that they be offered to God. Our doubts and resentments, our tears and confusions, these are offered together with our ecstasies and our gratitude for the amazing grace that makes whole our fragmented selves.

LIBERATED BY TRADITION

More and more churches today are moving toward the use of the classic eucharistic liturgy of Western Christianity. That is, not only those churches usually called "liturgical," such as Roman Catholics, Lutherans, and Episcopalians, but also Methodists, Baptists, Presbyterians, and others are increasingly embracing the fullness of catholic liturgy. Because of the ecumenical impulses of recent decades, and the commonality of liturgical scholarship, more Christians are "doing" a liturgy that gives full range to the diverse emotions, ideas, and conditions of men and women. As a consequence, worship is not designed by a minister to "meet the needs of the people" (as though the minister could even perceive such needs), but is an activity that can catch up all the needs, known and unknown, and respond to the paramount need of everyone, which is simply to worship God because God is to be worshiped.

There is and there ought to be a "givenness" to what we do in worship. Just as we have emphasized that the ministry is always the ministry of the Church, so our worship is always the worship of the Church. The great Abraham Heschel understood the givenness of the form of worship. People complained to him that the synagogue liturgy was not able to say what they meant. "The goal," he would respond, "is not that the liturgy say what you mean but that you mean what the liturgy says." The liturgy we do should have about it a sense of otherness. It is not simply the vehicle of our speaking to God, but of God's speaking his full counsel to us. It is not simply to facilitate our communication with one another but to confront us with the "cloud of witnesses" (Heb. 12) of other times and places who, through Christ, join us in the ritual renewal of our *sacramentum*.

Our form of celebration, then, is not something we improvise on the spot, nor is it something devised by a "worship leader" possessed of singular insight into "the needs" of the assembled People of God. It is the liturgy of the Church. This is not to say there should not be elements of spontaneity and familiarity in our celebration. There should be. But spontaneity should not be confused with eccentricity, or familiarity with chumminess. The worship folder at a recent church conference read: "Dropping our defenses and pretenses, we come together to encounter one another in the vulnerable love that acknowledges our interdependence in exposing the needs of our full humanity." No thanks, one is inclined to respond.

This conference happened to be mainly Roman Catholic, but in all parts of the Church one receives invitations to worship that must be declined. The above blather, which is not atypical, is not really an invitation to worship at all. It suggests sexual orgy more than

Christian liturgy. My defenses and pretenses have been painstakingly constructed over the years and are still very fragile. In exceptional circumstances of intimacy, I lower them with care; but to recklessly drop them at the bidding of people I met only that day smacks of a promiscuity that is downright indecent. As to "exposing the needs of my full humanity," I am not sure what it means but I think there is a law against doing it in public places. But of course the main reason this is not an invitation to worship at all is that worship chiefly has to do not with encountering one another but with encountering God.

Getting in touch with one's own feelings or with the feelings of others may be an appropriate enterprise under some circumstances, but it is only marginally related to worship. Martin Buber's I-Thou cannot so easily be displaced by I-Me and I-You. More accurately, it can be easily displaced but it should not be. This does not mean that worship is individualistic, something I do with my privacy in semipublic spaces. It does not mean that those with whom one worships are a crowd of strangers rather than a community of sisters and brothers. It does mean, however, that one does not worship the community. It does mean that the "significant other" is God, and the significance of others—as with one's own significance—derives from the love with which God makes us significant. To put it differently, the others are fellow travelers encountered on a journey. They are to be helpful to one another in every possible way, but finally they are bound together not by the pleasure they take in one another's company but by common commitment to reaching the journey's end.

It might be protested that this approach to worship as celebration could justify the kind of cold formalism that so many people claim to find oppressive. That is not the intention. The intention is to suggest that people may have a greater need for respectful distance than for cloying closeness. It is to suggest that liturgy should not turn the community in upon itself but should underscore the community's placement within the one, holy, catholic and apostolic Church that is met and beckoned by the radically Other. And it is to suggest that there is a very big difference between worship and therapy. The Christian message throws our questions into question;

it challenges not so much the way we meet our needs as the way we define our needs.

The head of one denomination's worship commission has declared, "Good liturgy is good psychology, and good psychology is good liturgy." Similarly, theologians have said that good theology is good sociology, and vice versa. One is reminded of the infamous remark by Charles Wilson, "What's good for General Motors is good for the country." Some distinctions are in order. Good liturgy may or may not be good psychology, depending upon which psychological sect one belongs to. But it is utterly illegitimate to assert that psychology, of whatever variety, should be normative of liturgy.

FLAUNTING IRRELEVANCE

It is surely important to make connections and linkages between Christian faith and other ways of defining reality. In seminary courses, conferences, and religious education materials, such linkages abound. "Christian faith and social change." "Christ in contemporary cinema." "The Spirit and psychological healing." "Synthesizing Christ and Marx." "Prayer and parent effectiveness." And on and on. Such linkages can be entirely appropriate. They can be, as their proponents claim, efforts to "relate" or to "apply" Christianity to all of life. But linkages have an insidious habit of turning into sponges. That is, they have a way of sucking up or absorbing necessary distinctions; they fudge contradictions and relax essential tensions. In relating Christianity to some other way of constructing reality, the other way too often demonstrates the greater power of absorption. The result, from the Christian viewpoint, is apostasy. To be sure, that is not the intention, but here as elsewhere intentions may have little to do with consequences.

Thus we must view with robust skepticism the proposition that good sociology, or psychology, is good theology, and vice versa. One suspects that those who say such things have a stronger idea of what good sociology (or psychology) is than they do of what good theology is. The reason for this is not to be found in a moral fault but in the very structure of intellectual discourse in our world. There are many more cultural pressures and "controls" reinforcing adherence to secular definitions of reality. Especially in university contexts—where people who make such statements are commonly to be found—there is powerful pressure to make one's work respectable to one's peers. There are few church contexts today in which there are effective controls over what is defined as "good theology." And the few churches that claim to have such controls usually have the worst theology of all because they insist upon a repetition of the orthodox party line, and such a mechanized repetition is quite the opposite of doing theology.

Our attitude toward worship is a good test, maybe the best test, of our resistance to the spongelike character of concerns for relevance. The early Christian fathers had a keen insight into the way that theology emerges from doxology. *Lex orandi, Lex credendi*—the rule of prayer is the rule of faith. If good theology is good anything else, it is good worship. This does not mean that every theological statement must be directly doxological, and certainly it does not mean that the liturgy should take on the form of a theological textbook. It does mean, however, that everything we say Christianity *is* must be related to and must be normed by that central act which is of the very *esse* of the Christian community: the acknowledgement of the sovereignty of God in Christ. The fact that we forget this is evidenced in little ways, by slips of the tongue, as it were. At a recent conference, a Methodist bishop said that our study of the Bible must be related "to the larger world." What he meant to say, one hopes, is that we should study the Bible more thoroughly, for the Bible encompasses all of and much more than what is ordinarily meant by "the larger world."

The apparent irrelevance of worship should not be denied but should be flaunted. In prayer, in intercession, in the water of baptism and the bread and wine of eucharist, in lifting our hearts in praise, we are dealing with the most real of real worlds. If we do not believe that, it is to be feared that we are not Christians at all. It must be added to this that, whatever significant contribution we as Christians have to make to a world that does not acknowledge our sovereign Lord, it can only be made through the confident and clear assertion of our Christian identity. All identities are constructed and sustained by differentiation. That means that it is not through our identity with the general culture but in our difference from it that we are Christians. Otherwise we are, in pathetic truth, the salt that has lost its savor, good for nothing but to be trampled underfoot. Our Christian concern for the world, our entering into the sufferings of the lost and the marginal, can be sustained only by our Christian difference from the world. Liturgy is the supreme articulation of that difference. We worship a different God.

Christian ministers are strangely troubled by doing the "traditional" thing in worship. With respect to lesser traditions, people have little difficulty in recognizing their responsibility to sustain and advance a particular history. It is hard to imagine someone in physics, for example, feeling uncomfortable with the claim that his or her responsibility is to sustain and advance the tradition of Thales, Kepler, Newton, Millikan, Bohr, and Einstein. It is likewise inconceivable that an actor would be insulted by the suggestion that he is in the tradition of Euripides, Shakespeare, Sarah Bernhardt, and Charlie Chaplin. Yet one regularly encounters Christian ministers asserting their creativity in terms of their independence from the Christian tradition. In truth, what they often mean by "the traditional way" is the limited tradition of a particular denomination or even of a local church. But liberation from such smaller and stifling traditions is precisely to be found in becoming *more* traditional. If we are to be free we must accept our responsibility as heirs of the many and diverse histories that make up the Christian tradition. The greatness of that tradition should be articulated and reflected in liturgy.

Again, H. R. Niebuhr said it well. His subject was theological education, but what he says applies to all of ministry: "Alongside tepid birthright loyalties to denominations and schools of thought, one encounters . . . the fervent convictions of new converts about the greatness of the common Christian cause. And amidst the confusions and perplexities of many men doing many things . . . the sense of the great tradition of the Church emerges in many places as the idea of a line of march to be taken up, of a direction to be followed, a continuing purpose to be served."[3] That line of march, that pilgrimage, is the theme of our gathering around the altar. It reaches back to the first covenant with Adam and forward to the consummation of Christ's return.

In 1965, during the confrontation at Selma, Alabama, an Episcopal bishop celebrated mass along the dusty roadside. It was an act of power, a symbol of liberation, precisely because it was the enactment of a tradition. There, at that most mundane of moments, the cloud of witnesses gathered around, brought together by the mystery of Christ among his people. Jerome and Francis and Aquinas and Luther and Francis Xavier and the brothers Wesley, they were all at Selma. It was excruciatingly relevant precisely because it was not a "civil rights liturgy" designed for the occasion.

Once again, the truth is underscored that prophecy must not be posited against tradition. And once again, Martin Luther King, Jr., is the chief exemplar of this truth in our time. He advanced the tradition because he, more than others, so firmly and imaginatively embraced the tradition. In his case he advanced both the Christian tradition of ministry with the oppressed and the American political tradition of democratic justice. He understood what so many today have forgotten, that relevance that is truly creative is on behalf of and not against a great tradition. By what authority does the prophet speak? If he claims to have direct communications from God, he is rightly suspect as a fanatic. If he claims to be possessed of superior conscience or intelligence, he is likely the victim of *hubris*. But if he calls the people to account for the tradition they profess in common, then he may be a prophet. He may be a prophet because, like most of the prophets of biblical times, he is first a priest. Because it cannot be judged by anything else we do, it is our role as minister in the worshiping community that is foundational to everything else we do. We worship God because God is to be worshiped.

AFTER THE SILLY SEASON

It is to be hoped that we are entering upon a better time for Christian worship. For many years liturgical renewal among Protestants took the form of appropriating the appurtenances of catholicity. Much of that was good and necessary; it created a new appreciation of the breadth and diversity of the great tradition. But in the several churches, the effort often succumbed to antiquarianism and aestheticism. Liturgical elites prided themselves on their knowledge of the arcane, and many confused the beauty of holiness with the holiness of beauty.

Among Roman Catholics, the liturgical renewal of the earlier part of the century seemed to triumph at Vatican II. But in the opinion of many, the triumph soon turned into chaos as liberation from particular restraints turned into the abandonment of the tradition itself. The critics often forget that many, perhaps the great majority, of the churches have been little touched by liturgical renewal in whatever form. But certainly they are right in believing that among those who saw themselves as the avant-garde of liturgical renewal a silly season ruled for a time.

For several years in the 1960s, I was the token Protestant on the board of the National Liturgical Conference. For many years the Conference and its annual Liturgical Weeks were major instruments in advancing the liturgical renewal espoused by Louis Bouyer, J. A. Jungmann, H. A. Reinhold, and others. By the beginning of the 1970s, the slogan of the Liturgical Week was e. e. cummings's "damn everything but the circus." If it was false and stifling to say that nothing matters but rubrical correctness, it is equally false and stifling to say nothing matters but the defiance of the same. Liturgical frivolity is as deadly as liturgical legalism—indeed, because it is harder to sustain, it becomes more forced. "Be spontaneous" is the most impossible of rubrics. When we compete with ourselves we quickly run out of acts. Yesterday's bright idea is bad enough, but it only makes matters worse to present it as today's. Thoughtful people begin to suspect that the spontaneous is not necessarily better than the considered. It is no longer entirely clear why a primal scream is more authentic than a Gregorian chant. After a while it becomes obvious that releasing balloons with the prescribed shout of joy is considerably less interesting than the elevation of the consecrated host. And so the silly season is, one hopes, reaching its end. Perhaps it has already ended.

Worship is the distinctively "Christian thing" that Christians do most frequently. It is statistically measurable and therefore understandably the activity on which survey researchers and pollsters focus. Of course religious vitality includes much more than "going to church." Preachers have always inveighed and will continue to inveigh against a "Sunday morning religiosity" that is unrelated to the whole of life. As much as it is necessary to warn against the separation between what we say on Sunday and what we do on Monday, the whole of life cannot be made fully consistent with what we celebrate in Christian worship. There is an inescapable disjointedness between worship and work, between life and liturgy. The liturgy does relate to all of life, but the relationship is more often one of contradiction than of consistency. The reason for this is that the whole of the world does not yet recognize Christ as Lord. What is celebrated and effected in liturgy is largely denied in the structures and experiences that make up everyday life.

In what is called everyday life, many false gods hold sway—money, sexual satisfaction, power, reputation. In unqualifiedly affirming the sovereignty of our God, the liturgy is an experience of "the real world" which the Christian must always struggle to actualize in a world that denies the reality. When we enter into a novel, especially one that includes elements of the fantastical, we exercise what is termed a literary suspension of disbelief. Something similar happens in liturgy. Except here it is belief that throws into question competing constructions of reality to which we too readily give credence. This does not mean that "the real world" ritually articulated in liturgy denies reality to ordinary experience. That is the doctrine of some Eastern cults, and those cults have become seductively attractive to Westerners who have wearied of the obligations and disappointments of history. No, the real world celebrated in Christian liturgy encompasses the whole world—including its loneliness, sickness, Auschwitz, and Cambodia. Again, the real world of liturgy is not another world but *this* world comprehensively understood under the lordship of Christ.

One very real danger is that the distinction between the sacred and the secular can be perverted into hermetically sealing off one "realm" from the other. If we deny the distinction, however, and conflate the two realms, both suffer. The sacred suffers because it floats off into a spiritual escapism that is no longer accountable to a wounded world in search of healing. And the secular suffers because it is turned in upon itself in its search for meaning and is deprived of the transcendent word of judgment and hope. It is awkward but it is unavoidable that we continue to employ distinctions such as that between the sacred and the secular. Finally, we are not talking about two spheres, or two realms, or two kingdoms. We are speaking, rather, of one realm that is ruled by God and his Christ, but we are speaking of it at a time when that rule is not yet fully actualized. Thus language about the sacred and the secular, the Church and the world, is related to the "now" and "not yet" of this historical moment that is still far short of the consummation. We should not be intimidated but should rather rejoice when people say that what we do in worship seems different, odd, out of touch with "reality." It should be that way. It is an inherent and necessary tension of Christian existence. Nowhere is the Church's sighting, signaling, and supporting of the Kingdom so explicit and intense as in the celebration of the King's presence among us.

THE JOY OF DUTY

Before ending this chapter, we should touch on yet another aspect of worship that is often neglected or even derided in the churches today. It has to do with *duty.* For years at St. John's in Brooklyn, our worship folder and publicity carried the statement, "God's People Are at God's Altar Every Week." The statement was meant to be both *de*scriptive and *pre*scriptive. From time to time, visitors suggested that this seemed somewhat legalistic. After all, we are saved by grace, are we not?—not by going to church. In response, I would make the case that the proposition is in fact liberating. Many serious Christians today are hungry for a distinctive "life-style." The covenant established by amazing grace must be embodied and acted out in visible form.

While many Christians talk about an "alternative life-style" today, they often have in mind some political, economic, or countercultural agenda that is either not attractive or not possible for most Christians. "God's People Are at God's Altar Every Week" is a beginning point for all Christians. It is surely not too much to expect of any serious Christian that he or she participate in the community's affirmation and renewal of its *sacramentum.* It is a duty—to oneself, to one's fellow believers, and to God. Of course it is easy to demean the Sunday morning congregation as people who are there out of a "mere" sense of duty. We should protest that "mere." I have always been puzzled by ministers who are so certain and so derisory about the motives of their people. Facing a congregation of ten people or of a thousand, I am consistently awed by whatever it is that brings them together. Habit? Fear of hell? The appearance of respectability? That and much more, no doubt. But also a search for meaning, for hope, for God. The truth is that we sometimes aren't sure why *we* are there, and we certainly don't know why *they* are there.

But I suspect that most of our people believe in some very deep sense that they *ought* to be there. We should not discourage that intuition. We should never, as though we were hucksters for a show, give them the impression that they are doing us—or God!—a favor by being there. Duty is not oppressive. It is the highest exercise of freedom to decide on what is our duty. In *The Professor of Love,* Philip Roth's hero gets his lover in a family way and this leads to reflection on duty. "On her own she decided to have that abortion. So I would not be burdened by a duty? So I could choose her just for herself? But is the notion of duty so utterly horrendous? Why didn't she tell me she was pregnant? Is there not a point on life's way when one yields to duty, *welcomes* duty as once one yielded to pleasure, to passion, to adventure—a time when duty is the pleasure, rather than pleasure the duty?"

The Westminister Catechism of 1647 puts it very well with its famous opening Question and Answer: "What is the chief end of man?" "Man's chief end is to glorify God and to enjoy Him forever." And, of course, the Psalms, the most used texts of Christian worship, abound in expressions of delight in doing one's duty. The Psalm writers are forever rejoicing and exulting in praising God and doing his will. How terribly Christians have misinterpreted living Judaism in this respect. It is said that the Old Testament is law and the New Testament is grace; that Judaism is a legalistic religion leading to self-righteousness and death, while Christianity is the religion of freedom and life. In fact, the God of Israel's covenant is our God, and it is precisely the measure of his grace that he holds us accountable to him and to one another. The alternative to accountability is not freedom but chaos, nothingness, and death.

"Lift up your hearts."

"We lift them to the Lord." Broken, doubting, tranquil, joyful, terror-ridden—whatever, we lift them to the Lord.

"Let us give thanks to the Lord our God."

"It is right to give him thanks and praise." It is what we feel like doing? It will solve our problems? It will change the world? Maybe. Who knows? But this we know: It is right. It is our duty.

9.
The Importance of Being a Preacher

For many Protestant Christians, *the* model of the Church is the Church as Herald. Thus the historian Wilhelm Pauck: "Nothing is more characteristic of Protestantism than the importance it attaches to preaching." The new understanding of the gospel that came out of the Reformation "led to such an emphasis upon the proclamation of the Word that henceforth the very reality of the Church was grounded in preaching."[1]

Preaching, however, was hardly discovered by the Reformation. It has always been and will always be—by whatever name—a central part of the Church's life. From Peter and Paul in the New Testament, through John Chrysostom, Ambrose, Augustine, and the preaching orders of the Middle Ages, the community has gathered to hear the Word proclaimed. And it has been gathered *by* the hearing of the Word. Admittedly, in recent centuries preaching as such has been downplayed by Roman Catholics. In part this was no doubt a reaction to what was viewed as an excessive or even exclusive emphasis upon preaching among Protestants. Of course there have always been outstanding Roman Catholic preachers, but they were usually seen as exceptions possessing a special gift. The preaching orders continued their work, and parishes regularly held "missions" in which high-powered preachers came in to induce the faithful to intensified Christian commitment. But for the most part, Roman Catholics went to church for the Mass and Protestants went to church for the sermon.

Since Vatican II, this too has changed among Roman Catholics. The sermon is no longer a brief interruption for parish announcements and moralistic exhortations to better behavior, but is seen as an integral part of the eucharistic action in which the community is confronted by the Word both proclaimed and celebrated. While homiletics does not yet have the place in Catholic seminaries that it is accorded among Protestants, priests have come to understand in the last decade or so that they are also to be preachers of the Word. At least in theory, preaching is no longer the exceptional vocation but the accepted responsibility of Christian ministry.

Also in this respect, then, there has been a remarkable ecumenical convergence. In Protestant bodies, too, there are hoary debates about the relative importance of Word and sacrament. Frequently and unfortunately, one was pitted against the other. If a person was enthusiastic about the renewal of the Church through the recovery of the weekly eucharist, he was suspected of an animus against the Word proclaimed, and vice versa. The recourse to the speedy either/ or is both simplistic and fruitless. It is the same problem we have encountered before when one model of the Church is elevated to the status of being *the* model of the Church. If someone says the sole purpose of the Church is to worship God, many will nod their heads in agreement. Say that the sole purpose of the Church is to serve human need, and many will stand up and cheer. Assert that the sole purpose of the Church is to preach the gospel, and it is welcomed by heartfelt amens.

If we cannot resist the compulsion to specify the singular and unique factor that makes the Church the Church, then surely that "factor" is Jesus the Christ. It is around him, *the* Word of God, that the community is gathered; without him, all that the Church does

—its sighting, signaling, supporting, and celebrating—makes no sense. One thing the community does is talk about him, and one form of talking about him is called preaching. Preaching is the members of the community talking about him to one another and to the world. In the latter case, preaching is often *evangelistic;* in all cases it is *evangelical.* That is, preaching is always the articulation of the *evangelion* of what God has done, is doing, and will do in Jesus the Christ. Worship, preaching, fellowship, and service are all integral facets of the community's life, and never should one be set against the others.

It is said that the most loving service to others is not *Christian* love unless it is accompanied by the verbal articulation of the gospel, and there is a measure of truth in that. One must as readily say, with St. Paul, that the most elegant and orthodox articulation of the gospel is, unless accompanied by loving service, a noisy gong and clanging cymbal. The point is that these are not the choices. Just as there is no *one* Christian life-style, so there is no one activity of the Church that should be stressed to the exclusion of others. We are rightly suspicious when we hear someone describe *the* purpose of the family in terms of its being an economic consumption unit, or an emotional support system, or a means to propagate the race. The sensible person counters that the purpose of the family is to be a family, which includes all of the above and ever so much more. We are right to worry about a family that never does things that families do: that never plays together or prays together or eats together or helps out in times of crisis. But we do not insist that the thing neglected is the one thing essential to being a family. Rather, we encourage the stirring up of gifts and responsibilities that are being neglected. So the purpose of the Church is to be the Church. In this community, too, gifts and responsibilities are neglected, and the ministry is the constant business of righting imbalances, curbing excesses, and poking at dying embers in order to bring alive and keep alive the full-orbed communion of Christian people. In this business, preaching is an instrument—a measure, a rod, and a poker, if you will—which itself needs regular attention if it is to do the job.

LETTING THE CHURCH PREACH

I have emphasized throughout that our ministries must be seen as ministries of the Church. This is urgently true also of our preaching. The great preacher P. T. Forsyth put it well at the turn of the century:

> The one great preacher in history, I would contend, is the Church. And the first business of the individual preacher is to enable the Church to preach. . . . He is to preach to the Church from the Gospel so that with the Church he may preach the Gospel to the world. He is so to preach to the Church that he shall also preach through the Church. That is to say, he must be a sacrament to the Church, that with the Church he may become a missionary to the world.[2]

The situations in which the Word is preached are as maddeningly various as is the Church itself. It is necessary to have our thinking jarred by this diversity so that we can then with greater modesty and greater confidence understand our particular place within the whole. The whole includes Greek monks on Mount Athos; Benedictine monks in England; Mexicans on their knees before our Lady of Guadalupe; Polish Blessed Bread; Australian aborigines singing Mass; Pentecostal healers handling snakes; Eskimos scratching the Ave Maria on whalebones; Chinese gongs sounding the Angelus; Wall Street brokers praying for free enterprise; guerrilla fighters invoking Christ the Liberator; German Advent wreaths; African tomtoms tolling a Requiem; Dutch Girl Guides catechizing Amsterdam prostitutes; Bowery derelicts exposing themselves to the risks of getting saved for the sake of a free bed; the burghers of Hamburg joining in "Nun danket alle Gott"; the white-robed choir of Black-conscious Bethany Baptist imploring Precious Lord to take our hands; Cardinals signing checks in Rome for the gnomes in Zurich; California nuns cleaning lepers in Seoul; Cowboy evangelists hustling truckdrivers on Route 66; Methodist elders urging people to come out for the parent effectiveness session this Thursday night; and on and on and on. All this and more, Jesus sees in his Church, and we must see it too. This is the Church of which we are preachers;

our ministries are located within this whole and exercised for some small but necessary part of it.[3]

In whatever part of this great Church one is preaching, it is imperative to keep the greater Church in mind. To put it differently, the whole is present in each of its parts. The Body of Christ is not divided, despite our efforts. Just as the Kingdom is present in the midst of you because the King is there, so also Christ is accompanied by his Body, the Church. Thus, preaching is not an individualistic enterprise. It is not like a star actor on a stage relating to an audience "out there," although, as we shall see, there are necessary elements of the actor's art involved in preaching. Preaching is communal, its tone tempered by the relationship between pastor and people. The totality of the relationship is not established by that moment of preaching, but that moment is interpreted, for better and for worse, by impressions and shared experiences of all sorts. There is a complicated sociological interaction, then, in the moment of preaching. But, beyond that, there is what is more properly described as a mystical communion.

It is a communion with, and accountability to, the greater Church on whose behalf one speaks. And there is the recognition of that Church in the faces of the people one addresses on Sunday morning. One looks out to that congregation, no matter how small or nondescript, and sees more than meets the eye. The preacher possessed of such a vision knows how pitifully truncated by comparison is all the sociologese and psychologese about group dynamics. More is in play here because Christ is in on the play. One must approach these people with great respect, indeed with reverence. The preacher dare never arrogantly suppose that he is bringing the truth to the unenlightened, or that he is the instrument relating the sacred to the profane. These are people related to God through Christ. They are by the grace of God a holy people, whether they act like or not, whether they always know it or not. Some of them, the preacher must not forget, are far more advanced in the spiritual life than he is. In ways that he may know nothing about, they have wrestled with angels and walked the way of the cross. They have been to mountaintops we have not scaled or even seen from afar.

To say, then, that our preaching is a ministry of the Church means that it is our ministry, our service, to address and to articulate the faith of the community. To be sure, we preach to convert, and every day in the Christian life is a day of decision; but we preach also to confirm and to celebrate the work of Christ among his people. Our purpose in preaching is not to create the Church; our Lord has already attended to that. Our purpose is to help the Church recognize and actualize what God has already declared it to be.

For some years now, it has been the conventional wisdom that the era of "the great pulpit" is past. To the extent that this is true, it may be because we have declared it so. In fact, however, one keeps on encountering great preaching, and in some places great preaching consistent enough to make a great pulpit. Of course how we define great preaching may change with the context. The great preaching of Riverside Church, New York City, will be quite different from the great preaching of the Assemblies of God Tabernacle on the outskirts of Modesto, California. It may seem like a cop-out to say that great preaching cannot be defined, you just know it when it happens, but so it is. In all great *Christian* preaching, however, at least this is true: It is an Emmaus-like experience in which the scriptures are opened and you recognize Christ, and in him, with a fresh sense of discovery, you see the truth about yourself and your world. "Did not our hearts burn within us while he talked to us on the road, while he opened to us the scriptures?" (Luke 24). Underscoring the unity of the verbal and sacramental Word, this experience prepared the disciples to recognize their Lord in the breaking of bread. Wherever this happens, there is great preaching.

Many who have written about preaching have remarked the inspired mistranslation of the King James Version when it speaks of "the foolishness of preaching." Of course, Paul was referring to the gospel itself as foolishness and scandal, but, had he the hindsight of two millennia, he might have included our presentation of the gospel as part of the foolishness. In his *Brief History of Preaching*, the Swedish Lutheran bishop Yngve Brilioth concludes on a note about "the absurd responsibility of preaching Sunday after Sunday."[4] As foolish and absurd as it may be, it has been done and no doubt will be done until the Kingdom comes. Those who have the responsibility of doing it should strive to do it with greatness.

I have heard professors of homiletics, who presumably have something to do with shaping the Church's preachers, declare that preaching is passé. What we do not wish or are not able to do, we say cannot be done. Or if it can be done, it is not relevant to our time, which is (don't you know?) revolutionary, unprecedented, and singularly incompatible with whatever has gone before. In preaching, as in so many other areas, we move from dubious social analysis to self-serving moral judgment. The family is disintegrating, therefore a little affair on the side is to be tolerated. Patriotism is almost nonexistent, therefore critical concern for the commonweal is outdated. Charity is resented as patronizing, therefore there is no need to give sacrificially to feed the hungry of the world. The merit system is a hoax, therefore it is unnecessary, perhaps even unjust, to strive for excellence. By such reasoning we smooth the way for the shoddy; we come to accept, even to champion, the second-rate. After all, the mediocre that boasts of making no effort to being anything other than mediocre has the merit of being "authentic" and "sincere"— and those are two very big gold stars in the jaded kindergarten of contemporary culture.

It is no secret that preaching has a bad name in some circles. A news correspondent dismisses Aleksandr Solzhenitsyn's prophetic warnings at a Harvard commencement: "After all is said and done, he is merely preaching." Mere preaching, so much for that! And a supine Church internalizes the contempts it picks up at the courts of culture from the ambassadors of other gods. Thus we are robbed of large parts of a Christian and humane vocabulary. When one loses words, the loss is not slight. They are not "mere words." We of all people should understand the connection between words and the Word. Yet one reads, this time in a popular Methodist magazine, about a local church that is reportedly undergoing spiritual renewal. The article declares: "Here there is no piety, no dignity, no form. Only freedom and joy." So readily do we internalize worldly contempt for values at the center of Christian existence. Without piety, or dignity, or the grace and restraint of form, what freedom and joy can there be? One quickly adds that it is not only Christian existence itself that is at stake but also the Christian contribution to a more humane world. Without devotion that rises above self-serving, without respect for the dignity of others, without the forms of deference and discipline, there is little hope for taming the beastliness of what people do to one another.

We must not let them take our words away, and certainly we should not lend them a helping hand in destroying the language of Christian identity. Of course some Christians are offended by any talk about "we" and "them"—as though there were no minions of the principalities and powers of the present time opposing the rule of the Christ; as though the difference between being a Christian and not being a Christian is not really that important. But the "we" is not against the "them"—it is ultimately *for* "them" so that we may all be "we" under Christ. Revitalizing Christian identity is not aimed at sealing us off from "the world"; our clear, coherent, courageous Christian identity is precisely our greatest contribution to the world. "If the salt has lost its savor. . . ."

THE PROW OF THE SHIP

We continue to preach and we continue to call it preaching. Preaching derives from *praedicare:* to proclaim publicly, to praise, to elevate. To elevate the lordship of Jesus Christ and with it the world that he claims as his own, surely this is our great contribution. In *Moby Dick,* Herman Melville's Father Mapple, in the little whaling town of New Bedford, climbs the ladder to preach from the high perch that is like the prow of a ship. "The pulpit," writes Melville, "is ever this earth's foremost part. . . . The world's a ship on its passage out . . . and the pulpit is its prow." To suggest that the pulpit is the prow as America and the world move out to the twenty-first century sounds, let us admit it, plain silly. Most observers, including most Christians, including perhaps ourselves, would snicker at the pretentiousness of the idea.

That the idea seems ludicrous, even to ourselves, is largely the fault of those of us who are preachers. Too often we do not believe in the sovereignty on whose behalf we are called to contend. We do not believe that Christ is "the new man for all men," the future of humankind. We are pathetically grateful for being permitted aboard the proud ship of the modern world. Out of deference to our former dignity, we are given comfortable cabins, and those in charge even let us wear officer's uniforms, thus maintaining the appearance that we belong to the class of politicians, bureaucrats, artistic entrepeneurs, social scientists, generals, and television commentators who have set the world's course on its passage to disaster. Our role is a shameful charade. Shameful not because it is demeaning to us but because we are party to the demeaning of the sovereign whose ambassadors we are. We cannot storm the bridge by physical force, and we should not try to. But we can dissent, protest, persuade, plead. We can preach.

Preaching will only be elevated and elevating by virtue of better preaching. Better preaching in this case means, among other things, more confident preaching; confidence not in ourselves but in the Lord whom we preach.

It is objected that such an emphasis upon preaching is self-serving. Whether in the national arena or in the local community, how do we elevate preaching without elevating the preacher? Does not the status of the ambassador rise with the status of the one whom he represents? I will have more to say about the engagement of the ego in preaching, but here it is enough to say that we should not let ourselves be terrified by the slit-eyed suspiciousness of a modern mindset that refuses to believe in anything beyond the self, that refuses to believe that the self can be taken captive to a higher call.

We are all Freudians now, more or less, of some form or another, and we should not be shocked by the ambiguity of our own motives. Even without benefit of Freud, Paul was keenly aware of his vulnerability to the criticism that his ministry was self-serving. His answer, which must also be our answer, is not that the criticism can be disproved but that the calling cannot be disobeyed. "For if I preach the gospel, that gives me no ground for boasting. For necessity is laid upon me. Woe to me if I do not preach the gospel! For if I do this of my own will, I have a reward; but if not of my own will, I am entrusted with a commission" (1 Cor. 9).

If some secular critics are disdainful of the pulpit's pretensions to be the prow of the modern world, it is my impression that many more are puzzled by the pusillanimity of the Church. At various levels of political, academic, and journalistic life, I have encountered thoughtful people who ask why it is that the Church seems to have so little to say. "Why is it," they ask, "that we, the secular solons, are shown such deference by church people? Why are church leaders so eager to accept our opinions, to try to be like us? Is it possible that the Christian capital of the West is so completely exhausted that there can be no new ideas, no new challenges, no new directions bearing a distinctively Christian mark?"

Not long ago, a Protestant church body thought to observe the American bicentennial by spending many thousands of dollars to bring together celebrities from academe and the communications media to discuss religion in the modern world. The brochure explained that it is necessary for the Church "to solicit the best minds of the time in order to find new ways to make Christianity relevant to our world." Solicitation is a more apt word than the sponsors of this event probably knew. It is not simply the oldest profession, it is the oldest form of religious decadence. In any case, one of the speakers, a noted humanist, observed that of course religion is on the wane as modern man becomes ever more rational, but there may nonetheless be a continuing role for the churches if they line up behind his favored causes for the improvement of the world. A few weeks later, the sponsoring body's publication carried a story on the meeting: "Church Has Role in Modern World." The gushing article left no doubt that we should be grateful for being permitted on board.

Preaching that applies for a license from unbelievers is no preaching at all. It elevates nothing. It reduces the gospel of Christ to simply another viewpoint that may or may not be "interesting" or "helpful." The preacher who cannot say with Paul, "I am entrusted with a commission," is, at best, in a perilous situation. We are entrusted with a commission from Christ and from the community that has accepted the commission of Christ. Sometimes, when the commissioning voice of Christ seems faint, we must dare to preach because the community calls us to preach. But finally, while they cannot be equated, the voice of Christ and the voice of his Church cannot be separated. Such is the promise that our Lord has made to those who follow him. Somewhere within the Body of Christ the will of Christ is articulated. There are different voices and we must choose; we can never be sure that we have chosen rightly, but ultimately our obedience is rendered to him who surely will judge all things rightly. That is the source of our freedom and of our joy in the ministry of preaching.

The Christian confidence proposed here is not to be understood simplistically in terms of what Richard Niebuhr described as the model of "Christ against Culture." If such a succinct phrase is necessary, the most appropriate one might be Christ *ahead* of culture. A simple preacher in rural Tennessee is the cultural and cosmic avant garde when he stands in his pulpit and declares, "Jesus Christ is Lord!" It is not enough, of course, simply to repeat such statements of Christian allegiance. The statements must be brought into relation—yes, even be made "relevant"—to other statements of meaning, to the claims of other gods. If relevance means transforming ourselves and the world, rather than conforming the gospel to things as they are, then relevance is not only permissible, it is mandatory.

Unfortunately, talk about relevance has been so prostituted by conformation that another word should be sought. Rather than a static noun like "relevance," it might be better to speak more dynamically of "engagement." Preaching must engage the world, and it must engage the world that is within ourselves and our people. Our engagement should be marked by intelligence, sensitivity, and courage. Our preaching should engage the culture appreciatively where possible, polemically where necessary, but always lovingly. Lovingly, because finally the gospel is *for* the world. It is only against the world where the world is against itself, denying its own promised future in the Kingdom of God.

If the gospel of Jesus turns out to be right, then Melville too is right: "The world's a ship on its passage out . . . and the pulpit is its prow."

A VERY PERSONAL MATTER

One of the most quoted statements about preaching in Protestant circles is the definition offered by the nineteenth-century Episcopalian bishop Phillips Brooks: "Truth through Personality is our description of real preaching." Today we are uneasy with the way the nineteenth century produced and venerated the great "princes of the pulpit." There are many reasons for our uneasiness. Our culture is uncomfortable with the category of greatness in any sphere. Some forms of egalitarianism require an animus against the elevation of excellence. In a post-Freudian era of psycho-suspiciousness, we are trained to "see through" the appearance of greatness, and if we don't actually see through it, to act as though we do. Then too, in religion and, more particularly, in the realm of politics, we have been sobered by the consequences of personality cults around the fraudulently great. The self, as many have observed, has become highly problematical. We are as likely to see truth *against* personality as truth through personality.

Our hesitancy about personality cults is not entirely new. The story is told that one Sunday at Henry Ward Beecher's Plymouth Church in Brooklyn there was a guest preacher. As he entered the pulpit in place of the idolized Beecher, there was an unseemly rush for the doors on the part of visitors. Raising his hand, the guest preacher announced, "All those who came here to worship Henry Ward Beecher may now withdraw—all who came to worship God may remain!"[5]

Now it should be obvious from everything said so far that we hardly favor an individualistic view of the ministry. The ministry, we have insisted again and again, is always the ministry of the Church. So the preacher stands before the people of God not because of his personality but because he has been called to preach to and on behalf of the Church. That said, there is yet much validity in Brooks's formulation about truth through personality. We ministers are not ciphers, or public address systems wired to a turntable playing the record of divine revelation. We are persons with distinct personalities. There is nothing profane about personality, as though it must be separated from our ministries lest it taint the truth to which we witness. On the contrary, we have not fully accepted our calling unless our personalities are fully engaged.

This way of thinking should not be strange to people who believe that the Absolute Truth of God himself became incarnate in the person and personality of an itinerant preacher from Nazareth. God's truth is strong enough to survive its passage through you and me. Indeed, in the wondrous foolishness of the gospel, we are precisely the conduits, if you will, that he has selected. As has often been remarked, it would have made a lot more sense to choose the angels.

In preaching, God employs our distinct and diverse personalities. Now, of course, especially young preachers, but not young preachers only, need preaching models. A certain amount of imitation is inevitable in the process of discovering one's pulpit personality (more on what is meant by "pulpit personality" below). Billy Graham, Fulton Sheen, Robert Schuller, William Sloane Coffin, and Clarence Jordan have no doubt been "done" in thousands of pulpits across the country. Better—because it reduces the risk of appearing ludicrous—to imitate a less well known preacher; but better by far to discover your own distinctive personality. The problem is not resolved by exhorting the preacher to "be yourself." He will, quite sensibly, respond, "Which self? My private self or my public self? And then which of my several public and private selves?" As they say, the self has become problematical.

Social scientists, Irving Goffman in particular, have written interesting things about "the presentation of self in everyday life."[6] More recently the discussion has included subjects such as "body language" and the signals we send by the way we dress. One dubious benefit of this discussion is to complexify what formerly seemed simple and self-evident. A clearer benefit, however, is to help us understand that the self, including the public self, is, within limits, constructed. To say it is constructed does not mean that it is phony, or artificial, or inauthentic. Again, the origin of "authentic" is *authentikos,* which has to do with being handmade. The question is not whether we have a public self as distinct from a private self, but whether we are the authors of our public selves or are plagiarists. To be sure, before we even knew we were borrowing, we were borrowing bits and pieces of other selves, beginning with our parents and siblings. But we put the bits and pieces together in our distinctive way, adding from dreams and imaginings, and finally we arrive at something we each call *my*self. And of course that self is always in process, being reconstructed and refined through experience.

For the preacher, the most public manifestation of the public self is in the pulpit. A parishioner says, "Our pastor doesn't really preach at us at all. He's just himself in the pulpit." That is usually meant as a compliment, but it is nonsense nonetheless. The person who says that has internalized the negative connotations surrounding the word *preaching*, which were discussed in the last chapter. What the person means to say is that the pulpit personality of the pastor is consonant with his impression of the pastor's *persona* in other contexts. When we say that a preacher has a "pulpit tone" that rings false, the problem is not that he has a pulpit personality but that he has somebody else's pulpit personality. Each preacher should get his or her own.

Queen Victoria complained of her Prime Minister, "Mr. Gladstone speaks to me as if I was a public meeting." The good lady had no doubt that Mr. Gladstone was being himself, he was just being the wrong self for the occasion. So the pastor who is "just himself" in the pulpit does not present his self as he does to his children while helping them with homework, or to his wife when getting ready for sex. Life, thank God, is various and the way we present ourselves to encounter life's variousness must vary too. The precise term for someone who always sounds and acts the same way is a dull person.

The preacher cannot afford to indulge in current notions about "the search for the true self." Such notions are afflicted by the well-known onion-peeling fallacy. One peels off one layer of the skin, then another, and then another, in search of the "real onion." The real onion, of course, *is* the layers of onion skin. So the self that is relevant to preaching is not discovered by internal explorations through feelings, soul, and psyche, but *through public experimentation with presentations of self in relation to the task of preaching.* Contrary to conventional wisdom, there is nothing dishonest or hypocritical in talking about a public *persona* or a public role. We should resist the assumption that a scream is more authentic than a sonnet, or a whisper more sincere than a public declamation. Such assumptions are linked to the now prevalent privatization of public meanings, the narcissism of cults of self-realization, and the sweet solipsism of people excessively impressed by their singularity. Such attitudes undercut the task of preaching. The great woe is not to not be yourself but to not preach the gospel. The great call is to be yourself preaching the gospel. As for hypocrisy, that is quite a different topic. Hypocrisy requires a great deal of effort, and most of us do not have the talent or energy to bring it off very well for very long.

TO RISK BEING VULNERABLE

Preaching, then, powerfully engages the self. This means the preacher is vulnerable. When we think of someone being vulnerable, however, we may at first think of someone who is exceedingly fragile and easily hurt, and that is not what I mean. I mean the preacher is vulnerable in the sense that he puts himself on the line, as it were, that he commits himself. He does not hide behind platitudes or a defensive tentativeness. A platitude is a borrowed truth that one has not made one's own and is therefore not responsible for. Defensive tentativeness is the kind of preaching that asks us only to "consider possibilities" or entertain "interesting ideas" but never runs the risk of raising a hackle. The hypertentative preacher may come across as a weak and vulnerable fellow, but in fact, like the platitudinarian, he has covered himself quite nicely. He is not really vulnerable to rejection because he has not said anything that is really his own.

The gospel belongs to Christ and his Church, to be sure, but the hearers should recognize that it also belongs to this preacher, that he is both possessed by and possesses this truth. He is not simply peddling tales picked up from others, he is communicating truth that is constitutive of his being, of his very and every self. The preacher is not vulnerable because he might be rejected as a person; he is vulnerable because the gospel might be rejected, in which he has invested his person. There is a certain school of philosophy, associated with Karl Popper, that claims a statement is not meaningful unless it can be falsified. It is an intriguing thesis which we cannot explore here, but something similar might be said about preaching. One has not said anything very meaningful unless it is vulnerable to falsification. The preaching of the timid soul who asks of us only to entertain interesting ideas is vulnerable to nothing other than being dismissed as dull. The preacher who insists that we wrestle with *his* truth, which he has wrestled from God's truth, is vulnerable to being rejected as a liar, fool, or false teacher. The stakes are much higher for him. A sermon that is lovely, uplifting, and "ever so meaningful" means very little unless it poses the question of truth or falsity. Is what is said true and, if so, so what? Preaching that does not pose questions and pose them urgently is not good preaching. The prow of the pulpit makes waves.

Passion is essential to preaching. Now passion means many things. It is emotion, but it is not emotionalism. Emotion is intense feeling in response to significant truth; emotionalism is borrowed feeling momentarily indulged. Passion is a sense of urgency. The hearer should know that here, clearly, is a person urgently trying to communicate something that is important to him. And, above all, passion means *pathos,* a kind of suffering. This is not to say that preaching should be oppressively morbid. Some splendid sermons are perfectly delightful, even playful. But the most delightful and joyous sermons should give evidence of a victory painfully won through *pathos.* In every sermon, whatever its tone, the preacher should be handing over a big piece of himself. It should be evident that the truth imparted—whether it leads one to the edge of despair or the mountaintop of ecstasy—was dearly won and is to be treated with respect.

Brilioth says of Tertullian that he preached with "restrained ardor." *Ardere*—to burn. Preach like a fire under control. Fires rage, and fires simmer, and fires dance; there are fires of wrath and fires of the passion we call love. Not for nothing were Isaiah's lips touched by a coal of fire. I have heard great preachers who, like great actors, have an awesome public presence. They are the kind of people of whom it is said that they walk into a room and, without their having said a word, the room is theirs. They fill the pulpit. And I have heard great preachers who, although they may be six feet tall, one has to look twice to make sure they are there. But once the sermon is begun, it is evident that the fire is there. Whether he speaks in tones stentorian or is barely audible, whether he is accompanied by grand gestures or with a crouch of intense concentration, it is soon evident that *here* is a preacher. Here is no smooth therapist, no peddler of religious palmsmanship, no friendly pusher of spiritual highs, no aspiring social critic, no seven o'clock news commentator on portentous events. No, here is a preacher who has been visited by the seraphim with a burning coal from the altar.

PEOPLE, PREACHER, AND LANGUAGE

Ardor usually connotes love. There is the love between pastor and people, and the love of both from God and for God. Preaching is part of the love feast of worship itself. The sermon is not something set apart from the liturgy, it is an integral part of the liturgy. It is offered up as the *leitourgia* of the people of God. The office of preaching and the office of hearing go together, the latter sometimes being more arduous than the former. The preacher regularly calls the people to attentiveness, not just because he wants a better audience but because they are engaged in a common work. In black churches this is done regularly and very overtly. The preacher may even stop and remonstrate with the members of the "amen corner" if they are not holding up their end of the common liturgy. "Preach it, preacher!" "Praise the Lord!" "Ain't it true!" "Amen, brother!" White folks are often puzzled and a little embarrassed by this kind of congregational participation. It must be understood that this express ardor is not simply response to the quality of preaching; the people are actually helping the preacher to preach. The amen corner is acclamation and it is intercession for the preacher. There is little chance for that kind of participation in most of our staid white churches. Yet the preacher will be on the lookout for the slight nod of the head, the eyebrow raised in question, the shadow of a smile, and he will know that the people are with him and for him. From the pulpit of Straitlaced Presbyterian, where in Sunday worship one would no more break forth than break wind, the sensitive preacher will elicit and encourage his amen corner.

The word *rhetoric* is hardly used today unless it is combined in "mere rhetoric." That is a great shame. It is a consequence of the same disease that separates joy and freedom from form and dignity.

True, already in classical times the philosophers criticized the *rhetor* who was prepared to employ his dishonest eloquence in any cause. But rhetoric means the art of expressive speech and, taken captive by the gospel, it is of the highest value. Preaching is the communication of truth through sanctified ego and sanctified rhetoric. It is not simply in the pulpit that rhetoric has fallen into disfavor. Survey the national political scene today and you can name scarcely one distinguished speaker. No Webster, no Clay, no Douglas, no Lincoln, not even a Woodrow Wilson, F. D. R., or John F. Kennedy. And now not even, to stretch the point some distance, a Hubert Humphrey. In the cultured mind, oratory is synonymous with pomposity. I daresay that most educated Americans cannot recall three lines from a political speech delivered in the last ten years. The times militate against a style that makes claims on other people's lives, or even on their attention. The mood is that of the low profile, of being cool, of small assertions and small risks, of playing it safe. It is a hard time for preaching.

Saint Augustine, a great preacher by all accounts, did not share our uneasiness with rhetoric.[7] He understood that the preacher's task is greater than the orator's; the preacher's desire is not simply to impress but to be understood. It is easier to move an audience to a momentary feeling or viewpoint than to instruct and inspire a community on the way of salvation. Perhaps this is one reason why many preachers find it easier to preach to a congregation other than their own. In another church, well-tested phrases and oft-used illustrations can be displayed with the freshness of new discovery. It is in the complex ambiguity of one's relationship with one's own people that the absurdity of the "absurd responsibility" of preaching becomes more evident. But if rhetoric is the art of expressive speech, rhetoric is all the more important in communicating with one's own people.

Augustine advocated the well-known definition of the speaker's task: *docere, delectare, flectere*—to teach, to delight, to influence. He explains with care how the preacher should make use of the three styles of address: *genus submissum, temperatum,* and *grande*—the restrained, the moderate, and the grand style. He cautioned that the grand style should be used with care. His caution is apt today. When employed by some, it is truly grand. When others attempt it, they sound a little silly—as though they are imitating someone they saw in a movie or in an historical documentary on educational television. Oratory that sounds pompous is bad oratory; rhetoric that sounds contrived is bad rhetoric; the antidote for both is better oratory and better rhetoric.

Augustine suggested that the preacher employs the highest rhetoric of all, what he called sublime speech. It was a form of speech aspiring to be worthy of its subject. To say it is sublime speech does not mean that it is solemn in the sense of excluding liveliness or spontaneity. To the contrary, the manuscripts indicate that Augustine and the congregation were in constant dialogue. It is noted where the people applauded, shouted their approval, or even asked questions. At one point the people applauded and Augustine responded, "I see my words please you. That is good. I have your applause, now I ask for your good works." Maybe this lively exchange, this sense of people and preacher doing their homiletical liturgy together, is related to the fact that Augustine and his people were African. Some black scholars have suggested such a connection between African origins and black preaching today.[8] But it is clear that in his writing on preaching, Augustine thought of himself as setting out principles that are universally applicable. Certainly the principle that we should appropriate all that is useful from rhetoric, the art of expressive speech, is one worthy of wider acceptance today.

I am no doubt biased by having pastored for so many years in black congregations where the use of language is more generally esteemed. That may have something to do with my being depressed by the debasement of language in our country. Listen to the politicians, the people on television talk shows, the academic lecturers, and, sorry to say, many preachers; every time they open their mouths the language is the less for it. To make matters worse, those who would improve the language evidence little understanding of what language is about. Books appear regularly on the proper use of the English language. Proper, in most cases, means accurate. Accuracy! One is taken back to seventh grade again, where Mrs. Johnson recited the rules of grammar which she observed so punctiliously and to such deadening effect. Accuracy indeed. Such books are one with the "ordinary language" philosophers of some while back who contended that the purpose of philosophy is to point out linguistic mistakes and the purpose of language is not to make them.

Not that accuracy is unimportant. But to say that the purpose of language is to be accurate is like saying that the purpose of sex is hygiene. Language is to enliven, to engage, to instruct, to challenge, to inspire. We human beings are, as the late Abraham Heschel insisted, the cantors of the universe. And language is our instrument. Language is not to be seen in a purely instrumental way, however. Language is to be celebrated. And the better it is celebrated, not so oddly, the more effective an instrument it will be for the praise of God and the edification of his people. We hear much today about the Church's obligation to contribute to cultural and social change, and that is good. A major contribution of the Church, and of the pulpit in particular, would be to rescue the English language from the sorrows of cruel and unusual punishment.

One comes upon real love for the English tongue among some Southerners and among Black preachers. One listens to black preachers like William Jones and Gardner Taylor in Brooklyn, or Samuel Proctor in Harlem, or Jesse Jackson in Chicago. Gardner Taylor begins by picking up a word, such as *reconciliation,* or *communion,* or *sisterhood.* First he just says it, but then you can see him warming up to it. Clearly he *loves* that word, and he's going to do wonderful things for it and to it. He tries just rolling it out of his mouth; then, staccato-like, he bounces it around a bit; then he starts to take it apart, piece by piece, and then put it together in different ways. And pretty soon you have a whole lot of people engaged in wondering and puzzling with Dr. Taylor, trying to figure out what this word and this idea of reconciliation is all about. They walk around the word, looking at it from different angles. Taylor gets on top of it and looks down, then he lifts up a corner and peeks underneath; you can see this is going to be a difficult word to get to know. He whispers it and then he shouts it; he pats, pinches, and probes it; and then he pronounces himself unsatisfied, and all the people agree. "It's time to look at what the great Apostle Paul has to say about this here word *reconciliation.*" And all the people agree.

There is a playfulness in all this, but the purpose is impressively serious. It may seem like taking the long way to get to the text, but along the way the preacher has tried out a number of conventional definitions and explanations of *reconciliation* and has, in fact, already covered a good deal of what he intends to say on the subject. It is one form of excellent rhetoric.

In some circumstances it is thought to be inexcusably racist to say that black folk have rhythm. But with respect to the linguistic rhythm of black preaching, it is true and it is enviable. When done well, it is both instructive and exhilarating, good pedagogy and good for the soul. Many white Americans are somewhat familiar with this rhythm, which frequently becomes a kind of chant, through the speaking of Martin Luther King, Jr. They remember his "I have a dream!" at the beginning of each strophe of the 1963 March on Washington speech. Or at Montgomery two years later, the accelerating repetition of "How long? Not long!" It is, unapologetically, a rhetorical device. But it is most emphatically not a "mere" rhetorical device. It is used to great effect with phrases that are most unremarkable in themselves. It requires a love for language, a fascination with words—how they are constructed and how they can be used. It is a love and a fascination that are powerfully in the service of the gospel.

We began this chapter by discussing the connection between the self and the task of preaching. Here too the black experience is instructive. Perhaps nowhere else in the Church is preaching connected with the public presentation of self in such an uninhibited manner. To its cultured despisers it is a "show"; to those who are open to understanding it, it is an exercise in the freedom of the gospel. There are no nibbling doubts about role-playing here, no "consciousness of the third eye" challenging the authenticity of what is happening—or, if these are there, they are firmly set aside. "Here are the people. I am the preacher. They came to hear me preach and I came to preach, so preach I will."

On Monday afternoons in Harlem, several hundred of the Black preachers of New York get together to confer on everything from fund raising to political patronage. One of them, or a guest preacher from another city, is chosen to give the sermon for the day. There is no doubt that he is supposed to "do his stuff" for the examination and edification of his peers. All stops are pulled, and this is followed by professional appraisal. It is not less "spiritual" for its being so workmanlike. Many white ministers might find it distasteful or even condemn it as exhibitionism. But I suspect that Chrysostom, Tertullian, Augustine, and maybe even George Whitefield would feel quite at home.

One does not wish to romanticize the state of black preaching. When it is good it is very, very good. And when it is bad . . . well, that too is true. An important aspect of equality is to remember that our black sisters and brothers are equal, and sometimes more equal than others, in manifesting the sins to which we are all heir. But the best of black preaching today puts together self and language in a way that can be instructive for all of us. Obviously it should not be imitated, but key aspects of it might well be emulated. Black preaching was born in and is carried by a particular cultural experience. But the principles that make it great, when it is great, are not that different from those specified by St. Augustine more than fifteen hundred years ago and observed by the worthier practitioners of the art ever since.

CONFIDENCE AND CONSOLATION

Because good preaching so intensively engages the self, it would seem immodest for anyone not to protest the allegation that he is a great preacher. Yet one suspects that most of us who exercise this "absurd responsibility" believe that we have, from time to time, preached truly great sermons. And one supposes that a great preacher is simply someone who has that experience more frequently, and who has his estimation of his preaching reinforced by others more consistently. It is hard to imagine that such a person is not conscious of his abilities in much the same way that athletes or artists are conscious of theirs. The art of preaching will be enhanced if we are more candid about the fact that preaching is, among many other things, an art. Our reticence in discussing it as an art may arise from personal modesty, or from a theology that so emphasizes the majesty of the Word that it seems almost blasphemous to apply the criteria of art to its communication. But it may be that our reticence is motivated neither by modesty nor by the majesty of the Word but by our unwillingness to engage in the discipline of hard study and training that is required to develop and sustain artistic quality.

Of course there are no pat formulas for great preaching. But the experienced preacher thinks he knows when he has delivered a really good sermon. Like all forms of public speaking—but more than others, because the range of subject matter is virtually unlimited—preaching can be a powerful aphrodisiac or, as it is said, an ego trip. One's own voice and person roll like a wave across a crowd, rebound from the back wall, and roll back, locking speaker and hearers in an embrace that is almost sensuous. It is very seductive. Descriptions of such speaking are heavy with the tones of will-to-power: "They hung on his every word"; "He had them in the palm of his hand"; and so forth. Of course egotism should be kept in check, but we should not be so terrified of its dangers that we mute the forces of effective communication. Like a concert pianist who knows he has given a fine performance, the preacher too can sit down after a sermon and feel the legitimate satisfaction of having done a good job. "Thank you, Lord, that seemed to go very well." As to the perils of ego tripping, most of us do not have the experience often enough to pose much of a threat to our spiritual health.

I have had the privilege over the years of speaking in almost every possible setting—political, academic, and churchly. I have spoken at rallies and conventions, in classrooms and auditoriums, and in churches of almost every denomination and description. Occasionally something extraordinary, almost magical, happens; more frequently you marvel at the patience of the people and hope they did not see the inadequacies as clearly as you did. But each time there is a risk; you do not really know what is going to happen. It is true that after a while you develop a degree of professional confidence. You are reasonably sure that the nightmares about falling flat on your face or being stricken dumb are not going to happen. An experienced concert pianist may be terribly nervous beforehand, but he is reasonably sure that when he walks out on that stage he is going to be able to find middle C. The question is whether his playing will be great or merely passable. The pianist and the preacher, and anyone else who is serious about what he is doing, can never be satisfied with the merely passable.

Each person's experience is as unique as is each person. Generalizations must be treated with caution. With that caveat, one ventures the generalization that all good preaching is intimately connected with the public presentation of self. Of course study and preparation and prayer and having something to say are each crucial, and we will return to these aspects. But when one stands before the congregation, one is keenly aware of the exposure of self. That can be frightening. One is tempted to look around for a fig leaf. Bombast or platitudes are fig leaves. Or, ostrichlike, one sticks his head into a written text, occasionally looking up to sustain the pretension that one is speaking to people instead of reading an essay. This is not, to my mind, what preaching is about, although perhaps some who are excellent pastors in other respects simply have no gift for preaching and thus must be resigned to reading in public.

But the preacher risks the exposure of self—a sanctified self, one hopes, but definitely self. You may have noticed that some preachers, when they face the congregation, pause for a moment. It is a moment designed not so much to collect thoughts as to establish presence. One collects oneself and the awareness of the other selves involved in the communal effort to come. During the times I was with Dr. King, I was struck by the way he did this almost consistently. Upon being introduced, or when the time came for the sermon, he would stand and wait, sometimes for ten seconds or more. It was what is known as a pregnant moment. It was a very active kind of waiting. His eyes would pass back and forth over the assembly, establishing his identity to them and theirs to him. Then, when all was quiet and it had been signaled that something important was about to happen, he would begin.

Now of course none of us is Martin Luther King, Jr. There was an aura and a sense of heightened expectancy that his presence brought to any meeting. It was quite different from the expectations at the beginning of Pastor Campbell's one hundred and eighty-seventh Sunday sermon at Elm Street Methodist. Yet I would suggest that such a moment before beginning to preach is of general value. It is a moment to establish contact and for people to settle down. And it is a moment of prayer. But it is also a moment of establishing one's "self," and of establishing for oneself and others the significance of what is about to happen. In this moment it is silently communicated that we are all about to set out on an adventure, that there is risk involved, and that everyone's help is required if what should happen is going to happen.

In that moment one may silently be saying to oneself something like this: "Well, here we are. It is presumptuous to think that I am going to proclaim the Word of God to you this morning. But if it is presumptuous, the responsibility for the presumption is shared. After all, it's not entirely my idea that I'm standing before you getting ready to preach. You did call me to do this. And I do believe, although I'm not always certain, that God has called me to do this. I'm not the world's greatest preacher, but I intend to do my best. In any case, you're here and I'm here and there's a job to be done. So let's get on with it." And then the sermon begins.

As I say, generalizations are difficult. I know a man who has been preaching more than fifteen years and is considered to be more than competent in his craft. He assures me that he is physically sick every Saturday night knowing that he must preach the next day. Frequently it happens that, immediately after the sermon and while the congregation is singing a hymn, he goes to the sacristy bathroom and throws up. Then he returns to continue the liturgy. That is one extreme. Quite different is a well-known evangelist who can, quite literally, at a moment's notice deliver a sermon of notable quality. Preaching would seem to hold no fears for him. Despite his remarkable facility, maybe because of it, his preaching does not seem facile. On one occasion, he was observed monitoring a television program of himself preaching. Turning to a friend, he casually remarked, "You know I never watch these programs without being inspired all over again." The preacher being edified by watching himself preach. It seems a little convoluted and perhaps even weird. Yet one can readily imagine Vladimir Horowitz listening to a recording of himself playing Chopin and remarking, "You know, he's very good." And maybe he means

Horowitz and maybe he means Chopin, but probably he means both.

So one preacher goes through fear and trembling, stricken by his smallness before the greatness of the task. The other may be equally impressed by the majesty of the Word and has no illusions that he is worthy of the task; but worthy or not, he does what he does well and offers up his inadequacies to God. They are both fine preachers. The important thing is that neither is paralyzed by the ambiguities of the engagement of self. They do what they are called to do.

Finally, there is a passage from Isaiah that has both troubled and comforted me over the years, as it has no doubt troubled and comforted many other preachers: "For as the rain cometh down, and the snow from heaven, and returneth not thither, but watereth the earth, and maketh it bring forth and bud, that it may give seed to the sower, and bread to the eater: So shall my word be that goeth forth out of my mouth: it shall not return unto me void, but it shall accomplish that which I please, and it shall prosper in the thing whereto I sent it" (Isa. 55, KJV).

When I was a boy in catechism, this was the passage we memorized as sure proof that preaching is very, very important. "The word shall not return void." I suspected then that that was a little too neat, almost magical; it didn't matter whether the sermon was prepared or whether it was delivered well. As long as "God's word" was spoken, the job was done and its effectiveness guaranteed. For a long time I thought the use of Isaiah 55 was the consolation of lazy and mediocre preachers.

And now *I* find consolation in the passage. Not because I am lazy and mediocre, although I am both at times, but because we finally do not know—we do not really know—when preaching is effective. Surely every experienced pastor has had occasions when people have said how much they were helped or changed by a sermon that the pastor had quite forgotten, or remembers with embarrassment. We do not know what is happening in this encounter called preaching. There is a great mystery involved. But the awareness of the mystery dare not be an excuse for neglecting the mastery of which we are capable. Our final reliance is on the promise that the Word shall not return void; our present obligation is to employ and refine every gift in our possession as we help in sending it forth on its mission.

10.
The Imperative Indicative

Why, when there are so many interesting things to say, must preaching be so dull? With respect to the preaching vocation, it is to be feared that many of us who might otherwise be conscientious will be brought before the judgment throne to answer the charge of betrayal by boredom. Pressed to offer practical advice about how to enliven the preaching enterprise for oneself and one's people, I would focus on two precepts: *simplify* and *experiment*. It is the advice I most often give myself in the time immediately after preaching, when the inadequacies of the sermon are most painfully lucid in my mind.

A good sermon is about one thing. That is the cardinal rule. Far from being simple, this is very difficult; simplicity is hard for most of us to achieve. The great preachers are unanimous in this discovery. In preaching, it has been remarked, purity of heart is to will one thing. John Henry Newman put it well: "Definiteness is the life of preaching. A definite hearer, not the whole world; a definite topic, not the whole evangelical tradition; and a definite speaker. Nothing that is anonymous will preach."[1] A "definite speaker" relates to what we have called the preaching "self"; a "definite topic" moves toward decision; and a "definite hearer" has to do with preaching as the communal doing of a common liturgy.

The inexperienced preacher and the experienced preacher hardened in mistakes try to convey the whole of their knowledge or feelings in one sermon. For some this means an every-Sunday tour from the Garden of Eden to the Gates of Paradise; for others it means the full exposure of their state of mind that week, which usually turns out to be confused. From an early moment in thinking about the sermon, one must persistently ask: "What is this sermon about? What do I *really* want to say? What do I hope it will do?" A good sermon is about one thing.

Simplicity means ruthlessly cutting away everything that does not contribute to or is not demanded by that one thing. An elegant introduction that is in search of a theme is to be brutally suppressed. An engaging illustration that will be remembered when the point it was to illustrate is forgotten must be cut off without mercy. Consign them to a provisional limbo, as it were, for it is through no fault of their own. And who knows? They may be rescued for service in the cause of some other sermon. If it does not support the cause of this sermon, it does not belong. Better to go into the pulpit bereft of elegant phrases, clever asides, profound literary allusions, and interesting tales than that the whole sermon should be condemned to uncertain purpose.

Simplicity does not mean simplemindedness. The deepest thoughts call for the greatest clarity. Clarity means also a clear succession of ideas, so that the attentive hearer can go back over the sermon and see the end in the beginning. Even in expository preaching, where the purpose is to expose the meaning of the text piece by piece, simplicity is not a wooden adherence to the obvious. It requires a lively imagination to expose surprises in the apparently self-evident. One of the most memorable sermons I have ever heard focused on the simple statement in the account of the flood: "And they that entered, male and female of all flesh, went in as God had commanded Noah; and the Lord shut him in" (Gen. 7:16). *And the Lord shut him in.* Noah could not shut the door of the ark against the cries of his neighbors begging to be let in. God's love is such that, even in his judgment, it is God who does the hardest things.

From the closing of the door of the ark, to the cross of Christ, to God's continuing pathos with his defiant creation—the connections are utterly simple in the service of a point both powerful and profound.

Much of the best of expository preaching, it should be noted, employs what might be called the "what if?" device. The biblical stories are so familiar to us that they tend to have about them the feel of necessity. "Well of course that's the way it was. Everyone knows that." But there is no "of course" about it. In the acts of God and man, there were and there are alternatives; otherwise there would be no freedom, and therefore no love. What if God had not shut the door? Would Noah have done it? Should he have? What if Judas had lived to seek readmission to the apostolic band? What if Paul had said that by faith, plus a reasonable number of good works, we are saved? What if Jesus had declined crucifixion in favor of clerical certification? The understanding of the path taken requires an awareness of the paths passed by. Not this, but that; not "of course," but amazement. And, in all, the *simplicity* of the storyteller's art.

THE DELIGHT OF EXPERIMENT

Simplify and *experiment.* There is a way of preaching that is truly yours. You are, as Newman says, "the definite speaker." But that way is always to be tested and refined; within it are many different ways of doing different things. If one has been preaching for forty years, preaching should still have about it something of an intellectual, artistic, and personal venture. Experimental does not necessarily mean tentative or uncertain. To the contrary, it requires a good deal of confidence to try something quite new. The uncertain preacher just tries to get through it without falling on his face. The master can venture variations on themes that are ever new. If the preacher is not at least a little curious about what will happen, that sense of dull predictability will no doubt be communicated to the hearer. Predictability diminishes joy, and in preaching, too, the general rule holds that what we enjoy doing we do well, and vice versa. Experiment is essential to the delight one should take in the craft of preaching.

Experiment can involve almost every aspect of preaching, from where one stands, to the gestures one employs, to the use of humor or the element of surprise in illustrations. Some pastors find that they are "freed up" by leaving the pulpit and preaching from the front of the altar or in the aisle. Many of us are inhibited in expressing our emotions and need to be encouraged to greater vulnerability in that respect. People need to *see* that we care about what we are saying. All this involves a good deal of self-consciousness about what we are doing. Not the self-consciousness of defensive fragility, but the self-consciousness of someone who has studied his craft. There is a kind of private delight in homiletical experiment. One does not announce to the congregation what it is you are testing in a particular sermon. What you are testing is for you to know and for them to guess; and if they did not even notice it but were more engaged in the preaching event as a result of it, all the better.

Experiment in preaching will avoid regular dependence upon visual aids and other gimcrackery in the pulpit. Such nonsense is not experiment with, but abandonment of, preaching—for preaching is the business of the spoken word. Such visual tricks are too often used in a pitch to the children. Many adults will say that they prefer the "children's sermons," with its little toys and tricks, but that is a preference not to be pandered to. There is a perilous cuteness about doing things for the kiddies in church. Some adults are entertained by it, but entertainment is a far remove from serious engagement in the proclamation of the Word. Preachers should resist the temptation to gain the attention of parents by gaining the attention of their children, for what that usually means is that parental attention is focused not on the sermon but on the phenomeonon of their children paying attention. Of course the children are part of the congregation and should be taken into account. It is sad that in so many churches they are sent off to Sunday School or some other activity, as though they have no part in the chief service of the People of God. But preaching should be aimed at engaging the whole congregation in reflection and decision; and if there are parts that elude the seven-year-olds, that is no fault. Perhaps families might even be encouraged to revive the custom in which the sermon was regularly discussed afterwards at home, and then parents can explain what the children missed. But it is much better for the children's attention to be held in church by the phenomenon of attentive adults; children should be able to see that worship is a communal venture they grow up into, not a kiddies' hour they grow out of.

So experiment definitely does not mean the introduction of novelties and entertainments to compensate for the failure of preaching. It does mean that the preacher is conscious of his craft and deliberative about the ways in which a change of tone or gesture or illustration can better effect communal engagement. I earlier mentioned the way in which some preachers use a pause at the beginning of the sermon to establish mutual "presence" and to signal the importance of what is to happen. Similarly, a brief pause in the middle of the sermon or at some other point along the way can effectively reestablish presence and purpose. This takes a degree of confidence, for the uncertain preacher is eager to get through it, lest he lose the point or the people's attention. But a brief silence can be used to regain the initiative, to recollect the point, and to reenlist the drifting hearer. To the inexperienced speaker, any pause seems frighteningly long, but it does not seem so to the hearer. Such a pause does not signal loss of control but a reassertion of control and direction.

Certainly in preparing a sermon, but also in the course of preaching it, one is conscious of different homiletical modes. There is the forensic mode, in which one sees himself as a lawyer arguing a case before a jury. There is the conversational-reflective mode, in which one invites the hearer to join in an exploration of a question or subject posed. There is the narrative mode, in which the points are more winsomely made for their being made indirectly, as in the drama about who would close the door of the ark. There is the lecture mode, which need not be deadly simply because so many lectures are that way. There is the manifesto mode, in which the preacher articulates a carefully wrought statement of position that obviously invites response. And, of course, there is the expository mode, in which the pieces of the text are probed and taken apart and then, when put together again, the whole presents itself in unsuspected freshness. Among these and other modes one makes a choice to be tested and refined in a particular sermon. It is, of course, an ongoing experiment, and more than one mode may be employed in the same sermon.

Admittedly, some may find suggestions such as these inhibiting, artificial, and contrived. Where is the spontaneity in preaching? Obviously, I can only speak with authority from my own experience, but that experience is for the most part confirmed by numerous conversations with other preachers and by the literature. And that experience is simply this: That the sermons that seem to me, and apparently to others, most spontaneous and lively are the sermons in which I most deliberately and definitely knew what I wanted to do and how I wanted to do it. It sounds cynical to say that the appearance of artlessness is an art, but there is a measure of truth there. The more gracious truth is that when you have fixed your purpose, laid your plan, and eliminated what is extraneous, then you are most free to do what is at hand to be done.

AIDS TO BEING CONTEMPORARY

Preachers need also to hear good preachers. Books of sermons were once very popular, but publishers have eased off from them in recent years—because, some say, there is not much great preaching; others say they simply don't sell. It is hard to know which is cause and which effect. A contributing factor may be the new availability of cassettes and other recording devices by which one can hear sermons as they were actually delivered. In addition, there are today numerous "homily services" offering complete sermons for every Sunday and feast of the year. They are especially popular among Roman Catholics and were originally justified in terms of helping priests who had not been trained to the discipline of every-Sunday sermon preparation to comply with the new preaching regulations. Unfortunately, they have now in many instances become a substitute for such preparation. I confess that for some years I wrote sermons anonymously for several of these services. One whimsical satisfaction in that connection is that there was in Brooklyn a

Roman Catholic parish that was the exception to the ecumenical cooperation St. John's had with Catholic and other churches. The priest of that parish thought me a dreadful radical and community troublemaker and did nothing to disguise his hostility. It was therefore with some satisfaction that I discovered that he had for some time been preaching, all unknowingly, sermons I had written.

Homiletical aids of various kinds have been around from the beginning, at least as far back as Ambrose's adaptation of Cicero. In the Middle Ages there were numerous *artes praedicandi,* little aids to preaching filled with hundreds of *exempla,* or illustrations. What are in fact *libri exemplorum* are still issued by some religious publishing houses today. The endurance of such aids no doubt witnesses to their utility. More helpful to the preacher, I suspect, is some kind of regular and considered response to his preaching beyond the at-the-door comments such as, "That was a beautiful sermon, Pastor." Some churches have a coffee and discussion group after the service, in which people share with the pastor their ideas on the sermon. Other pastors have a Bible study scheduled for earlier in the week, in which the sermon text for the next Sunday is studied. And in those traditions that follow a pericopal system, it is not uncommon for neighboring clergy to get together on Monday or Tuesday to begin work on the text.

At an early point in looking at the text, the question arises about its relation to "the present situation." In discussing that question one must, I suppose, take into account Karl Barth's oft-quoted and oft-misunderstood statement about preaching with the Bible in one hand and the daily newspaper in the other. The metaphor no doubt has its uses but, as a general thing, the lust for contemporaneity should be kept in close check. It has been said of some styles of liberation theology that they preach with the newspaper in one hand, a gun in the other, while standing on the Bible. Substitute a bottle of tranquilizers for the gun, and one has the picture of much current preaching of the peace-of-mind variety. We could do with a lot more preaching that keeps both hands on the Bible. If we are true to the biblical text, the contemporaneity of it will be evident enough.

Paul Scherer, a great teacher of preaching, has difficulties in saying that a biblical situation is "just like our situation." He quotes John Knox: "My primary experience is not that of *learning* something about the past, but of *recognizing* something in the present." Scherer comments, "I am unable to recall any biblical situation of which that cannot be said. Far from being 'like,' in a very real sense every Biblical situation *is* our situation—though the two may in no instance ever be identified."[2]

The apostolic word *is* our situation. In discovering that word and the Word to whom it bears witness, we see ourselves more clearly than through the study of the newspaper or other contemporary sources. The great "contemporary" questions of fear, hope, disappointment, love, ecstasy, sickness, and death are all there. If one does not, for example, find every instance of betrayal and reconciliation in the parable of the prodigal son, one has not adequately expounded the parable. We carry within our minds the connections with the contemporary, as do our hearers, and reference to such connections need therefore only be oblique and suggestive.

The distinctiveness of Christian preaching is compromised, and the just expectations of our people disappointed, if we regularly focus on such connections directly and prescriptively. I do not say this because addressing contemporary problems, especially social issues, can be controversial. To the contrary, we should not ordinarily address them too directly or prescriptively, because that does not lead the hearer to the deeper controversy with the will of God. The preacher who presumes to declare from the pulpit what should be done about disarmament, or capital punishment, or teenage crime can be readily dismissed as "too conservative" or "too liberal," depending on the taste of his hearers. In any case, his views on the subject are frequently not as interesting or as informed as what people might receive through magazines, or television, or books. Again, our goal in preaching is not relevance but engagement.

The connections with the contemporary emerge obliquely, suggestively, and troublingly from immersion in the text. The hearer is not so much challenged to come to terms with the preacher's viewpoint as with the one who is rightly acknowledged as Christ our Contemporary. We are the more persuasive the more we make it clear that we have not confused our opinion with the

Word of God. With respect to the particular answers to all problems, ancient and contemporary, we invite the hearer to join in the search for a divine will that always eludes our certain apprehension. This does not mean we end on a note of uncertainty; rather, we begin and end with the assurance of a hope that transcends our differing perceptions of what ought to be done.

PREACHING FOR DECISIONS

Preaching that engages people in a search, that is an invitation to venture, is not the opposite of preaching for decision. The adventure is composed of many decisions, and every sermon should call for decision. It is a decision for Christ, as they say, but not as though one had been a pagan until that moment. Decision is like the dying and rising again that, as we considered earlier, is the daily drama of Christian existence. Each sermon should call for a decision with respect to some further dimension of Christ's teaching and rule. Do I believe that? Is that really true? Will I do that? Do I want that? Such are the questions that should engage the hearer in the course and conclusion of preaching. As the sawdust trail is to a revival meeting, so the walk to the eucharistic altar is symbolic of a response to the sermon's challenge. The decision about a particular point may be ambivalent and tentative, but the decision to immerse one's uncertainty in the blood of the Lamb is emphatic.

Christian decision is composed of many decisions. Some biblical scholars have taught us to make a sharp distinction between the *kerygma* and *didache* in the New Testament. The *kerygma* of God's saving acts and the *didache* of the discipled life cannot in practice be so sharply distinguished; certainly they must never be separated. It is ironic that Rudolf Bultmann, with his program of demythologizing, and the revival tent fundamentalist are both inclined to concentrate on the *kerygma*, almost to the exclusion of the *didache*. The converted life is the life of many conversions, some major and some seemingly minor. And, in the curious ways of the Spirit, the seemingly minor may turn out to be the major. For example, there are men who, so far as we can tell, would undergo a much more foundation-shaking transformation of life if they stopped demean-

ing and domineering their wives than if they once again "surrendered their hearts to Jesus," which they seem to do with ease. Examples can be multiplied.

The debate over what it means to preach for decision is not new.
In the nineteenth century, Dean Church wrote in criticism of a
certain style of evangelical preaching:

> What it failed in was the education and development of character.
> . . . It shrank, in its fear of mere moralizing, in its horror of the idea of
> merit or of the value of good works, from coming into contact with the
> manifold realities of the spirit of man: it never seemed to get beyond the
> 'first beginnings' of Christian teaching, the call to repent, the assurance
> of forgiveness: it had nothing to say to the long and varied process of
> building up the new life of truth and goodness: it was nervously afraid
> of departing from the consecrated phrases of its school, and in the
> perpetual iteration of them it lost hold of the meaning they may have
> had. . . . At length it presented all the characteristics of an exhausted
> teaching and a spent enthusiasm.[3]

Preaching that aims only at that one big conversion, that decisive
surrender, inevitably ends up exhibiting the signs of "an exhausted
teaching and a spent enthusiasm." The variousness of what we are
becoming in each new day must be surrendered, and the meaning
of surrender must be explored in relation to each new particularity,
each new possibility, each new temptation. Conversion is dramatic
discontinuity, a breaking of shackles, it is death and resurrection;
and conversion is also the quiet decision to continue on a pilgrimage
that began with the promise to Adam and will end in the return of
the Second Adam. Each sermon, then, should invite a further decision along that pilgrim way.

Richard R. Caemmerer, who taught so many of us at Concordia
Seminary, St. Louis, proposed that every sermon should be composed of three parts: goal, malady, means. The goal—whether it be
a "faith goal" or a "life goal"—is where you want to get; the malady
is what prevents us from getting there; the means is the gospel that
overcomes the malady and bestows, as a gift from God, the opening
to the goal. Similarly, Paul Scherer considers the nuances in
preaching for decision and was critical of sermons that neglected

"the indicatives of the Christian faith, where all the imperatives are born." The imperatives are born from the indicatives. In our preaching we do not so much prescribe behavior; rather we are midwives of the imperatives that issue from the indicatives of our proclamation.

Earlier we considered the pretentiousness and imperiousness of pastors who prescribe a certain mood for worship, as though it were not our duty to offer all our moods, both fair and foul, to God in liturgy. So in preaching for decision, the focus is not on the decision but on that about which decision is called for—more precisely, the focus is on him who calls for decision. We do not so much tell people how they ought to respond to Christ, or even that they ought to look to Christ alone; we simply hold up Christ. This is the outcome of all our study and all our preaching, to hold up Christ, his office, his teaching, his benefits. The subject is inexhaustible, for he is the Lord of life in all its variousness, the monumental and the quotidian, the political and the private, the beautiful and the unseemly, the spiritual and the secular.

PREACHING WITH AUTHORITY

To say that preaching should be indicative is to say also that preaching should be doctrinal. To be a minister of the Church means to set forth the classic points of reference by which the Christian community interprets reality. Such points of reference are doctrines, and the most essential of them are dogmas. One almost wants to scandalize by saying that preaching should be dogmatic. For it is as true now as when John Henry Newman wrote it more than a hundred years ago: "Many a man will live and die upon a dogma; no man will be a martyr for a conclusion."

The problem is not that dogma is outdated, it is that most of the great dogmas are unknown. We have not made them our own because we have not thought them through and prayed them through. It is probably true that many ministers have made more their own the dogmas of sexual fulfillment, racial equality, or American superiority than the dogma of the Holy Trinity, for example. Seminary graduates frequently declare themselves liberated from the dogmas they never learned. And because our modern minds are so skittish about doctrine and dogma, the people of the Church are, for the most part, theologically illiterate. They cannot know whether they believe or not because they do not even know what Christians are supposed to believe.

Several years ago, Dean Kelley's *Why Conservative Churches Are Growing* depicted the hunger of people for religious authority. Because they do not find that authority in their own churches, they gravitate toward those who equate authority with authoritarianism and dogma with dogmatism. Jesus impressed people because he spoke with authority, but he was not authoritarian. He engaged people in reflection, inquiry, and self-examination leading to repentance and newness of life. Authoritarianism, like dogmatism, does not call for engagement but for submission; it invites not the birth of thought but the end of thought; it does not provoke to pilgrimage but encourages the laying down of our burden in a false and premature sense of arrival.

Dogmatism and authoritarianism will always have their appeal, as the Grand Inquisitor of Dostoevsky's *Brothers Karamazov* understood so well. The antidote, however, is not a timorous tentativeness but preaching that is marked by genuine authority. Genuine authority comes from truth that we have made our own. How many churchgoing Christians are aware that the great ecumenical creeds they recite on Sunday reflect a theory of reality that is comprehensive, intellectually rigorous, majestically nuanced—a theory that by comparison makes most of the regnant philosophies of our time seem like almost accidental collections of careless guesswork? Not many Christians would suspect it, in large part because they have not heard it set forth from their pulpits. Thus, Christianity remains for many an amalgam of sentiment, nostalgia, psychic uplift, and bland moralism. Many of these people suspect that there must be more to it than this. But they come seeking the bread of truth and are offered the stones of ignorance or even pious unbelief. These are the people who, in their hunger, are prey to the dogmatists. Of the new authoritarians, they say, "At least they know what they believe!"

The preacher owes at least this to his hearers: that they know what he believes and why—and, sometimes, what he has a hard time believing and why. But his primary responsibility is to hold forth the indicative. All the imperatives, all the emotions, all the decisions emerge from the indicative, and the indicative is doctrine. Not doctrine necessarily in the narrow systematic sense, although systematic exposition is too easily scorned by many, but doctrine as the great Christian teaching which is the story of God's reckless love, centered in the dying and rising again of the sovereignty now disputed.

Jesus came proclaiming that the Kingdom of God is at hand and called people to repentance. The Kingdom is the indicative, repentance the imperative. If Christian people are not acting upon the imperative, it is in large part because they do not understand the indicative. This is the great task of preaching, to set forth the truth that the Kingdom of God has appeared, is now coming, and will be consummated in Jesus the Christ. The imperative "therefores" in response to this assume a prior understanding of the "this" to which we are to respond. The preacher will not hesitate to implore the people to be worthy of the calling to which they are called; he will, in love, berate them for failing to be what by the grace of God they are (although he will not stoop to the "hellfire and brimstone" style that people so love because it makes them feel so good to be told—in a very generalized way, of course—that they are bad). But above all the preacher will focus on the indicative; at the center is not *our response* to Christ but, quite simply and complicatedly, Christ himself.

PREPARING THE PREPARATION

A word should be said about the preparation of the sermon and about the sermon as preparation for ministry. We are again reminded that preaching is not a solo performance but a communal venture. This is true in the actual moment of preaching among the people of God, and it is true in terms of intended consequences. We must never think that all the teaching and persuading and leading is done by the clergy, as though the pastor simply bestows knowledge and inspiration and thus activates the laity in carrying out the mission. But it is a false and fearful ministerial modesty that reduces the pastor to a mere "facilitator." The truth is that there is scarcely a local church that has a sense of lively celebration and mission that does not also have strong pastoral leadership. Strong pastors do not always have lively churches, but lively churches, almost without exception, have strong pastors. A strong pastor, in the sense meant here, is characterized not by the authority he exercises over the laity but by the authority with which he empowers people for mission. Preaching, at its best, is empowerment. Such a preacher has internalized and made his own the understanding articulated in the familiar words of the 1954 assembly of the World Council of Churches:

> The time has come to make the ministry of the laity explicit, visible and active in the world. The real battles of the faith today are being fought in factories, shops, offices and farms, in political parties and government agencies, in countless homes, in the press, radio and television, in the relationship of nations. Very often it is said that the Church should "go into these spheres"; but the fact is that the Church is already in these spheres in the persons of the laity.

Conviction about the many ministries of the Church does not make the ordered ministry of spiritual leadership less important but more important. It is a truly awesome thing to be held accountable not only for our own ministries but for many ministries. In preaching, as in all our work, our best is required and, especially in preaching, our best means preparation. A common rule of thumb is that every minute in the pulpit should be preceded by an hour in the study. Given the length of sermons in most churches today, that means twelve to twenty-five hours a week in sermon preparation. That formula may be somewhat mechanical; twenty hours a week in actually writing a sermon seems excessive. The polishing of phrases can get in the way of the one thing one intends the sermon to do. But twenty hours a week in study that is preparatory to preaching is not at all excessive. That is, if one is thinking early in the week about the text for next Sunday, all of one's reading, reflection, puzzling, and conversation is directly or indirectly aimed toward that end. That means that at least by Tuesday morning one's conscious work on next Sunday's sermon is under way. Let me put it more strongly: If by Tuesday morning you have not begun consciously working on Sunday's sermon, *you are behind schedule.* If you sit down Saturday afternoon or evening to begin the next day's sermon, you are probably hopelessly behind schedule.

One well-known preacher takes three weeks of the summer in which he devotes almost full time to developing the themes for his sermons of the whole year ahead. That is an heroic discipline and no doubt has much to recommend it. But even if one were to do that, the sermon of a particular Sunday reflects the labor of the prior week. On Saturday the preacher might write up what he has worked on all week, but that is a matter of harvesting. Pity the preacher, and pity more the people, when planting, growth, and harvesting are regularly clumped together in a few hours set aside for sermon preparation.

In most congregations the pastor is also the chief teacher of the community. Being unprepared in the pulpit is as reprehensible as the teacher who is unprepared in the classroom; indeed, considering what is at stake, much more so. This does not exclude spontaneity; it does exclude irresponsibility. Spontaneity may be the movement of the Spirit at the moment; it has nothing to do with the irresponsibility that wastes the many moments that should have been used in preparation for that moment. A favorite rhetorical trick on some speaking circuits is for the speaker to lay aside his manuscript very dramatically and declare that he has decided to speak not from his prepared remarks but from his heart. It is reported that some speakers have actually carried two manuscripts to the podium, one to lay aside and one to read from the heart. Such tricks have no place in the pulpit. A Christian congregation has a right to expect that their preacher and teacher has thought, read, pondered, puzzled, and prayed over the matter at hand and that he is now prepared to share the harvest.

Seminarians and very young pastors sometimes boast among themselves about their ability to "wing it," to produce a passable sermon on sudden notice. That is excusable in the inexperienced; maybe the experience of winging it a time or two is even salutary; it is part of gaining the confidence that one will be able to find

Middle C when he goes on stage. But as a regular thing, it is a betrayal of the preaching task. Pastors who boast of how little time they spend in sermon preparation may be unusually glib, but they are, I suspect without exception, saying more about their people's patience than about their own preaching ability.

We do not need to take up the age-old debate between preaching traditions that emphasize the written text, on the one hand, and others that view even the sketchiest outline as evidence of distrust in the Spirit's guidance. I do believe that for the first five or ten years of ministry it is a very good thing to write out the sermon in full, whether or not one takes the manuscript into the pulpit. Quite apart from whether one has a manuscript and from what he does with it, the Sunday sermon should be the product of many hours of preparation. By Tuesday one has the text and the several themes it suggests firmly in mind. Before Wednesday is out, one has selected one theme from the several possibilities. Now we know what it is we are going to preach about next Sunday. The rest of the week is letting everything flow into the arguments, illustrations, and construction of the sermon.

This idea of "flowing in" assumes, of course, that sermon preparation is not limited to what you do sitting at a desk. The preacher is thinking about his sermon all the time. Preparation involves a great deal of creative woolgathering, picking up little bits and pieces from unexpected places. Pastoral calls, counseling, family chatter, all may be homiletically suggestive—once that theme is firmly fixed. Although this can be problematic, even one's prayers and devotional reading begin to focus in relation to the theme. Here again, the value of preaching by a pericopal system is demonstrated. That is, the set lessons and themes of the Church's seasons and feasts prevent one's thinking, praying, and preaching from getting stuck in a subjective rut. The Church's system of lessons, among its many other virtues, challenges the preacher to growth by dealing with biblical texts and aspects of the faith that he might otherwise neglect.

While the sermon's preparation, then, engages all one's thinking and doing that week, there is no substitute for the hours spent in actual study. Study involves working on the biblical text and context, in the original languages if one is able, consulting commentaries and relevant works of theology, history, and whatever. Such study is not aimed at impressing the people with snippets of erudition, although there is nothing wrong with a congregation suspecting their preacher of literacy. The preacher who exhibits the process of his research from the pulpit, however, is like the carpenter who leaves his tools lying around after the house is finished. The purpose of such study is not to impress but to learn, and to make the subject at hand truly one's own. Not, of course, that one attains mastery over the mystery of divine truth. But the theme is truly your own when you have immersed yourself in it, understood some crucial aspects of it, and know that you have something important to say about it.

A word should be said about the use of historical and textual criticism in sermon preparation. For reasons having to do with intellectual honesty and serious search for the biblical meaning, many of us employ critical methodology. That fact should not be treated as a "professional secret" to be kept from our people. This only leads to confusion and suspicion. If methodology does not affect our exposition of the scriptures, it is hard to understand why we should bother ourselves or others about it. The obverse side of the problem is preaching that sets forth more method than meaning. This again is an instance of leaving the tools lying around. The real goal and, I suspect, the too rare achievement is to employ methodology in a manner that illuminates the meaning. I have heard preaching, for example, that explains the different schools of Johannine theology in a way that enhances rather than detracts from the biblical word. But in the training of many clergy there was little effort to bridge the gap between the study and the preaching of a text, between classroom and pulpit. As a general rule, *if the mention of critical methodology in a sermon does not clearly help the text to say what it means, any reference to it will seem to imply that the text does not mean what it says.*

"MODERN" DEMANDS VERSUS STUDY

Many pastors report that they do not have time for serious study at all. Or they count the hours dawdled over news magazines and professional manuals as study. Frequently it is the same pastors who say they do not have time for prayer. It is to be feared that the person who does not have time for study and prayer does not have time for Christian ministry. A great temptation of ministry is hollow activism. One tries to convince others, and oneself, that one is doing something important because one is always so busy. A suburban pastor confessed to me that he recently caught himself quickly putting aside a theological book he was reading when a parishioner came into the office. He hastily began working on some parochial reports that were on his desk, remarking that they had to be in that day, and, of course, impressing the member with the burdens of ministry. To his credit, he recognized this as a charade to be confessed. Others are less fortunate. "Is the pastor busy?" asks the caller. "No," says the church secretary, "he's just reading." No, he's not busy, he's just thinking. No, he's not busy, he's just praying.

There used to be a sharp difference between those Christian traditions that emphasized a "learned ministry" and those that flaunted their sanctified illiteracy. Fortunately, that difference is diminished today, and that may be one of the happier aspects of the "professionalization" of the ministry that has in many ways been so debilitating. "Book learnin' " is not the term of opprobrium it once was in some churches. There are, to be sure, still vestiges of the old suspicions. A television evangelist offers a snide aside about today's "fancy churches," observing that none of the twelve disciples went to college. That evangelist manages a multimillion dollar media enterprise and jets about in apostolic simplicity. His intellectual mastery of technology, finance, and communication is apparently no threat to his primitive Christian purity; that purity, it would seem, could only be compromised by equal seriousness in the study of scripture and theology.

Even though many of us were not brought up in the myths of anti-intellectualism, we succumb to the temptations of hollow activism. We do not want to be thought bookish or excessively devout. "A good pastor," we hear it said, "cares more about people than about books." Well, yes, and no doubt there are people who escape into books to get away from people. It is not so often remarked that others escape into golf, boating, cars, or building the county's biggest Sunday School. These are more "normal" preoccupations that threaten no one. It is different with books and disciplined reflection and prayer. Learning and holiness can seem threatening to others. Martin Luther, John Wesley, John Henry Newman, and a host of others have testified that they would not have been able to do what they did had they not spent hours each day in study and prayer. But there are few cases on record of ministers being given bigger churches because they were noted for their sanctity.

No one can doubt that the New Testament, in both word and apostolic example, enjoins the highest spirituality upon Christian ministry. But today we hear it said that the New Testament sets an impossible ideal, that the ministry today is much more complex than it was in those simpler days. In truth, however, the leadership of the churches in the apostolic era was probably a much more various and demanding task than almost anything we know as formal ministry today. We may think that "church administration" is a modern phenomenon, and its demands upon time are frequently resented by contemporary clergy. But the sheer administrative work required in the early Church must have been enormous. A first-century convert, whether Jew or Greek, became almost completely dependent upon the new community. It was an association that comprehended every aspect of life. Disputes had to be settled, members protected from persecution and loss of job, visiting Christians shown hospitality, authorized letters of recommendation issued to Christians traveling to another city, finances divided up according to needs, communications maintained with apostolic authorities, and of course there was the regular care of the poor, especially the aged, the widows, and the orphans. One gains the impression that meetings were always being called on both a scheduled and emergency basis.

This communitarian period of the Church's life is often idealized as an early form of Christian socialism, and so it may have been. As Oscar Wilde once remarked, "The trouble with socialism is that it leaves you with no free evenings." Pastors who today complain about the number of meetings and the demands of administrative trivia might like to think that once upon a time, in the pure and primitive days, these things were not so, but they likely were more so. Or at least we might think that then the meetings were more urgent and purposeful. Perhaps so, but we can infer from Paul's writings to the Corinthians, for example, that surrounding their crises there must have been countless hours of committee wrangling, personal pettiness, sleazy power plays, and other nuisances that, then and now, can so drain the ministry of its joy.[4] In the face of all this, the intellectual and spiritual vitality of the New Testament Church had to be sustained. The bishop, evangelist, or catechist had to have worked through the truth of the gospel and made it his own. He could not rely upon borrowing somebody else's truth by using platitudes that had been made venerable by centuries of Christian tradition.

Reflection, study, and prayer have always had to compete against the imperious claims of other activities. The imperiousness of the claims is reinforced by the fact that such activities are usually more visible, often more immediately satisfying, and almost certainly more likely to be applauded by others. Church officialdom is more likely to take note of a pastor mighty in raising money than of a pastor mighty in prayer. We complain that we do not have enough time. One answer is to learn to do expeditiously what has to be done in order to get on to what must be done. What *must* be done is largely determined by our own setting of priorities. When as a young priest, Archbishop William Temple deplored the fact that there was so much to do and so little time in which to do it all, his wise father responded, "William, you have all the time there is." *You have all the time there is*—it is a thought worthy of more than a moment's reflection. Finally, before God, we are responsible for what we do with all the time there is.

Of course we will show up for Sunday services. *Of course* we will not miss the church council meeting. *Of course* we will see that the parish newsletter is written. *Of course* we will visit members in hospital. Of course—because if we did not do these things we would be in default of contract. But the same cannot be said of spending even two hours a day in prayer and study. It would seem that we are more frightened of being found in default of contract than in default of calling. A recent survey of a large church body, the Lutheran Church in America, indicated that fully twenty-five percent of the clergy did not pray each day. For many more, prayer was brief, sporadic, and squeezed in between other more pressing obligations. There is no reason to believe that the situation in this church body is all that different from others. No professional "skills" or "competencies" can compensate for this hollowness at the heart of things.

One should not make preparation sound excessively solemn or onerous. There is joy and delight in crafting the sermon, just as the painter may rejoice in what takes shape from the work of his own hands. But with the joy and delight of creativity there is intermixed a great deal of anguish, dissatisfaction, and the strong temptations to toss it all over, to try winging it once more, or to use that sermon that came in the mail after all. At one level we are all afflicted, more or less, by the sin of sloth; at a more profound level we, like Jonah of old, are in rebellion against the vocation by which we are embraced. Melville spoke of the pulpit as the prow of the ship. In another nautical metaphor, the pulpit has often been described, even constructed, as the big fish that swallowed Jonah. For example, in the *Walfischkanzel* in Reinerz, Germany, the pulpit is a huge, elaborately and grotesquely detailed fish, and the preacher takes his stand in the wide gaping mouth. Whatever their physical design, our pulpits too are like that. After nights and days of doubts and darkness, of protest and probing, of running away and being brought back, we too are tossed up to the people as reluctant prophets, preachers of judgment and hope.

11.
The Pursuit
of
Holiness

"Are you now ready to take upon you this Holy Ministry.... Will you adorn the doctrine of Our Savior by a holy life and conversation?"

"Yes, with my whole heart, the Lord helping me through the power and grace of His Holy Spirit."

In these or similar words, a minister promises at ordination to live a life in the pursuit of holiness. To "adorn the doctrine of Our Savior by a holy life and conversation" is a general phrase subject to many interpretations. It means at least the following:

1. The minister is called and pledged to be an exemplary person.
2. The pursuit of holiness is a lifelong process of actualizing what we already are in Christ.
3. There is not conflict but complementarity between the special vocation of the minister and the vocation of all Christians.
4. Holiness is not an abstract perfection but obedience in mission.
5. The pursuit of holiness is not so much the observance of limits as the exercise of freedom.

The purpose of this final chapter is to clarify these five propositions with special reference to the particular temptations of Christian ministry posed by activism, ambition, sexuality, and money.

THE EXEMPLARY PERSON

Wherever one looks in Christian history, the community is concerned about the quality of its leadership and develops ways to select and designate its leaders. In the New Testament this concern is evidenced in many ways, from the "casting of lots" in Acts, through the extended Pauline discussions of apostleship and other roles such as prophet and evangelist, and on to the more "catholic" instructions of the pastoral epistles, where most scholars find the beginnings of the classic episcopal governance of the Church. From the earliest community onward, it is evident in all church orders that the person consecrated or set aside is chosen not simply for certain skills but for personal qualities of holiness.

At an ordination in the Roman Rite, the bishop invites the congregation to testify to the candidates' "fitness for the priesthood." He announces: "If any one has any objection to urge against them, let him come forward boldly and speak." Then, remembering our common fragility and the charity without which life together is not possible, the bishop cautions the potential challenger: "But let him not forget the state of his own soul." Every Christian rite for ordering to ministry includes some exchange between people and ordaining authority with respect to the worthiness of those being ordained. In the early Church and in some parts of the Church today, the people cry out *Axios!* ("He is worthy!"). If one is honest about the quality of the Church's ministry both past and present, it is obvious that some have viewed this ritual as little more than empty form. Few serious expectations are attached to it. But it is a solemn thing to promise the pursuit of an exemplary life. It is nothing less than a vocation to holiness.

This promise can be understood in less elevated terms. After all, at a very minimal level, other assocations and their professional leadership have "ethical standards." Lawyers can be disbarred for unethical conduct and, until the recent changes brought about by abortion practice, medical doctors swore themselves to the Hippocratic oath. Any group has an interest in seeing that its leaders do not undermine or bring into disrepute the purposes for which the group is established. Thus politicians take an oath of office, and even business corporations prescribe a clear set of expectations for the behavior of their executives. But these commonsense understandings between leadership and constituency fall far short of what should be intended in Christian ministry.

The sociological and structural base of the community's expectations regarding the ministry is inescapable and must be taken seriously. But that is not the whole of the matter; the community invests in its ministry a spiritual commitment and hope, and rightly expects that investment to be honored. Similarly, there is a particular interest in the *public* behavior of the minister. In some traditions the priesthood is simply designated as "the office of public ministry." There is understandable concern about the one who will preach, teach, and otherwise act in a representative capacity on behalf of the community. This might be described as a strategic concern for the quality of ministry and, like the sociological and structural, it still falls short of the vocation and pledge to holiness.

To adorn the gospel with a holy life is a pledge that engages the very core of the person. One is not only to behave in an exemplary manner but to be an exemplary person. "Therefore be imitators of God, as beloved children. And walk in love, as Christ loved us and gave himself up for us, a fragrant offering and sacrifice to God" (Eph. 4). The injunction is of course addressed to all Christians, but the ministry of the Church is to exemplify its meaning for all Christians. We are to walk in the light and do all things as in the day; there is to be a coherence between public and private person. These are hard sayings and it is little wonder that rites of ordination and consecration include prayers for a special measure of the Spirit's aid to those who are "set aside."

Today talk about "imitating" another person has unhappy connotations of mimicry and false consciousness. The intention is better caught in the word *emulate.* Most of us have encountered at crucial points in our lives people whom we try to emulate. Such encounters more often than not have a strong bearing upon our decision for the ministry to begin with. Admittedly, emulation probably involves a degree of imitation. We imitate the tastes, mannerisms, and even the gestures of the person we admire. This is a common and probably necessary experience that usually occurs in adolescence. The pastor is properly concerned about the impression he makes upon young people. It should be noted as an aside that much that passes for youth work in the churches is led by adults who are perennial adolescents, pandering to young people in order to gain their acceptance. We do not owe to young people, and one suspects they do not really want, our effort to be accepted as senior citizens in their world. The chief obligation and gift to young people is the model of an adult life worthy of their emulation.

In writing to the churches, Paul is effusive in his use of maternal and paternal imagery to describe his relationship to the Christians for whom he is responsible. He does not hesitate to hold himself up as an example of one who follows *the* exemplar, Jesus Christ. The office that is entrusted to us inescapably carries with it that obligation and privilege of exemplification. The ongoing task is to strengthen the coherence between "office" and "person"; in other words, the person is to "adorn" the office. The language of adornment may seem superficial and even effete. Another way of putting it is that the coherence between office and person increases the *credibility* of that which the office represents. It has been said that saints are people whose lives prove that Christ is risen. That may be saying too much, but their lives are hard to explain apart from the risen Christ. So it should be said of ministers; their lives do not prove that they are representing someone else, that they are ambassadors of the Christ; maybe they are, maybe they aren't. We will see, and the whole creation will see along with us. But they do seem to be ambassadors, signaling a promise and a possibility from a future that is both far off and closer than each breath we draw.

In the third century, Origen excoriated bishops who failed to act as religious examples and sympathetic physicians of the soul but were rather worldly minded, pursued earthly occupations and affairs, longed for wealth, were haughty, quarrelsome, and self-assertive. They loved to be flattered, said Origen, and were less conscientious in the conduct of business than secular officials. As men in charge of penance, they were alternately harsh and impermissibly complaisant; and if anyone tried to bring them to account for their sins, they formed cliques and, if need be, anti-churches, so that they could hold on to their office. Clergy brag about their seniority, says Origen, and try to secure the best offices for friends and relatives. They refuse to take advice from their equals, much less from a layman or a pagan, and are, in sum, just like the Pharisees of old. This, von Campenhausen notes, is the first time in Church history that the comparison is made between the Christian clergy and the New Testament's unflattering portrait of the Pharisees.[1] It would be far from the last time.

Corruption takes many forms. The nuanced and eminently respectable slide into unbelief is the most common way in which we give up on the pursuit of holiness, probably without even knowing that we have given up. Corruption can also be more blatant. In my early years in Brooklyn, I was approached by the pastor of a large black church who invited me to join him in a scheme in which he worked with real estate interests to blockbust white neighborhoods and move more successful blacks into segregated suburbs. He preached racial integration while privately working to expand the all-black ghetto; he preached the responsibility of upwardly mobile blacks to help stabilize and strengthen the neighborhood while privately encouraging them to buy homes in suburbia. He received up to three thousand dollars as a "kickback" on each home purchased. He was amused by my shocked disapproval, writing it off to my youth, and reminding me that while man did not live by bread alone, it sure did help. In another instance, a white minister active in reform politics privately pointed out the lucrative connections between political influence and the manipulation of real estate prices. He admitted to having done quite well and even quoted Reinhold Niebuhr in justification of his "ethical realism."

Of course these are gross examples, at least bordering on the criminal. Most ministers do not have such temptations, or opportunities. It is said that everyone has a price. Nobody knows whether it is true of him until he has been offered that price, and most of us are never offered it. But these are the conscious and overt corruptions. More common and subtle are other ways in which we confirm the wisdom of the warning that a bishop should not be a "lover of money" (1 Tim. 3). Especially among Protestant clergy, there is the question of wedding and funeral practices, for example. The Yellow Pages of any metropolis contain a listing of "Marrying Sams" available any time day or night at an appropriate fee. Similarly, clergy have their names listed with large funeral establishments, on call for a price. One hears such clergy rationalize their avarice with talk about "opportunities to preach the gospel" and "to help people in need." One pastor solemnly declares his conviction that no body should be lowered to the grave without a farewell blessing. His concern, needless to say, does not extend to accompanying the corpses of derelicts to potter's field. In truth, marrying and burying for money is a form of prostitution. Where there is no significant pastoral relationship with the persons involved, such "ministry" is no more than a purchased service. One is merely selling the panache of piety, reducing Christian truth to sentimentality and the veneer of respectability.

The troubling words of Jesus about the love of Mammon (Mammon is almost personalized as a false god) remain terrifyingly pertinent today. The warnings in James and elsewhere against kowtowing to the rich should be pondered by every minister when he thinks about who are the "important" members of the congregation. One of my father's sterling memories is that as a very young pastor in northern Canada he refused to admit to communion a wealthy member who had been convicted for political corruption and, contrary to my father's certain knowledge of his guilt, had publicly denied any wrongdoing. This man and his relatives accounted for more than half of the church's offerings, and they all threatened to leave unless the pastor backed down. My father stood firm, insisting that the man admit his fault publicly and be received back into the fellowship as a forgiven sinner. The man refused, many members left, and, after a time of great financial difficulty, the congregation revived and was much the stronger for the ordeal.

In many churches today such a course of events is simply inconceivable. There are no adequate procedures for "church discipline" to be exercised by the pastor, deacons, or others in the congregation. Or if such procedures do exist, they have long since fallen into desuetude. According to today's canons of ministerial training, my father should have invited the fellow to a private session in "values clarification" rather than calling for public repentance of public sin. Today the pastoral course he chose would be widely condemned as legalistic. Any serious approach to church discipline is no doubt susceptible to legalism, but one wonders if the alleged fear of legalism today is not really a fear of offending contemporary sensibilities by suggesting that it is sometimes possible to draw a line between right and wrong. Witness the recent instance in which an Amish believer sued his church for censoring his behavior by the discipline the Amish call "shunning." The plaintiff, although he lost in court, won considerable outside sympathy. Not, of course, that the outsiders were interested in the integrity of the beliefs and practices of the Amish community, but because it is thought to be a civil right not to be publicly accused of sin. The demolition of the difference between good and evil is the secularized bastardization of Luther's *simul iustus et peccator*. The pursuit of holiness and the vitality of the churches in our day require a recovery of the practice of Christian discipline.

Such discipline can be recovered, of course, by retreat to narrowly intentional communities. That way lie the dangers associated with "sectarianism," to be sure, but it is good to remember that sectarianism has frequently been a renewing force for the larger Church. Most of us are not in such narrowly intentional churches, however, and so the recovery of evangelical discipline is that much more difficult. Discipline does not mean fulminating against drunkenness, sexual deviance, and crimes in high but distant places. These are cheap shots. In most churches today it takes little courage to come out against what passes for "permissiveness." Unless, of course, the permissiveness protested is indifference to the sins, crimes, and cruelties of those in a position to threaten directly our financial and professional security. Let the minister, then, be no lover of money. The love of money may not be the root of all evil, but it is a root exquisitely intertwined with so much that makes ministries less than exemplary.

For many people, Sinclair Lewis's Elmer Gantry still casts a shadow of suspicion over Christian ministry. Journalists relentlessly press the Gantry syndrome in connection with very prominent ministers, eagerly sniffing about for that financial motive that "explains what he is really up to." Much of this is outrageously unfair, and yet it reflects a popular intuition about the connection between money and integrity that is not too far removed from the teachings of the gospels. Most of us do not "sell out" by making crooked deals, or even by consciously compromising principle in order not to compromise financial security; we pay our tribute to Mammon in the minutes and hours spent in worrying about money and the things that money can get.

There are few decisions that a young pastor or pastoral couple make that are more important than the attitude toward money. One should as early as possible determine the top income one would ever want or strive to have. Of course there has to be a degree of flexibility in such a decision, but the question of money and the dangers it poses should be kept under the closest scrutiny. Otherwise the desire ineluctably grows, avarice feeds upon itself, and one ends up as the victim of an appetite that is in fact insatiable and consumes by worry, guilt, and discontent the hours and days that were once consecrated to ministry. This is not the place for bromides about the wickedness of a consumer society; what we call the consumer society has likely been the greatest engine of economic distributive justice in the history of humankind, but the consumer*ism* that accompanies it is undoubtedly an enormous spiritual danger. For each of us, the answer to the peril is not—at least not chiefly—in calls for changing the economic system but in a pursuit of holiness that signals triumph over the ambiguities of prosperity.

It is not likely any time soon that ministers will be required to take an oath of poverty. Yet there is today a happy rewakening to the liberation of living in simplicity of life, of breaking free from consumerism's grip. Very early we must determine whether we are going to live "the good life" of our own design, worked out in fear in trembling toward our destiny and our calling from God, or whether we are going to live the massified "good life" proffered on television and in the countless catalogues that constitute the daily reading of millions. And money is, of course, often related to career advancement. The late Saul Alinsky, famed guru of community organizers, once met with a group of seminarians interested in ministries among the poor. "The first thing you got to decide," said Alinsky, "is whether you want to be a priest or be a bishop. If you want to be a bishop, you might as well leave now because you'll never do anything else." Too many of the bishops of our churches, because they wanted to be bishops, never did or ever will do anything else.

I know a pastoral couple who have six children and live in gracious simplicity on a total income of nine thousand dollars, and another couple with three children and a combined income of thirty thousand dollars whose lives are debilitated by economic anxiety. The reader can no doubt think of similar comparisons. The difference is not in economic needs. The difference is that one family is living its own good life and the other is living somebody else's good life. It is often said that it is much easier for celibates and single clergy, but that is not necessarily the case. Cars, traveling, expensive recreation and gimmicks can create a similarly debilitating economic pressure, and they often do. Whatever one's circumstance, unless one is born with or has discovered some special immunity, he is under pressure by the seductions of Mammon. This rule of thumb deserves at least respectful attention: If there is any dimension of ministry that you did or did not choose to pursue primarily for financial reasons, you probably chose wrongly. The pursuit of holiness is an exercise of freedom from bondage to Mammon, who, together with sexual fulfillment, is among the most imperious gods of the present age.

In biblical thought, holiness is the essential attribute of God, and God is unqualified freedom. His freedom takes the form of love, by which he first created all things and now engages his creation in faithful pilgrimage toward perfect union with himself. The Church is the community that knows and signals what the whole creation is about. The ministry is to exemplify that mission of the Church. The minister is to lead Christians in being different. The pursuit of holiness is nothing less than the pursuit of God, and it is a very uncomfortable business for us, as it is infinitely more so for him. In his classic description of the holy, Rudolf Otto spoke of the "numinous," the mysterious quality of the divine that is "wholly other." The numinous is on the one hand "tremendous"; it frightens and repels. On the other hand, it is "fascinating," irresistibly attractive and engaging. People who exemplify holiness share, although perhaps in small part, that numinous quality. They are both attractive and threatening. The degree of freedom they manifest from the usual strictures and worries of life is powerfully appealing. It is at the same time threatening, a kind of implicit judgment on the way most of us have ordered our lives, or disordered them. Whatever our personal qualities or lack of qualities, we ministers are formally designated to bear a tradition that reflects and aspires to holiness. To lead in the pursuit of holiness—this is what the Church, at least ritually, says it wants us to do; and we are always surprised when people actually do it. The common ambivalence about the holy, its terror and its attractiveness, pervades also our own thinking.

There are signs of a welcome recovery of concern for "spiritual formation" in ministerial training today. Such training should help people to work through and to live with the ambivalence of holiness, the inescapable oddity of the ministerial vocation, the unavoidable "difference" that we are to exemplify. In some seminaries the talk is still about training "enablers," "facilitators," and the like. But what is needed is not the training of religious technicians but the formation of spiritual leaders. It is important for seminaries to impart skills and competencies; it is more important to ignite conviction and the courage to lead. The language of facilitation is cool and low-risk. The language of priesthood and prophecy and the pursuit of holiness is impassioned and perilous. We cover our fearful choice of the low-risk option with egalitarian talk about the priesthood of all believers. But those who have been touched by the burning coal from the altar, and whose touch has been ratified by the call of the Church, must not pretend that nothing special has happened to them. Such pretense is not humility but blasphemy; it is not modesty but ingratitude; it is not devotion to equality but evasion of responsibility. It is fear, the fear of being different. And when we are afraid to act upon the difference to which we are called, we inhibit others from acting upon the difference to which they are called.

To be exemplary is, by definition, to be different. What we make of the "difference" that ordered ministry makes is another matter.

It can be a difference behind which we shield ourselves from genuine encounter with others. It can be a difference in the negative sense of more total conformity to the conventions and prevailing habits-of-soul in the group whose judgment we fear. Or it can be a difference in the intensity of venture, a challenge to the spiritual lethargy that now holds the churches in thrall. But whatever difference it makes, the difference should not be denied.

ACTUALIZING THE HOLINESS THAT IS OURS

The pursuit of holiness is not the quest for the Holy Grail. It is not a matter of looking for something that we do not have or of achieving something that we are not. It is rather a question of actualizing the gift that is already ours. This touches on the ancient and venerable debates about the relationship between free will and salvation, between nature and grace, between justification and sanctification. For those who subscribe to the Reformation emphasis on *sola gratia* and *sola fides*, any talk about the pursuit of holiness is bound to be problematic. An equal problem today, however, is that many do not know or do not care about these debates that are readily relegated to the ancient history of Reformation and Counter-Reformation polemicism. This is deeply regrettable, for if our thinking about the pursuit of holiness is not grounded in the atoning work of God in Christ it is little more than moralism, a vain quest for perfection, a certain formula for either self-righteousness or despair.

Salvation by grace or salvation by good works, that is the way the choice is often posed. The prior assumption, of course, is that one's ultimate concern is salvation. Unless one believes that salvation is indeed at stake, everything we say about Church and ministry is gutted of its supreme urgency. Salvation may mean the search for a gracious God or the search for ultimate meaning; the terror-filled quest for the forgiveness of sins or the struggle for a new order of justice and love; the hope for eternal happiness or the probing for a truth that rescues our lives from inauthenticity. Whether we use traditional or more contemporary language, it is salvation that is at stake. However expressed, salvation is the difference between life and death; to speak significantly of salvation is to affirm that what we are and do now is of cosmic and eternal consequence. The most elementary Christian assertion, without which no truth can properly be called Christian, is that salvation is the present gift of God in Jesus the Christ. In Christ life appeared and has overcome the forces of *thanatos*—of meaninglessness, of lostness, of every evil. That is the life into which the Christian is incorporated in the community of faith.

Good works, or the pursuit of holiness, are the consequence, the continuation and actualization, of the gift already given. Good works cannot be the enemy of grace, for that which is the enemy of God's grace is by definition not good. Only those works are good that adorn and enhance the love of God in Christ. Thus Tertullian said that the virtues of the pagans who are without Christ are in fact only "splendid vices." To put it differently, virtues that are set against the grace of God in Christ are fatal virtues.

As we noted earlier, Paul proclaims that we are reconciled to God through Christ, and at the same time he urges us to be reconciled. This connection between indicative and imperative, between justification and sanctification, is frequently described as "paradoxical." Unfortunately, referring to something as a paradox has degenerated into a bad theological habit by which we excuse our saying incompatible things without having to think about them very much. Better than the language of paradox is the language of pilgrimage. The pursuit of holiness is active engagement in the "now" and "not yetness" of Christian existence short of the Kingdom come. The indicative and imperative of salvation are not contradictory but speak to the continuity of the life lived in hope. The biblical assertion is that each human life is a response to vocation and destiny, which is God's gift to us even before we are born. With Isaiah we declare: "Listen to me, O coastlands, and hearken, you peoples from afar. The Lord called me from the womb, from the body of my mother he named my name" (Isa. 49). Sanctification is becoming what, by the grace of God, we are.

In ministry, as in life, we never arrive, for our ministries and our lives point beyond themselves. It is true, as they say in the abortion debate, that the fetus is merely a potential human being; but it is wrong to say "merely," for we are all potential human beings, growing into the fullness of humanity that is Christ. This note of preparation, of anticipation, of potentiality, should mark the whole of our ministry. This too is what Jesus meant by the necessity of being born again and becoming like a little child. The illusions of completeness and of having arrived must die, so that each day we begin anew the life of Christian hope. The pursuit of holiness means that our ministries are ever in process of formation.

The New Testament word for moral consecration or holiness is *agiasmos*. It is derived from the active verbal form and thus signifies "sanctifying" rather than "sanctification." The phrase *agiasmo pneumatos* might be better translated "Sanctifying Spirit" rather than "Holy Spirit," for it does not connote the moral status of the Spirit but rather what the Spirit is *doing*. The grace of God, then, is not compromised by good works; good works are the grace of God. The grace of God is an active gift, not just the static status of "being saved." To put it differently, we are saved and we are being saved. As important as understanding what the grace of God *is* is understanding what the grace of God *does*. "For the grace of God has appeared for the salvation of all men, *training us* to renounce irreligion and worldly passions, and to live sober, upright, and godly lives in this world, awaiting our blessed hope, the appearing of the glory of our great God and Savior Jesus Christ" (Titus 2:11). The pursuit of holiness is the Christian ever in training.

In the pursuit of holiness, a sense of urgency is combined with a sense of modesty. This may at first seem contradictory. We are inclined toward an "all or nothing" attitude; our efforts are geared to satisfaction; if the success of the enterprise is not clearly in view, we will not waste our time on it. The way of the pilgrim is quite different, however. He urgently presses on, not because this day's journey or even this lifetime's journey will bring him to the destination, but because he travels by promise. The success of the enterprise was signaled in the raising of Jesus from the dead; the full actualization of that triumph may be far, far distant. Our sense of urgency is premised not upon our chronological closeness to the consummation but upon the fact that this time, no matter how close or how far, is the only time we have; it is the piece of the pilgrimage for which we are accountable.

Without this modesty about our moment in time, the pursuit of holiness can easily lead us astray into the illusions of gnosticism. As we know from the pastoral epistles and post-apostolic literature, the gnostics were decidedly immodest. They claimed to possess a liberating and superior "gnosis" or knowledge that put them above the limitations of history. Their belief that perfection is now available to the initiated and that the creation is fundamentally evil led either to moral libertinism or, more commonly, to rigorous asceticism. Because creation is evil, they had no use for the "orders of creation." For those whose consciousness had been raised into the true gnosis, the distinction between male and female was of no consequence, secular rules of governance and civility were irrelevant, and the family was held in contempt. All these, they believed, were of the "old order" that had passed away; they are oppressive and inhibiting remnants of a way of life that holds no interest for those who have been liberated. Against the gnostics, the pastoral epistles counsel respect or piety *(eusebeia)* toward what is good and just in the existent order (2 Tim. 2).

Our ecstasy is not to be confused with the consummation; faithfulness is the courage to live by the Absolute within the preliminary but necessary orders of history. Faithfulness is facing up to the disputed nature of the sovereignty we profess. This does not mean passivity. To the contrary, the representatives of the disputed Sovereign will be persecuted (2 Tim. 3:12), because they render only qualified respect to the existing structures that others worship, since they assert a transcendent freedom from the securities by which others are bound. The pursuit of holiness means that, against the "realists" of that time and ours, Christians live in eschatological hope; and against the gnostics of that time and ours, Christians understand history as the still incomplete actualization of that hope. This is the joining of urgency and modesty that, with respect to the world as it is, rules out both realist conformity and gnostic escape.

Spiritual ecstasy can be empowering as well as delusory. Just as we should not be so impressed by the perils of good works that we neglect doing good, so we should not despise but rather welcome the experience of the presence and power of God in our lives. For those who would seriously pursue holiness, the classic reference in this connection is still the little book by Brother Lawrence, *The Practice of the Presence of God.* There are Christians, and ministers who are exemplars of holiness, who claim never to have experienced the ecstasy of the Divine Presence. There is no reason to feel sorry for them; indeed, it may be that their everyday consciousness of God is what those of us who are less spiritually gifted know only occasionally and therefore think so extraordinary. Be that as it may, I have known intermittent moments, sometimes sustained for several days, in which the presence of God bears in upon me with such terror and fascination as to be almost unbearable. In such times it seems evident beyond doubt that the reality of God is more certain than the existence of the material objects surrounding me. This desk is more doubtful than his glory, this window more to be questioned than his love. Obviously such statements are filled with epistemological and other problems which we cannot enter into here. The point is that such moments can be empowering. They should be received and recollected with gratitude. No matter what future doubts or unbelief may assail us, the remembrance of such moments gives us pause before abandoning a love once so surely possessed; it keeps us open to the possibility that we once glimpsed the real world of which this world is part; and it precludes the decision of despair that divorces the perceived from the promised.

Having tasted such goodness, one cannot help praying with the Psalmist, "Restore unto me the joy of thy salvation" (Ps. 51). And the joy is restored, but not necessarily in the form of experiences revisited. Such experience is to be gratefully received but not to be relied upon; welcomed but not demanded; desired but with a desire short of lust. The joy is restored in the objective word of assurance; it is celebrated more in the knowledge of Christ for us *(pro nobis)* than in the experience of Christ in us *(in nobis).*

As with the children of Israel in the wilderness, there are dry and difficult times in ministry. There are stale periods when mystical vision is smothered, prophecy seems pretentious, and even the apocalyptic sounds prosaic. One learns not to panic at the appearance of monotony. But neither should one be casual about the rot that can set in and finally rob ministry of its joy and venture. For very few people is life lived consistently on the felt edge of new discovery. Most of us know and expect the feeling that we are meeting events and ourselves coming around again in all too predictable a fashion. As preachers, for instance, we are properly depressed to hear ourselves repeating ourselves. The answer is not to feign excitement about exhausted ideas and emotions. There are few things so distasteful or so unpersuasive as forced enthusiasm. The better answer is to be prepared for such periods of weariness and to respond to them with a disciplined program of prayer, study, and hard thought.

On this score the wisdom of the saints has been confirmed in lives beyond number: When we least feel like praying, we most need to pray; when study seems unfruitful, we need the more intensely to study; and when thinking is dead-ended, think again. In times of spiritual and intellectual drought, the great temptation is to believe that renewal can be found in noise and action. This is the activism to which so many ministries fall prey. It is a frenetic effort to justify our ministries by doing things. Whether it is in parish programing, or evangelism, or community organization, activism is an attempt to forget the drought by expending energies; the result is to intensify the thirst and thus to intensify the need to forget. Or it takes the form of the stereotypical salesman, celebrity, politician, and media evangelist—hollow men and women who need their daily fix of admired hyperactivity in order to assure themselves that they are alive and that it matters that they are alive.

Activism is a form of decadence. Decadence is the decay that hollows out the forms of life, leaving them devoid of meaning and, even more fatally, flaunting such hollowness as virtue. As Paul put it, we boast of our shame. Mindless activism reduces the Church to a comfortable Rotarianism where grace is hustled at bargain prices, or it replaces the pursuit of holiness with the pursuit of narrow political, social, or psychological goals. Of course there are other forms of decadence. There are timorous, abstractly overintellectualized and overaestheticized ministries that give the appearance of churchy games played by curators of the monuments to past pieties. And, as discussed earlier, there is the decadence that confuses institutional failure with the Way of the Cross. But surely the most common and respectable form of decadence is the activism that becomes more frenetic as the direction of ministry becomes more uncertain.

In times of staleness, then, we need not to break out but to break in, to enter more deeply into the center of self and God and to renegotiate once again the terms of ambassadorship. We should neither deny our weariness nor defy it with the quick fix of self-willed enthusiasm and action. Rather, like the Psalmist, we entrust it to God, making no secret of what is no secret to him, unleashing the deep to call unto the deep, knowing that he is the cause both of our complaint and of our hope. There is no substitute for this renegotiation. If we accept substitutes, we end up in fraudulent ministries, and the fraud sooner or later becomes apparent to us, if not to others. "As a hart longs for flowing streams, so longs my soul for thee, O God" (Ps. 42). We must hold out for that, and learn to hold on while holding out. Spiritual integrity consists not in being satisfied but in being insistent.

We have said that activism is a form of forgetfulness, an alternative pursuit to the pursuit of holiness. A less respectable but perhaps equally common form of ministerial forgetfulness is the sin of sloth or acedia. It is a spiritual torpor and apathy that is not to be confused with ordinary and sometimes healthy laziness. Laziness can be enjoyed, like the extra hour of sleep stolen from an occasional morning; we tell ourselves that that call can be made at ten just as well as at nine. Laziness can be leisure created, delight's defiance of the schedule's harassment. Laziness is a reward bestowed on oneself, sinking into the hammock of a summer's afternoon, with a cool drink and half-believed self-assurances that that meeting was not very important anyway. In fact, you comfort yourself, it will probably do them good to get along without you for once.

Such "laziness" can be liberating. It is quite different from sloth. If it could speak, laziness might say, "I know I should be doing this or that, but I'm just too lazy today." Acedia, to the extent that it could articulate itself at all, might say, "Should I really be doing that? Why? What difference does it really make?" Laziness is time resistant to the pressure of duty; acedia is the temper that undermines the duty. Laziness can be defiance; acedia is pure forgetfulness. Laziness is, at least in part, a decision; acedia is an addiction. Laziness is on friendly terms with time, using it to a different purpose; acedia is the enemy of time, consuming it in nothingness.

Acedia is all of Friday consumed in getting out the Sunday bulletin. Acedia is three hours dawdled away on *Time* magazine, which is then guiltily chalked up to "study." Acedia is evenings without number obliterated by television, evenings neither of entertainment nor of education but of narcoticized defense against time and duty. Above all, acedia is apathy, the refusal to engage the pathos of other lives and of God's life with them.

The sin of acedia is hardly unique to the clergy, but the temptations can be peculiar and severe. Unlike most other occupations, the meaning of what we do has to be largely reconstructed by ourselves day by day. In this sense our situation is like that of the writer or creative artist. Nobody tells the novelist what the next chapter must be or can even convince him that the novel is worth doing. The reliance upon what is called inner-directedness is frightening. So, if we are honest about it, the external demands and definitions of what is required of us as ministers are often quite minimal. In many —perhaps most—situations, one can "get away with" doing very little. Ministers resent the old jibe about their only working one day a week, but we may protest too much. In truth, many full-time pastoral positions are not full-time in what is externally or structurally required of them. This is not to say that we cannot fill the time. Here, too, Parkinson's Law applies: Work expands in proportion to the time available for doing it. But filling time is not a very fulfilling ministry. Nor would I suggest that many ministers are not fearfully overworked. But here we must understand that hyperactivity and sloth are twin sins. They are both escapes from the daily renegotiation of our ambassadorship, from the daily resumption of the pursuit of holiness. Acedia is activism grown weary. Activism is the effort to justify ministry by busyness, which is no justification at all, while acedia has given up on the search for justification.

Acedia, like activism, feeds on the fear of uncertainty. The remedy is the courage of uncertainty, knowing clearly that everything we do and everything we are is premised upon a hope not yet actualized. We should not try to shore up the believability of what we do by borrowing legitimations from other professions and other enterprises. Again, nothing can vindicate the Church and our ministries in the Church but the coming of the Kingdom of God, and that vindication is assured in the Word which is the Risen Christ. The pathos of the present moment and of all history is God's working out of the vindication of his own holiness. By entering into that pathos we join him in his work. That God is the Holy One of Israel and that Israel, including the Church, is the signal of the future of all humankind—that is the most important single truth in the whole of creation. All of our prayer, meditation, study, teaching, and loving service are to articulate that truth. In light of that truth we dare to call the Church a holy people (1 Peter 2, following Exod. 19). Thus the pursuit of holiness is the actualization of who we are; but even more ultimately and to the minds of many absurdly, it is the actualization of who God reveals himself to be. Any understanding of the pursuit of holiness that falls short of this extravagant claim is only moralism and leads either to self-righteousness or to despair—which is to say, it leads to death.

ORDINATION AND THE VOCATION OF THE CHURCH

The vocation of the Church is to sustain many vocations. The ordained minister, the one set aside and consecrated, is to illuminate the vocation of the Church and the vocations of the many people who are the Church. That means that ordination is not exclusionary but exemplary. Such a statement is easily made, but it is and always has been hard to live out in the life of the Church. The popular suspicion persists that the minister is more fully a Christian than "ordinary" members of the Church. Ordination, it is thought (even if it is unsupportable theologically), represents "first-class" spiritual status. Of a religiously serious adolescent it is said that perhaps he should be a priest. As though religious seriousness can only be usefully employed (or protected?) in holy orders. In some traditions it is said of someone who is ordained that "he went into the Church." As though we did not all enter the Church in baptism.

The idea of special vocation has always been a problem in the Christian community and probably always will be. Maybe it always should be. The early Church wrestled and wrangled over the relationship between charisma, function, and office. On this question the evolutions and revolutions of two thousand years are still clearly reflected in the theologies and polities of the churches that today comprise the Church. Some Reformation traditions posited the "priesthood of all believers" against any notion of special priesthood. Yet these traditions, too, live with the ambivalence and tension of a formally designated and consecrated ministry. And even the more "catholic" streams that have underscored office and jurisdiction are tempered by the knowledge that the Church, as the People of God, is prior to the Church's ministry.

The idea of special vocation also engages common human anxieties and resentments about who exercises authority over whom. These considerations are exacerbated by Jesus' many cautions about not seeking power over one another, about the first being last, about the leader being servant of all, and so forth. Thus even in the papacy's periods of greatest pretension and power, the popes paid at least lip service to the proposition that they were only "the servants of the servants of God." Still today the tension is symbolized dramatically in the Maundy Thursday liturgy, when the pope humbly washes the feet of children and beggars. The tension is no less for Protestants. A prominent Southern Baptist preacher, a pillar of rectitude rewarded by prosperity, drives to his gigantic air-conditioned church in his air-conditioned Cadillac, preens himself in his impressive pulpit, and allows as how he is the chief of sinners. To the unsympathetic it looks very much like an exercise in pretentious modesty.

One is reminded of the story of the rabbi who on the Day of Atonement publicly lamented his sins, declared himself totally unworthy, a nobody. The cantor, not to be outdone, picked up the theme, confessing that he too was a nobody. The sexton, not to be entirely left out, deplored his transgressions, concluding that he too was a nobody. The rabbi, turning to the cantor, says, "Nu, so who does he think *he* is to be a nobody?" Complexity is compounded for those who own a lord who forbids them to lord it over one another, who pray eloquently in public to a lord who condemned the display of piety, and who speak of conquering the world for a Christ whose victory consisted in being conquered by the cross. It is all very confusing.

The simpleminded would cut through the confusion and what they view as the hypocrisy of ecclesial office by abolishing the notion of a special ministry altogether. But this, as we know from abundant historical experience, hardly resolves the problem. For the community is still left with differences of gifts *(charismata)* and functions, and if these are not to be exercised in an arbitrary and tyrannical way, they must be regularized and held accountable to the community in clearly designated offices. Thus we have the irony that office, which has so often been the source of authoritarianism, is also essential to freedom. This ironic twist was already evident in the second century in connection with the Montanist sects. Montanus and associated "prophets" claimed a Spirit-led authority that was posited against the allegedly spurious authority of the Church and its formal ministry. In this sense, Montanism would seem to have been the party of freedom against "the institutional Church." But in the hands of a Tertullian, for example, it became evident that freedom was the last thing Montanism had in mind. Tertullian insisted upon the most severe moral rigorism, declaring this to be of the very essence of Christianity. His attack upon the office of bishop came precisely because the bishop, claiming to be empowered to forgive sins, was the last structure of freedom, the last authority that could admit to the fellowship of the saved those who did not conform to the tyrannical demands of the new "prophets." Interestingly, when Montanism was finally condemned, it became an obscure rigorist sect in which "succession" to the prophets was legitimated not by appeal to the Spirit but by possession of office. In fact, the Montanists ended up adding several more ranks to the catholic hierarchy before wandering off into historical oblivion, still quarreling over authority.

The twentieth century offers many examples of the same phenomenon. New sects arise against the formal and presumably stultifying churches. Charismatic leaders, usually claiming special Divine guidance, declare a new freedom which, quite predictably, degenerates into a new tyranny. The worst tyranny, whether in politics or religion, is the purely personal authority claiming to be directed by special forces of God or history, for such authority is arbitrary and finally accountable to no one. That the early Church escaped this process can be attributed in large part to the understanding that emerged about the relationships between charisma, function, and office. The singularity of the person and work of Jesus was unquestionable; the singularity of the apostolic office, legitimated by being an eyewitness to the Risen Lord, was agreed upon; and from then on it was understood that authority rested not upon repetition of these events but upon fidelity of witness to this gospel tradition and its meaning for the world.

To speak of office in the Church, then, is to speak of modesty and accountability. This does not mean that the official ministry of the Church may not succumb to temptations of pretension and power. But when it does, it can be brought to account precisely because it is an office; that is, its function is publicly designated or authorized, it does not exercise authority by virtue of private inspiration. When the minister's authority is called into question, it is usually a mistake to appeal directly to the authority vested in him, as though he were pulling rank. This only intensifies resentments. He should not speak of the rights that are his by virtue of office but rather of the mandates to which he has pledged obedience. This is more than a tactic to be employed in pastoral politics, as it were. It is of the very essence of interpreting ministerial office in terms of the pursuit of holiness, not in terms of the assertion of privilege or power. Lay people are as a rule respectful of ministry that is manifestly pledged to holy obedience, but they are quick to challenge what appears to be simply an assertion of right.

As a practical and pastoral matter, it is counterproductive to press the claims of office at points where there may be ambiguities. The office is demeaned when, usually on marginal issues, it is embroiled in a contest over who "runs" the local church. Whether the vacation church school is held in July or August, or whether priority should be given to repairing the roof or buying a new carpet, these questions are far from the heart of Christian ministry. The pastor with perspective knows that he has his hands more than full with the attainment of excellence in worship, preaching, teaching, pastoral care, and all that is involved in the pursuit of holiness. He will not be distracted from these tasks which are clearly his. And he can be assured that, as a strategic question, the more he plausibly demonstrates spiritual leadership, the more will his counsel be respected on every question of concern to the life of the church.

Paul persistently emphasized the diversity of gifts. The New Testament nowhere supports a leveling egalitarianism in the life of the Church. Rather the whole Body is strengthened as each part becomes more fully what it is called to be. The pursuit of holiness is not a zero-sum game, as though there were only so much holiness to go around. One member's gain is not another's loss, but rather a gain for the whole Body, making it more whole. The destiny or vocation of each member is not limited but infinite, the possibilities of actualization inexhaustible. In other words, the pursuit of holiness is premised upon the belief, indeed the Divine promise, that there is a complementarity of excellences. The vocation of each member is unique, and each member should sustain all other members in discerning and pursuing their peculiar callings. Conflicts arise only when people try to pursue vocations that belong to somebody else.

Some theologians have recently suggested that we should rethink the traditional idea of vocation that has undergirded the dignity of daily labor. Many jobs in the modern world—especially those that are tedious, menial, and devoid of inherent meaning—should not be dignified as vocations. Rather, they contend, such labor should be seen for what it is: a necessary evil in a sinful creation far from the Kingdom of God. Such arguments should be resisted. Without denying that much labor seems demeaning and "alienating," we should be cautious of our own subjective and class biases in judging the work of others. What seems tedious and menial to us may provide great satisfactions for others; and as for the inherent meaning of an endeavor, is that not brought to the work by the Christian's understanding that it is done for the glory of God? Of course some Christians may be employed in work that is unrelated to their vocation, which is why our responsibility is to help people discern as well as sustain the commitments proper to them. If what a Christian is doing—whether as an advertising executive, homemaker, or government bureaucrat—cannot be done for the glory of God, it ought not to be done at all, at least not by that person. The exercise of discernment means that at times there will be decisions for change. When change is not possible, and when what one is doing is not intrinsically reprehensible, the Christian seeks to discern vocation within the givenness of his life, which in that case includes his occupation. The idea of vocation does not involve an abstract conceptualization of who we think we truly are or would like to be, but rather involves the search for and fidelity to the will of God in the lives that are ours. It is desirable that occupation be subject to autonomous choice; but if in some circumstances that is not possible, it is no disaster, and it is no release from our call to pursue holiness. Many of the crucial determinants in our lives, beginning with genetic endowment and family origins, are not subject to autonomous choice, yet, for all that, our lives are no less ours. Fidelity means the pursuit of holiness in the lives that are ours, not in the lives that we wish were ours.

The ministerial vocation, then, is not exclusionary but exemplary, not in competition with but complementary to the vocations of others. The minister should persistently lift up, enhance, and exalt instances of lay vocations pursued with courage and faithfulness. In the local church the excessive attention given those who compete for the pastor's vocation and its responsibilities detracts from the public celebration of those who pursue their own vocations. We should gladly and publicly make clear that, while we are called to be spiritual leaders, we are not necessarily in the lead in the actualizing of God's call. The Sanctifying Spirit in the lives of others may be making much more headway than in our own lives, and we should urge sisters and brothers on to even greater progress, knowing that we are all enriched by their advance. Concern for the vocations of laypersons also requires great sensitivity to the myriad ways in which their dignity and integrity are under assault in the everyday world. Jesse Jackson, the black preacher in Chicago, leads the congregation in the antiphonal chant, "I am somebody!" Something like that should be happening in all of our churches. Admittedly, there are self-important Christians who think they are somebodies on entirely the wrong grounds. Such grounds need to be cut out from under them by the sharp sword of the Law, with the purpose not of demeaning them but of recalling them to the "reconstituted somebodiness" that is ours in Christ.

And it is good to keep in mind that, as the synagogue sexton reached for status by claiming to be a nobody, those who flaunt their importance may inadvertently be exhibiting a deep sense of their unimportance. In the leadership of the church, the pastor who encounters hostility and conflict may on rare occasions be forced to conclude that he is confronted by sheer evil, by the demonic. In such instances his hope lies in whatever rites of exorcism are available to him, or in rugged perseverence, or in talking to the bishop about a transfer. But, as a general rule, the operative assumption is that such conflict results from people seeking an importance and a vocation other than their own. The appropriate action is for the pastor to recall them to their own vocation and strengthen them in it by the exemplary pursuit of his vocation.

Finally, the complementarity of vocations requires that we really want, that we really pray for, the Sanctifying Spirit in the lives of others. We should pray and pray urgently for the success of other ministries. If we are afraid of competition from the church up the street, our own ministries will become defensive holding actions. Above all, we should be praying for our own people. Many times a week, people ask the pastor to pray for them or for their loved ones. "Yes, I will pray for you," he responds. But what if he doesn't? Perhaps he should say to such people, "No, I'm sorry but I don't pray." Such a healthy jolt might get intercession written into the minister's contract, as it is already and most certainly in the calling. A grand old pastor who died several years ago first impressed upon me the importance of praying for one's people. He would go into the church or some quiet place alone, taking with him the list of all his parishioners, and devote no less than an hour a day to praying for them one by one.

It does not matter whether one is in a "prayerful mood," whatever that may be. And all inhibitions about whether or not prayer "works," whatever that may mean, must be rejected as temptations from the Evil One. We are not likely to announce on a Sunday morning that we are not in the mood to preach, or that we have our doubts about the efficacy of preaching, and therefore there will be no sermon this morning. It is to be suspected that we preach because the people know and care if we do not preach, while only God knows and cares if we do not pray. The ministry of intercession is an integral part of our own pursuit of holiness, and it is the clearest evidence of our faith in the complementarity of all vocations within the Body of Christ.

ABSTRACT PERFECTION VERSUS
OBEDIENCE IN MISSION

We are commanded to be perfect as the Father is perfect. The meaning of that is exemplified in the life of Christ, which is the life of obedience. To speak positively of obedience today is to be profoundly countercultural. The valid suspicion of talk about obedience is grounded in the experience of authoritarianisms, both past and present. Obedience is confused with "blind obedience," which is morally odious. Obedience is confused with conformity, with going along, with asking no questions. But obedience really means responsiveness; it is related to the Latin *audire,* to hear, to listen, to respond appropriately. Obedience is not the surrender of responsibility but the acceptance of responsibility for what we respond to and how. Obedience is not conformity. Indeed, we must refuse to conform in order that we may obey. Conformity means accepting a direction or destiny that belongs to someone else; obedience is the actualization of our own destiny.

Obedience, then, is not the enemy of freedom but the exercise of freedom. Contrary to much popular thinking, we are not most free when we are least responsive to the commands, invitations, and directions which beckon us. Liberation is not the absence of duty but deciding which duty is ours. We are liberated by that which we accept as obligation. Again, we are freed when we discover the pleasure of duty rather than the duty of pleasure. There is no more onerous bondage than to be liberated from any obligation that is truly ours. The discovery of our true selves is the emergence of ourselves in free decision and fidelity to the obligations that are ours. The pursuit of holiness is not the pursuit of an abstract perfection—whether that be the perfection of our "authentic selves" or the perfection of moral behavior. The pursuit of holiness is rather a lifetime of responsive listening, of obedience, to our vocation.

This insight is powerfully expressed by Dietrich Bonhoeffer in his poem-prayer, "Who Am I?" written during his imprisonment. He reviews the ways in which he is perceived by others—by his family, by jailers, by church and government authorities, by fellow prisoners—and the ways in which he perceives himself. Of all these different and sometimes contradictory perspectives, he asks, which is the real me? It is impossible to tell; there is a measure of truth in each. Then Bonhoeffer concludes triumphantly, "Thou knowest, O Lord. I am thine!" Who am I, really? I am the one who, in the particularities and confusions of this one life, lives in responsive listening, in obedience, to you, O Lord.

We want to be known for who we really are, not for the "roles" we play. But that way of thinking is dead-ended. Who we are is defined by that to which we are obedient. Imagine a first-century person in Galilee wanting to know Jesus for who he really is, apart from what he came to do. Always he *is* the one who came to do the will of the Father. To know him is to know his work, to know him is to follow him. There is no other way. He does not wish to be known, indeed he cannot be known, apart from his mission, apart from his obedience, apart from his cross.

"Am I not free? . . . Though I am free from all men, I have made myself a slave to all, that I might win the more. . . . I have become all things to all men, that I might by all means save some" (1 Cor. 9). This offends contemporary sensibilities. It is compromise, it is false consciousness, it is inauthentic existence. But Paul knew that the self that we are, when separated from the loyalties, commitments, and obligations that we have freely accepted, is an abstracted and false self. Today's human potential therapies that thrive on such separation are dead wrong—that is, they are lethally wrong. "You are what you think you are." "You are what you want to be." "You are what you feel you are." No, we *are* what we are called to be in obedience to the vocation we have accepted as ours. "I do it all for the sake of the gospel, that I may share in its blessings." We *are* what the gospel promises we will be.

The pursuit of holiness means singleness of heart. We all live far short of that purity of heart that wills one thing; it is important to remember that and thus to know that we live by grace. Just as important to remember is that the one thing we should will is not some abstract moral perfection for ourselves but the perfect rule of God, the Kingdom of God. What the particulars of the perfect rule of God might be eludes us at this preliminary point in history. But, for each of us, that perfection is discovered in part by single-minded, single-hearted obedience to doing what he has called us to do. Anything that divides our hearts and minds, such as ambition, is to be seen as the enemy.

From ambition we should draw back as from lethal poison. But, it is countered, we should be ambitious for doing good. If the attainment of some position of greater power and influence can increase the good we can do, what could possibly be wrong with that? It is a seductive line of reasoning. It is the reasoning that underlies the corruption of careerism in the ministry, that makes it almost automatic that successful ministries move on to successively larger churches until they are crowned by executive posts, honorary doctorates, and the bishop's mitre. Whoever ministers in one place with an eye on the next is ministering with a divided heart.

Of course, few people stay in one place their whole lives; we have to make decisions when changes are proposed to us. We say that we move on to "greater challenges for the Lord"; but such challenges are usually shadowed by the suspicion created by the greater satisfactions offered. A good general rule by which to test our singleness of heart is that, when faced with choices, we give greater weight to the one that will require the greater sacrifice. And another general rule: Choose the one that others would be less likely to choose. Were these rules more honored, the Church would have more exemplary ministries in the inner cities, among the rural poor, with a great host of society's marginal people. Does this mean that pastors of large and prosperous churches, denominational executives, seminary deans, and bishops cannot be saved? Of course not. With God all things are possible. There might even be legitimacy in the sentiment attributed to one pope, "Since God has seen fit to give us the papacy, let us enjoy it." But only when, after great resistance, one is forced to conclude that God has given it. They carried a protesting Ambrose to the church in order to make him a bishop. The corruption of the present-day Church would be greatly reduced were more of its leaders compelled to office by obedience rather than attracted to office by ambition.

THE OBSERVANCE OF LIMITS OR
THE EXERCISE OF FREEDOM

Activism, ambition, money, and sexuality—these are among the chief forces dividing the ministerial heart, crippling the pursuit of holiness, and compromising the vocation to exemplary life. The temptations are quite different in the ways they affect the relationship between ministry and people. Activism, for example, is often approved and rewarded. There are seldom severe strictures against ambition and the love of money, unless they become overweeningly overt. But with respect to sexuality, sensitivities are heightened and censures are strong. In Christian thinking in this area, the line between prejudice and piety, between fear of God and fear of the unfamiliar, is hard to draw.

But here too the pursuit of holiness cannot be dominated by fear or by negative limitations. The question is not, "What can I get away with?" but "What am I called to do in order to actualize what, by the grace of God, I am?" In short, here too we are called to the exercise of freedom in the courage of uncertainty. The freedom of obedience always comes hard. Much easier is conformity to clear-cut rules and unchallengeable prohibitions. Especially in the interstices of the erotic, where are engaged our deepest longings for companionship, for loving and being loved, for ecstatic loss of self in another, here we would readily surrender our freedom. Freedom can be surrendered either in comformity to the expectations of others or in conformity to our own passions. Legalism and libertinism are but two sides of the coin we pay to be freed from freedom.

Obedience is responsive listening for the will of God. On the basis of the Spirit's promise to the Church, we listen for God's speaking also through his people. The pursuit of holiness means living in sensitivity to the sensitivities of God's people. In sensitivity to their sensitivities, but not in subservience to their prejudices. Again, holiness is not some bland and respectable "goodness"; it is the radically disturbing pressing on to the Good. It challenges more than it confirms; it fascinates and it terrifies.

In the service of satisfying passion, we can call upon an almost infinite reservoir of rationalization. After all, our peccadilloes are precisely that: small infractions that hurt no one. In discussion of social policy today, we hear much about "victimless crimes." In public policy the concept is dubious, in ministerial ethics it is disastrous. We are to live as in the day, so that we need not fear exposure to the light of all that we do. It is a hard saying. And woe to us if we offend one of these little ones whom he calls his own. It would be better for us that a millstone be hung about our necks and we be cast into the depths of the sea. It is a very hard saying.

Moral theologians have made much of the distinction between "giving offense" and "taking offense." We should not submit to those who use their weakness as a weapon. We dare not let our lives be inhibited by those who would take offense at every infringement of their prejudices. We dare not because we have no right to surrender our freedom, and because we should not confirm them in their petty legalism. To offer people our subservience is to deny them the strength of our obedience. This is nasty in its complexity, this relationship between freedom and obligation. It is also majestic. Refusing to surrender our freedom on the side of legalism or of libertinism, we conclude with the seventeenth-century poet: " 'Tis glorious misery to be born a man." (Walking the edge of subservience to current fashion, one spoils the cadence by adding mentally, "or a woman.")

"Ich kann nicht anders," Luther declared at Worms, lighting up the modern world with an exemplary instance of the freedom of obedience. "I cannot do otherwise": The emphasis is upon the *ich,* which is not mere feeling or what is usually meant by conscience but is a judgment born from self-understanding. This is not individualistic whimsy or self-assertion; contemporary twaddle about

"doing your own thing" could hardly be more foreign to Luther's intent. He holds himself accountable to those who differ, calling on them to correct him by scripture, by witness of the tradition, or by clear reason. Barring such correction, he has no choice but to obey, to exercise freedom in the courage of uncertainty. In a similar vein, the civil rights and antiwar movements raised the question of civil disobedience, and it was argued that this was not really disobedience but obedience of a different order.

It is often remarked that the gospels have relatively little to say about sexual sins, and that is true. In the reported words of Jesus there is at least ten times as much on the dangers of money and the oppression of the poor by the rich. One must point this out when the discussion of Christian ethics is too confined to sexuality and one would direct attention to issues of social justice. At the same time, however, we cannot belittle the emphasis upon sexuality in the New Testament. Almost all the scholars agree that the biblical passages on holiness and sanctification are closely and inseparably connected with sexuality. Typical are the warnings of Ephesians 4 against "immorality and all impurity. . . . For it is a shame even to speak of the things that they do in secret." So pervasive is the emphasis that it is said that Paul and the pastorals are "obsessed" by sexuality. The same critics who make that claim sometimes also assert that the New Testament writers, living in a pre-Freudian era, could not appreciate the pervasiveness and nuances of sexuality in human behavior. It is hard to have it both ways.

Or it is said that the New Testament writers were "culturally conditioned" and that therefore their ideas about sexuality need not be taken too seriously. This is a curious argument indeed. Does it mean that *we* are not culturally conditioned, or that we are conditioned by a superior culture? Both propositions are implausible. Or perhaps we are looking for principles that transcend culture. But that is what the earlier gnostics thought they had found, enabling them to be disdainful of the beliefs and rules and orders of a given time in history. True, ours is a living tradition, and the Spirit is leading the Church into fuller truth, illuminating the meaning of obedience in this moment. To cite the most common example, our attitude toward human slavery may not be Paul's, yet we are confident that it is obedient to New Testament teaching in relation to our historical moment. The Sanctifying Spirit is not to be confused with the spirit of the times; yet those led by the Spirit are to be creatively responsive to the questions and opportunities posed by the times.

If it is proposed that the Spirit is leading the Church to change its understanding of the exemplary life, it must be clear that what is being proposed is not greater permissiveness but truer obedience. This intent is not always manifest among those who propose changes in attitudes towards celibacy, homosexuality, marriage as a lifelong union, and other dimensions of sexual behavior. At the same time, it is far from clear that those who resist such changes are interested in true obedience, as distinct from conformity.

The purpose here is not to treat these questions in detail. Books have been written on them, and the debates will no doubt continue for some time. The point here is the connection between the pursuit of holiness and the minister's pledge and call to live an exemplary life. If that pledge and call are agreed upon, then what is being debated today is the definition of the exemplary life. The question is not what is permissible but what is exemplary.

It is urged, for example, that marriage as a lifelong union is no longer exemplary. Quantity of years should give way to quality of relationship. Satisfaction is a higher virtue than longevity. Divorce, it is said, might not only be permissible but might be an exemplary release from a union no longer pleasing to God. One argument employed is that we are in a new situation in which people live much longer. It is argued, "When our grandparents said 'until death do us part,' they knew it wouldn't be very long." But in fact, a healthy twenty-five-year-old person in the year 1900 had about the same life expectancy as a healthy twenty-five-year-old person today. What has changed is not life expectancy but what we expect from life. In most churches, until very recently, ministerial divorce was considered a severe, if not disqualifying, fault. That is no longer true in some churches. It happens that divorced clergy, even twice-divorced clergy, acknowledge this as evidence of tragic failure from which they have learned. Thus, it is suggested that fault is turned into exemplary growth and restoration in the fellowship of forgiven sinners. One might argue that such instances do not challenge but reinforce the ideal of marriage as a union of lifelong fidelity. To acknowledge the breaking of the promise is to acknowledge the promise.

It is commonly said that rising divorce rates signal that marriage and family are no longer held in high esteem. As we know from the rate of remarriage, however, people may think too highly of marriage, or at least expect too much from it. People get married again, and maybe again, in search of a partnership that lives up to their ideal of what marriage should be. In this cultural context it is understandable that people do not pledge themselves to one another as long as they both shall live but as long as they both shall love, in the sense of feeling about one another the way they felt when they decided to get married. What has changed is the understanding of love and fidelity, and the relationship between the two.

Marriage as a social institution is not under attack, but the Christian understanding of marriage certainly is. It is deeply regrettable that some ministers are quite prepared to accommodate cultural shifts, letting couples adjust the marriage rite to suit their intentions. Unless one views the church as a service agency for performing social rites, there would seem to be absolutely no reason for a minister to preside at a ceremony that is not clearly understood to be a rite of *Christian* marriage. One may tolerantly view various forms of cohabitation and sexual union, and the tolerant usually plead for greater "honesty" about human relationships, but it is precisely because it is profoundly dishonest that a minister should not call something a Christian marriage that is not that. It is not a Christian marriage simply because it is called that or because the people involved are Christians.

To qualify as a Christian marriage, which is to be held up as exemplary, it would seem that those involved should take seriously the *mysterion* and *sacramentum* that are so clearly evident in the biblical concept of two becoming one flesh and, most particularly, the concept of the union between Christ and the Church. At the very least, this requires a definition of love that has more to do with fidelity than with compatibility. If Christians wish to enter upon some other form of union and desire the blessing of the Church on that union, pastoral judgments may differ. But honesty requires that this not be confused with Christian marriage. In recent years this question has been discussed, even heatedly debated, in connection with the "marriage" of homosexuals. But were we more candid, the question would be raised in connection with a large proportion of marriages at which we ministers preside.

One hears ministers describe the performing of marriages as one of the uninteresting routines of their work. That seems distressingly wrongheaded. Preparing people for marriage is a ministry that touches their lives at what will quite possibly be the single most important decision they will make in their adult lives. It is an awesome undertaking. As we have seen that God's integrity consists in his faithfulness, so the marriage pledge is a unique testing of the integrity of the persons involved. Almost always when presiding at a marriage, I am strongly tempted to interrupt the proceedings to ask once again whether the couple really know what they are undertaking. Of course that is the point of the prescribed questions in the rite, but one fears they are often asked and answered as mere formalities. They are certainly just that if the minister views marriages as a bothersome routine rather than as a singular opportunity to touch the lives of people at a point when they most often need, and more often than not welcome, concerned ministry. And those who do not welcome it can always get married elsewhere. The minister has nothing to lose but his fee, and maybe an upset family. But that is a small enough price to pay in defense of ministerial integrity.

Divorce and the failure to minister to others in marriage both raise serious questions about exemplary ministry. Another issue that receives little public discussion but is no secret in the ministerial club is the frequency with which ministers have extramarital affairs. There are no adequate statistics, but discussions with clergy and with bishops (who usually handle such problems with discretion when they become an issue) suggest such affairs are happening more often than they used to. Whatever its basis in fact, there is a long tradition of rumored female attraction to clergy, whether single or married. Of course clergy may be indulging in wishful thinking on this score. Nonetheless, the relationship between the sacred and the sexual is well established, as witness the biblical condemnations of erotic temple cults in both the Old and New testaments. (I am unaware of any studies of extramarital affairs involving female ministers, although those who oppose women's ordination frequently cite the ambiguities of cultic eroticism as one reason for their opposition.) In any case, the male minister's affair with a church member or someone else is nothing new.

No matter how compassionate one may be toward human needs and compulsions, such affairs are not mere peccadilloes. To make light of them as "a little thing on the side" is to trifle with other persons and to foolishly underestimate the degree to which the erotic engages and divides oneself. Marital infidelity threatens, if it does not demonstrate, the loss of personal integrity, puts the public credibility of one's ministry into jeopardy, and establishes in one's life a dark corner of the night that shadows the whole of one's work. We may protest the "hypocrisy" of people being outraged by this when it is so commonly done by others. (Although not nearly so commonly as the apologists of the "sexual revolution" would have us believe.) But again, hypocrisy is the tribute that vice pays to virtue. Ministers are not "just like everybody else." Ministers who plead to the contrary simply fly in the face of everything that the Church—and that they in their more sensible moments—intend by Christian ministry. Is the burden of being different unfair? Not really; not if we have freely affirmed the vocation and pledge to adorn the gospel with a holy life.

The purpose here is not to affirm conventional morality; it is to affirm concern for the Church and the role of the ministry in the Church. Unconventional and minority views have a venerable record of sometimes turning out to be acclaimed as right. What is exemplary in the realm of sexuality is subject to change. If one's effort is to redefine the exemplary concept of marital fidelity, that could be a worthy intention. That would seem to require that one's behavior be public, if it is to have any effect on changing attitudes. One should then, to borrow a phrase from another debate, come out of the closet. But in fact the defense of marital infidelity, when it is made, is usually framed in terms of satisfying irresistible needs or of winking at the marginally permissible; in short, it is defended in the language of limit observance rather than of the exercise of freedom in the pursuit of holiness. If we are unfaithful in this way, we have, at least in that one area, abandoned the pursuit; and of course the nature of compromise makes it difficult to contain the corrosive damage to that one area.

There are several issues affecting sexuality where the received definition of the exemplary is being directly, publicly, and forcefully challenged. This is evident in debates over feminism, clerical celibacy, and homosexuality. The first touches on ministry most directly in connection with the ordination of women. Sensitivities on this question are very delicate, and it is hard to say anything without being misunderstood by one faction or another. Perspective requires that we keep in mind that, despite all the furor expended, the ordination of women and even more the full exercise of pastoral leadership by women is a relatively isolated phenomenon.[2] The number of women currently in theological seminaries and seeking ordination may dramatically change this circumstance in some churches. But at present there is not enough evidence to know in what ways, if any, women in the ministry will change the definition of the exemplary with respect to marriage and family life. Today, with a high degree of frequency, the ordained woman is married to an ordained man, and the chief change seems to be that the church gives some kind of canonical status and maybe a salary to the one who is, in effect, assistant pastor. Obviously this could change where the work of the woman takes priority over that of the husband. To date, congregations have been reluctant to receive and bishops have been reluctant to appoint women to positions of pastoral leadership. Depending on one's view, this is is mere prejudice and should be overcome, or, it is a thoughtful intuition about the right order of the world and should be respected. The point here is that, however this question develops further, the discussion should focus not on individual rights or on what can be permitted but on the definition of the exemplary life to which ministry is solemnly pledged.

The question of clerical celibacy continues to be much controverted, notably but not exclusively in the Roman Catholic church, for the obvious reason that that is the only church where it is mandatory. (It is mandatory for bishops in Eastern Orthodoxy, but that is another question.) Only a few years ago, many thoughtful writers declared it inevitable that Rome would change its requirement of celibacy, probably sooner than later. Today that confidence seems to be waning. Some Roman Catholics, while inclined to favor making celibacy or marriage optional, worry that such a step could spell the end of celibacy, making it the marginal and sometimes suspect phenomenon that it is in most Protestant churches. Since our culture deems marriage "the normal thing," the celibate would be put on the defensive with respect to his or her deviance from normality. As is well known, many thousands of priests and religious have left the active ministry over the past decade and more. While the exodus seems to have been stemmed, the number of new vocations in seminaries and religious orders is also dramatically reduced. The celibacy requirement is frequently cited as the chief reason for this decline.

Among some of those who have remained in active ministry, one response to the "celibacy crisis" has been the discussion of what is called "sexual celibacy." It is contended that the celibate is not asexual but simply handles his or her sexuality in a different way. To the extent that this is a commonplace recognition of the pervasiveness of sexuality in human life, it would seem to be unexceptionable. Some of the literature on sexual celibacy, however, reminds one of nothing so much as the old manuals on how far one can go in "necking" and "petting" before committing sin. It is not a very seemly discussion for adult people. The focus is on the limits of permissibility rather than on the pursuit of holiness. Certainly it stretches the limits of credulity among Catholic lay people and among other priests and religious. Yet there is a painful dilemma here, and one cannot help being sympathetic to people who "discovered" dimensions of their sexuality some years after they had pledged themselves to the celibate life. I have been very moved by conversations with priests and nuns who felt compelled to leave their ministries. For example, more often than not, priests do not question that they had—and still have—a vocation to the priesthood, but they lack a vocation to celibacy. Thus the Church has made it impossible for them to exercise their priestly vocation. The force of that argument is weakened, however, by the fact that, if they had a vocation to priesthood in the *Roman Catholic* church, it was clear from the beginning that celibacy is in practice, whether it should be or not, a requirement for being a Roman Catholic priest. The question of marriage and celibacy is of importance not only for Roman Catholics but for all ministers, and indeed for all Christians. Following Max Thurian of Taizé *(Marriage and Celibacy)*, I believe it is a mistake to speak of people being "called" either to marriage or to celibacy.[3] Marriage and celibacy are both abstract states when separated from the particularities of persons and work. Both marriage and celibacy are to be understood in terms of a prior vocation. They are implied, as it were, in a prior decision. One is called to live one's life with a particular person, and that implies marriage. Or one is called to a work that can only be done or can best be done in the state of celibacy. Note that I do not say it can best be done by "remaining" celibate, as though celibacy were simply the consequence of not getting married. Celibacy is rather a positive decision implied by one's perceived vocation.

Thurian argues, and I believe he is right, that conventional thought is skewed in a way that demeans both marriage and celibacy. Marriage is denied the dignity of Christian vocation if it is viewed as simply the natural thing to do. Similarly, celibacy is demeaned if it is understood merely in terms of canonical requirement or personal disposition. Historically, both marriage and celibacy have been honored as exemplary forms of Christian life. One hopes that will remain true in the future.

That distinction between sensitivity and servility toward common attitudes is important in yet another area where the definition of the exemplary life is being directly and publicly challenged. In the last few years, several churches have been formally petitioned to ordain declared and practicing homosexuals. The official responses to date, while reflecting heightened sensitivity to the nuances of the question, have been in the negative. Some observers believe that the wave of "gay rights" activism has, at least in the churches, been turned back or contained, and that may be the case. The attitude of the Christian community today would seem to range from condemning homosexual practice as an "abomination" to a practical approach of discreet toleration, but without formal approval. The second approach can be and is criticized as "hypocritical" or as a fearful refusal to face the question. Its defenders counter that some ques-

tions permit of no satisfactory answer and therefore cannot be offi-
cially "resolved." The issue, they suggest, is best left to common
sense, compassion, and pastoral discretion. They readily admit that
this is an inadequate response, but then those who have come to
terms with life's ambiguities know that this is hardly the only
problem for which there are no adequate solutions.

Homosexual activists are understandably dissatisfied with this
approach. They insist that formal statements and policies should be
moved farther along the spectrum of attitudes toward homosexual
practice: It is not a perversion to be condemned or a deviance to be
tolerated or an exception to be acknowledged but an alternative to
be approved. While the churches have declined to acknowledge even
"model" homosexual relationships (relationships of stability and
sexual fidelity, similar in some respects to heterosexual marriage)
as an exemplary Christian life-style, the issue cannot easily be
shelved. At least for a time, it will be kept alive by "gay caucuses"
in the several churches and by a few local churches specifically
designed to minister to the "gay community." (Highlighting the
idea of the Christian minister as exemplar, one notes that one such
congregation in New York City censured its minister for sexual
promiscuity and other indiscretions.) Whatever one's attitude toward homosexuality, it should be admitted that the activists have
rendered a service in underscoring the exemplary nature of ministry. That is, by pressing for the ordination of declared and practicing
homosexuals, they were making clear on behalf of all Christian
homosexuals that what is wanted from the Church is not a license
to sin, or mere "understanding," or a suspension of ethical judgment, but formal affirmation of an alternative path in the pursuit
of holiness.

If there is now a pause in activist pressure, it may be a good time
to evaluate the results of several years' furor over this issue. One
suspects that such an evaluation would conclude that, as with most
controversies, it has brought mixed blessings. For the young person
with very ordinary youthful anxieties about his or her sexual orientation, the public discussion has perhaps relieved the nightmare of
being alone and hopelessly "different." At the same time, some
young people may have been incited to "come out of the closet"

prematurely, declaring their homosexuality as their primary identity when in fact it is but a part of "normal" ambivalence about sexual orientation. Also on the negative side, the popular awareness of homosexuality does not seem to have had much impact upon popular disapproval; thus it has put under a cloud of suspicion some unmarried persons who in fact are not homosexual. Then too, there may be merit in the society's becoming more generally aware of the very large subculture of the "gay world." This subculture is usually depicted as decadently sleazy, narcissistic, and promiscuous. Apologists contend that, to the extent this picture is accurate, the "gay world" is that way because of societal disapproval and repression. Their opponents answer that society disapproves because the subculture is that way. Obviously, this kind of argument can go on for a long time. But with respect to both social policy and the Church's mission, it is a plus that people are aware of a world of values and behavior that involves many thousands of Americans, including innumerable members of the Church. Whatever else may happen, one hopes there will be no return to the miasma of ignorance, prejudice, and fear that has too often marked the Church's view of homosexuality in the past.[4]

In its countercultural role as radical critic, the Church has an enormous contribution to make in relativizing, and thus shattering, the tyranny of sex over so many lives in our society. Like consumerism, indeed as a species of consumerism, sexual satisfaction is presented as a categorical imperative. American society is in a constant state of what moral theology used to call "sexual commotion." This imperious commotion should be challenged by a community that is heir to a much more comprehensive and subtle understanding of what it means to be human. We must insist that virginity is not a perversion, restraint is not inhibition, desires are not necessarily needs to be met, biological capacity contains no imperative to action. Against the myriad manuals for sexual fulfillment, the Church's witness should be clear that persons are never to be subordinated to performance, nor love to lust.

Perhaps all times are times of sexual commotion; ours being different only in that the commotion is culturally celebrated and established as social and psychological orthodoxy. Of course the

Church is caught up in the commotion, but that need not mean it is captive to it. Fidelity, homosexuality, changing sex roles, marriage and celibacy—all are questions that will continue to claim the attention of the churches. The Christian contribution is to understand these questions not in terms of liberation from limits but in terms of that true liberation which is the exercise of freedom in the pursuit of holiness. If the Church and its ministry have the nerve for it, the commotion can be tempered and transformed by a new vision of the exemplary life, and that could be the real sexual revolution of our time.

CONCLUSION AND BEGINNING

At whatever point we are in ministry, whether we are just starting out or are veterans of visions lost and visions only partially fulfilled, we are at a point of change, of formation, of potentiality, of promise. The harder we work at this ministry, the less easily satisfied we are with ourselves. The more we know the value of the treasure, the more keenly we know the earthenness of the vessel. "We are afflicted in every way, but not crushed; perplexed, but not driven to despair; persecuted, but not forsaken; struck down, but not destroyed; always carrying in the body the death of Jesus, so that the life of Jesus may also be manifested in our bodies" (2 Cor. 4).

At the beginning and at the end of every day, we offer up our ministries. We are responsible for the offering, and God is responsible for the consequences, and his is the infinitely greater responsibility. We tinker and tune and experiment and resolve and fail and try again, in the happy assurance that, when all is said and done, it is the awesome recklessness of his love and not our ambition that called us to the seeming absurdity of this work. Because of our infidelities, we have a lot to answer for. Because of his promise, God has a lot more to answer for. "Even when we are faithless, he remains faithful—for he cannot deny himself" (2 Tim. 2). We affirm our place in the tradition of fidelity, and of infidelity, that is the Church. In that tradition we proclaim the presence of the One who seems to be absent. We are the stewards of the mysteries of his presence, and of his absence.

The pursuit of holiness is holding out for the fullness of God's rule in our lives and in our world. And it is learning to hold on while holding out. Christian ministry is freedom's exercise and aspiration. It is Martin Luther King, Jr., on the eve of his death in Memphis, Tennessee: "I'm not fearing any man. Mine eyes have seen the glory of the coming of the Lord!" And it is Paul in 1 Corinthians 4. Once again he has painstakingly tried to explain what his ministry is all about. Once again he suspects that he has failed to be entirely persuasive. He has done his best and he hopes the Corinthians will think better of him than they did before. And then he adds: "But with me it is a very small thing that I should be judged by you or by any human court." Then this statement of most perfect liberation: "I do not even judge myself. . . . Do not pronounce judgment before the time."

Let no one judge before the time. At that time it will be revealed to us and to all that we were indeed the ambassadors of a sovereignty then no longer disputed. That is the promise, and that promise alone is the source of freedom for ministry.

Notes

CHAPTER 1. THE THUS AND SO-NESS OF THE CHURCH
1. Wolfhart Pannenberg, *Theology and the Kingdom of God* (Philadelphia: Westminster, 1969), p. 72 ff.
2. David L. Norton, *Personal Destinies* (Princeton, N.J.: Princeton University Press, 1977), p. 15.
3. Ibid., p. 58.

CHAPTER 2. MINISTERING BY HOPE BEYOND APOLOGY
1. Hans von Campenhausen, *Ecclesiastical Authority and Spiritual Power* (Stanford, Calif.: Stanford University Press, 1969), p. 3.
2. Ibid., p. 10.
3. The complex ways in which the early Church appealed to the apostolic are critically analyzed in Robert L. Wilken, *The Myth of Christian Beginnings* (New York: Doubleday, 1971).

CHAPTER 3. A CHOICE OF MODELS
1. Paul Minear, *Images of the Church in the New Testament* (Philadelphia: Westminster, 1960).

2. Robert McAfee Brown, *Frontiers for the Church Today* (Oxford: Oxford University Press, 1973).

3. Avery Dulles, *Models of the Church* (New York: Doubleday, 1974).

4. Martin E. Marty, *A Nation of Behavers* (Chicago: University of Chicago Press, 1976). Marty elaborates the metaphor of a "religious map," by which sensibilities and behavior can be located.

5. H. Richard Niebuhr, *The Purpose of the Church and Its Ministry* (New York: Harper & Row, 1956), pp. 23–24.

6. Dulles, *Models of the Church*, p. 118.

7. John Courtney Murray, *We Hold These Truths* (New York: Sheed and Ward, 1960).

CHAPTER 4. AUTHORITY FOR MINISTRY

1. Bernard Cooke, *Ministry to Word and Sacraments* (Philadelphia: Fortress Press, 1976). An excellent example of the "anti-institutional mood" as expressed in current Catholic thought.

2. H. Richard Niebuhr, *The Purpose of the Church and Its Ministry* (New York: Harper & Row, 1956), p. 25.

3. Robert McAfee Brown, *Frontiers for the Church Today* (Oxford: Oxford University Press, 1973), p. 97.

4. Daniel Day Williams, *The Minister and the Care of Souls* (New York: Harper & Row, 1954), p. 90.

CHAPTER 5. RECONCILIATION AGAINST RESIGNATION

1. John T. McNeill, *A History of the Cure of Souls* (New York: Harper & Row, 1951).

2. Daniel Day Williams, *The Minister and the Care of Souls* (New York: Harper & Row, 1954), p. 99.

3. On the question of whether such concerns do dominate the religious agenda in some current thinking, see Avery Dulles, *The Resilient Church* (New York: Doubleday, 1977), especially Chapter 4 on the Hartford Appeal. See also essays in *Against the World for the World,* ed. Peter Berger and Richard Neuhaus (New York: Seabury Press, 1976).

4. Williams, *The Minister and the Care of Souls,* p. 101.

5. Krister Stendahl, "The Apostle Paul and the Introspective Conscience of the West," reprinted in *Paul Among Jews and Gentiles* (Philadelphia: Fortress Press, 1976).

6. Robert Coles, "New Forms of the Sin of Pride," *The New Review of Books and Religion,* December 1977, p. 3.

7. The treatment of character and the perduring self is indebted to the work

of Stanley Hauerwas. See especially his *Character and the Christian Life* (San Antonio, Texas: Trinity University Press, 1975).

8. For a thoughtful critique of putatively neutral "values clarification" from a Christian perspective, see Kevin Ryan, "Moral Formation: The American Scene," in *Moral Formation and Christianity*, ed. Franz Bockle (New York: Seabury Press, 1978).

9. H. Richard Niebuhr, *The Purpose of the Church and Its Ministry* (New York: Harper & Row, 1956), p. 35.

CHAPTER 6. SACRAMENT AND SUCCESS

1. Norman Dietz, *The Lifeguard and the Mermaid* (Orient, N.Y.: Dietz Publications, 1977), p. 9.

2. Bernard Cooke, *Ministry to Word and Sacraments* (Philadelphia: Fortress Press, 1976), p. 39.

3. See, for example, Juan Luis Segundo, *A Theology for Artisans of a New Humanity*, 5 vols. (Maryknoll, N.Y.: Orbis Books, 1975). For a thorough critique of this radically utilitarian view of the Christian faith, see Richard J. Neuhaus, "A Theology for Artisans of a New Christendom," *Commonweal*, July 4, 1975, pp. 243–46.

CHAPTER 7. THE SEARCH FOR COMMUNITY

1. K. Morrison, *Tradition and Authority in Western Christianity* (Princeton, N.J.: Princeton University Press, 1969), p. 162.

CHAPTER 8. TO CELEBRATE THE MYSTERY

1. See Constant Jacquet, Jr., "Women Ministers in 1977," National Council of Churches, March 1978. Of the approximately ten thousand women ministers in the U.S., the great majority are in groups such as the Salvation Army, the International Church of the Foursquare Gospel, and various Church of God groups. If one looks at the whole Christian community in a global context, the phenomenon of women's ordination is of course even more isolated.

2. Ernest Becker, *The Denial of Death* (New York: Macmillan, 1973).

3. H. Richard Niebuhr, *The Purpose of the Church and Its Ministry* (New York: Harper & Row, 1956), p. 102.

CHAPTER 9. THE IMPORTANCE OF BEING A PREACHER

1. Wilhelm Pauck, "The Ministry in the Time of the Continental Reformation," in *The Ministry in Historical Perspective*, ed. H. Richard Niebuhr and Daniel D. Williams (New York: Harper Row, 1956), p. 110.

2. Quoted in *Preaching in the Witnessing Community*, ed. Herman G. Stuempfle, Jr. (Philadelphia: Fortress Press, 1973), p. viii.

3. This listing of Christian diversity draws on a similar listing in Malachi Martin, *The Final Conclave* (Briarcliff Manor, N.Y.: Stein and Day, 1978), p. 13.

4. Yngve Brilioth, *A Brief History of Preaching* (Philadelphia: Fortress Press, 1965).

5. Niebuhr and Williams, eds., *The Ministry in Historical Perspective*, p. 283.

6. Irving Goffman, *The Presentation of Self in Everyday Life* (Garden City, N.Y.: Anchor Press, 1959).

7. Brilioth, *A Brief History of Preaching*, p. 50.

8. The question of the African roots of black preaching and worship is discussed in a number of works: Henry H Mitchell, *Black Preaching* (Philadelphia: Lippincott, 1970); Bruce A. Rosenberg, *The Art of the American Folk Preacher* (Oxford: Oxford University Press, 1970); and Charles V. Hamilton, *The Black Preacher in America* (New York: William Morrow, 1972).

CHAPTER 10. THE IMPERATIVE INDICATIVE

1. Quoted in *The Preaching of John Henry Newman*, ed. W. D. White (Philadelphia: Fortress Press, 1969), p. 28.

2. Paul Scherer, *The Word God Sent* (New York: Harper & Row, 1965), p. 8.

3. W. D. White, ed., *The Preaching of John Henry Newman*, p. 13.

4. John Knox speculates about the everyday ministry in the New Testament Church, in H. Richard Niebuhr and Daniel D. Williams, eds., *The Ministry in Historical Perspective* (New York: Harper & Row, 1956), p. 10 ff.

CHAPTER 11. THE PURSUIT OF HOLINESS

1. Hans von Campenhausen, *Ecclesiastical Authority and Spiritual Power* (Stanford, Calif.: Stanford University Press, 1969), pp. 252–53.

2. Constant Jacquet, Jr., "Women Ministers in 1977," National Council of Churches, March 1978.

3. Max Thurian, *Marriage and Celibacy* (London: SCM Press, 1959).

4. One of the most helpful statements on the Church and homosexuality was issued as a pastoral letter by Francis J. Mugavero, Roman Catholic bishop of Brooklyn, N.Y.: "Sexuality—God's Gift," *The* (Brooklyn) *Tablet*, February 12, 1976, and reprinted in *Insight: A Quarterly of Gay Catholic Opinion*, Spring, 1977.

Index of Names